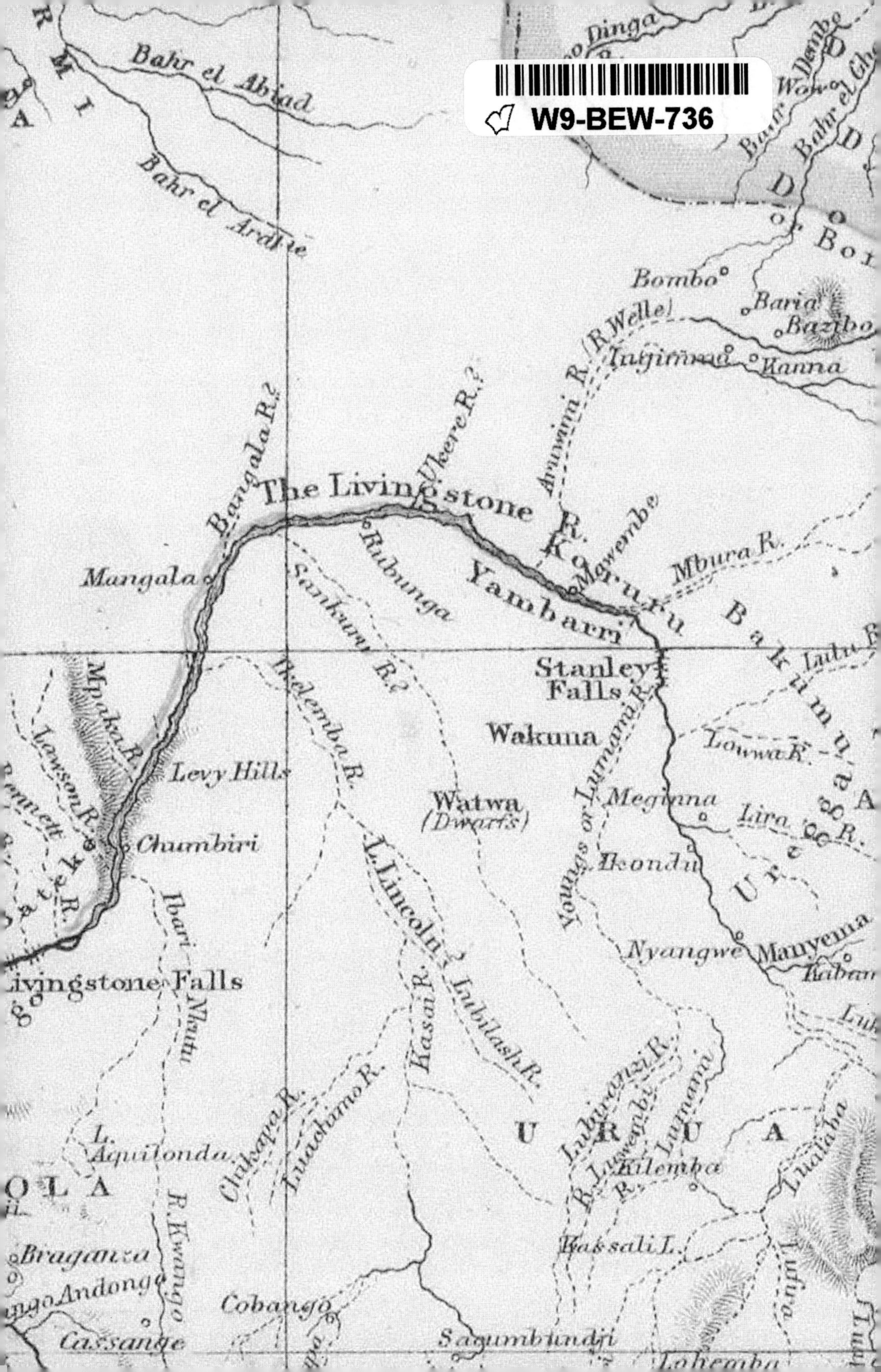
Bahr el Abiad
Bahr el Arab
Dinga
Bahr el Ghazal
Bombo
Baria
Bazibo
R. Welle
Tingimma
Kanna
Bangala R.?
Ukere R.?
Aruwimi R.
The Livingstone R.
Mawembe
Mbura R.
Mangala
Rubunga
Yambarri
Koruru
Bakumu
Stanley Falls
Lulu R.
Wakuma
Lowwa R.
Levy Hills
Watwa
(Dwarfs)
Meginna
Lira R.
Chumbiri
Ikondu
L. Lincoln
Youngs or Lumami R.
Uregga
Nyangwe
Manyema
Livingstone Falls
Kasai R.
Lubilash R.
Luachimo R.
Chikapa R.
Lubiranzi R.
R. Luwembi
Lumami
U R U A
L. Aquilonda
Kilemba
Lualaba
Kassali L.
Braganza
R. Kwango
Lufira
Andonge
Cobango
Cassange
Sagumbindji

Congo

Congo

The Miserable Expeditions
and Dreadful Death of
Lt. Emory Taunt, USN

ANDREW C. A. JAMPOLER

NAVAL INSTITUTE PRESS
ANNAPOLIS, MARYLAND

NAVAL INSTITUTE PRESS
291 Wood Road
Annapolis, MD 21402

Library of Congress Cataloging-in-Publication Data
Jampoler, Andrew C. A.
  Congo : the miserable expeditions and dreadful death of Lt. Emory
Taunt, USN / Andrew C.A. Jampoler.
     p. cm.
  Includes bibliographical references and index.
  ISBN 978-1-61251-079-8 (hardcover : alk. paper) —
ISBN 978-1-61251-270-9 (ebook) 1. Taunt, Emory H.—Travel—
Congo River Valley. 2. Congo River Valley—Discovery and
exploration. 3. Congo (Democratic Republic)—History—19th
century. 4. Congo (Democratic Republic)—Colonization. 5.
Belgium—Colonies—Africa. I. Title.
  DT639.J36 2013
  916.751022—dc23
                              2012050876

∞ This paper meets the requirements of ANSI/NISO z39.48-1992
(Permanence of Paper).
Printed in the United States of America.

21 20 19 18 17 16 15 14 13   9 8 7 6 5 4 3 2 1
First printing

Book design and composition: Alcorn Publication Design

To Chrissy and Bart, and Jason and Jennifer

Going up the river was like traveling back to the earliest beginnings of the world, when vegetation rioted on the earth and the big trees were kings. An empty stream, a great silence, an impenetrable forest. The air was warm, thick, heavy, sluggish. There was no joy in the brilliance of sunshine. The long stretches of the waterway ran on, deserted, into the gloom of overshadowed distances. On silvery sandbanks hippos and alligators sunned themselves side by side. The broadening waters flowed through a mob of wooded islands; you lost your way on that river as you would in a desert, and butted all day long against shoals, trying to find the channel, till you thought yourself bewitched and cut off forever from everything you had known once—somewhere—far away—in another existence perhaps.

JOSEPH CONRAD, *HEART OF DARKNESS*

Contents

Illustrations and Maps

Illustrations

Maps

Congo

1

The Congo: A Study of the Negro Race

Fatal Africa! One after another travellers drop away. It is such a huge continent, and each of its secrets is environed by so many difficulties—the torrid heat, the miasma exhaled from the soil, the noisome vapours enveloping every path, the giant cane-grass suffocating the wayfarer, the rabid fury of the native guarding every entry and exit, the unspeakable misery of life within the wild continent, the utter absence of every comfort, the bitterness which each day heaps upon the poor white man's head, in that land of blackness, the sombrous solemnity pervading every feature of it, and the little—too little—promise of success which one feels on entering it.

> *Dorothy Stanley (ed.)*, The Autobiography of Sir Henry Morton Stanley, G.C.B.

1

The American poet Vachel Lindsay first performed his masterwork "The Congo: A Study of the Negro Race" in 1914, six years after the Belgian government annexed the Congo Free State, the vast equatorial African expanse that had been for more than thirty years the personal property of Leopold II, king of the Belgians. By the time Lindsay began chanting his odd poem aloud to audiences, the Congo had largely passed from newspaper front pages and public consciousness. It would not reappear in either place for decades.

Helen Bullis, the *New York Times* book review's poetry critic in 1915, called "The Congo" a "splendid flourish of imagination," having first found in it a hallucinatory "touch of hashish-dream." For the most part, however—and especially after 1920—contemporary poets were mystified or embarrassed by Lindsay's extraordinary work, which he presented in dramatic recitations that were the performance art of the day. Moving about the stage and waving his arms, he recited,

Then I saw the Congo, creeping through the black,
Cutting through the forest with a golden track.

Then along that riverbank
A thousand miles
Tattooed cannibals danced in files;
Then I heard the boom of the blood-lust song
And a thigh-bone beating on a tin-pan gong.
And "Blood" screamed the whistles and the fifes of the warriors,
"Blood" screamed the skull-faced, lean witch-doctors . . .
From the mouth of the Congo
To the Mountains of the Moon.
Death is an elephant
Torch-eyed and horrible,
Foam-flanked and terrible . . .
Listen to the yell of Leopold's ghost
Like the wind in the chimney.
Burning in hell for his hand-maimed host.
Hear how the demons chuckle and yell
Cutting his hands off down in Hell.
Listen to the creepy proclamation,
Blown through the lairs of the forest-nation,
Blown past the white-ants' hill of clay,
Blown past the marsh where the butterflies play:—
"Be careful what you do.
Or Mumbo-Jumbo, God of the Congo,
And all of the other
Gods of the Congo,
Mumbo-Jumbo will hoo-doo you . . ."

In part, the poem was Lindsay's reflection in rhyme on the recent death in Equatorial Africa of the Reverend Robert Ray Eldred, forty, a missionary of the Disciples of Christ, who had drowned the previous September while attempting to swim across the Lokolo River. Eldred's death near the village of Eyengo followed by less than a year that of his wife, who suddenly fell feverish and died November 1912 in the church's mission upriver at Longa. Lindsay later explained that a church sermon about the Eldreds' sacrifice had prompted him to imagine the distant site of their tragedy, a place where Christian missionaries and other foreigners had been dying early of disease, injury, and poor judgment for nearly five centuries.

This quoted extract from the poem, minus Lindsay's instructions to the reader about how it is to be recited aloud (in one place "solemnly chanted," in another "shrilly and with a heavily accented metre"), is from the first stanza of three, "Their Basic Savagery." The other two stanzas of the poem are titled "Their Irrepressible High Spirits" and "The Hope of Their Religion." The last stanza ends with the twelve apostles who, while seated on high in bright white suits of armor, "thrilled all the forest with their heavenly cry, 'Mumbo-Jumbo will die in the jungle.'" Meanwhile, beneath their thrones and along the banks of the river,

> The vine-snared trees fell down in files.
> Pioneer angels cleared the way
> For a Congo paradise, for babes at play,
> For sacred capitals, for temples clean.
> Gone were the skull-faced witch-men lean.
> There, where the wild ghost-gods had wailed
> A million boats of angels sailed
> With oars of silver, and prows of blue
> And silken pennants that the sun shone through.
> 'Twas a land transfigured, 'twas a new creation . . .

Acknowledging the durability of ancient gods and practices, Lindsay imagined a solitary vulture orbiting this triumphant scene, crying "in the silence the Congo tune, / Mumbo-Jumbo will hoo-doo you."

Impoverished, ailing, and infested by mental demons, estranged from wife and children by his bizarre suspicions, Lindsay committed suicide in December 1931 by drinking drain cleaner. (The *New York Times* and other newspapers that published an obituary attributed his death at age fifty-two to a sudden heart attack. That era's journalism conventions precluded mention of suicide.) But he lives on, thanks to the Internet, where he can be seen and heard reciting "The Congo" as he presented it to audiences nearly a century ago.

2

The Congo River, Vachel Lindsay's "golden track" into the equatorial West African highlands, was discovered by accident in 1482. Its first European explorers, Portuguese sailors, were trying to open a blue-water route to the treasures of the Orient. They had been seeking such a route, a shunt around the ancient caravan tracks across Asia controlled at their western terminals by the Ottoman Turks, for more than fifty years.

In 1434 a sailor remembered as Gil Eanes sailed beyond Cape Bojador (26° 8' north latitude), making the Portuguese the first Europeans to reach this far south along the west coast of Africa, an achievement in the face of the contrary currents and winds that had until then given these waters the daunting name *Mare Tenebroso*, the "Sea of Darkness." A half-century went by before another Portuguese, Bartolomeu Dias, managed in 1487 to pass 35° south latitude and to round the continent's southernmost tip, which he called the "Cape of Storms," *Cabo Tormentoso*. (In one of history's most successful marketing efforts, that place was soon rebranded by the Portuguese king as *Cabo de Buon Esperanza*, the "Cape of Good Hope.") Success finally came to the Portuguese in May 1498, when Vasco da Gama sailed wearily into Calicut, on India's southwestern coast.

During the decades between Eanes and Dias, sailors edging their way cautiously down the West African coast passed a succession of rivers as they probed uncertainly toward the bottom of the continent, the Indian Ocean, and their distant goal: the Senegal and the Gambia, bracketing Dakar on Africa's western bulge; the Niger, circling in a great arc past Timbuktu into the shoulder of the Bight of Benin; and, nine hundred miles farther south, the Congo, discovered by the Portuguese sailor Diogo Cão in 1482 during the first of his two voyages off West Africa.

Cão's initial contacts with the natives of the lower Congo's kingdoms— he got as far upriver as Matadi, where he left a stone marker— were remarkably benign. For a brief time after 1492, when the king of Kongo converted to Catholicism and took the name João I, it was possible to imagine a very different future than the one that ultimately emerged from these first encounters. Instead, beginning in the sixteenth century the depopulation of the Americas found its solution in African slavery, which forever poisoned the white man's relations with the Congo.

Europeans arrived in the New World like an extinction meteor from space, with a cataclysmic impact on native peoples and societies that culled populations, shattered cultures, and changed everything forever. The chief instruments of change were not the usual suspects, weapons and religion, but smallpox and measles, against which none of the indigenous populations had any natural immunity. Estimates of the lethal impact of these viruses on the peoples of the Americas vary, ranging from a conservative third to as high as nine of ten. Some think that as many as 100 million of an estimated total population of 120 million died. By the early seventeenth century, professional slavers were moving thousands of substitute laborers across the Atlantic annually, legally through the eighteenth century, illegally a few decades later. The number increased dramatically over the years.

The slavers' many miserable victims—the midcontinent's first volume exports of natural resources—transported themselves overland, herded in coffles from the interior to catchment facilities ("barracoons") on the Atlantic Coast or just off the Indian Ocean coast, on the island of Zanzibar, where they were confined and collected for shipment to Europe, the Americas, Araby, and beyond. Native Africans spared capture and export as chattel remained behind to watch their home continent parted out to foreigners.

That partition was swift and thorough. Ernst Ravenstein, of the Royal Geographical Society, wrote in the *Statesman's Year Book* (Macmillan, 1891) that of Africa's 11.5 million square miles and 127 million inhabitants, only 2 million square miles and 24 million people still remained "unappropriated" by Europeans as the century approached its end. Great Britain and France controlled nearly half of the "appropriated" land and people, with the Portuguese, Spanish, German, Italian, and Turkish African colonies together spanning more than 3 million square miles of what was left and collectively encompassing a further 24 million natives. The Congo, Ravenstein wrote, added to these totals an additional 827,000 square miles and 15 million people entirely under European control.

3

The Congo's runoff is fully fifteen times that of the Nile, Africa's longest river. One and a half million cubic feet of water flow every second out the sluice that's the Congo's exit to the Atlantic Ocean, between Banana Point— shaped like a slender, drooping tentacle—near the north shore of the river's mouth and Shark Point on its south shore in neighboring Angola. The flow is so fast that the river has no delta. Instead, over the ages its torrent has dug some pits in the bed of the lower river nearly six hundred feet deep and gouged out a V-shaped submarine canyon in the continental shelf off West Africa almost five hundred miles long and fully four thousand feet deep. The flow, dark as bile where it first touches the ocean because of vegetable tannins, floats a layer of fresh water on the surface of the South Atlantic out many miles from the coast.

In 1877 a U.S. Hydrographic Office guide to navigation along the west coast of Africa, H.O. 48 (for the most part a translation of contemporary French sailing directions), told mariners that nine miles seaward of its mouth the waters of the Congo were still quite fresh, and out fully forty miles from the coast they had "only partially mingled with those of the sea; while the discoloration caused by the fresh water has been known to extend 300 miles off, where the current also has been reported to be perceptible." H.O. 48

also warned coasting sailors that the outflow of the river was marked by "floating islands, consisting of bamboo and *débris* of all kinds, which are met with far out at sea. These floating masses are sometimes so compact that it is impossible for a vessel to make headway through them without the assistance of a fresh breeze."

Vachel Lindsay badly underestimated the length of the Congo. It's not a thousand miles long but nearly three times longer measured from its source. (Straightened and relocated, the river would stretch from San Diego, California, to well beyond Bangor, Maine.) His poetic imagery suggests the Congo meanders gently through a verdant world. And in some places, especially along the long island-filled and reed-lined reach between 21° and 18° east longitude or in lake-like Pool Malebo, it flows toward the Atlantic through just such a bucolic setting. Elsewhere, for example deep in the narrow gorge between Kwamouth and Langa-langa, the river's character changes. There it pushes downstream over a rocky bed with great force and speed, piling up washboard waves against a contrary prevailing wind. This is the only reach where it's possible for dugouts to move on the Congo propelled by the wind. Many do, heading upriver beneath a single square sail improvised from all manner of cast-off plastic or fabric bagging.

Altogether the Congo and its twenty-three principal tributaries constitute a more than nine-thousand-mile-long network of routes into the heart of Africa, but it's a network obstructed very near its start on the Atlantic by an extended, impassable chokepoint. The Congo falls nearly 1,300 feet in the 1,400 miles between today's Kisangani and the ocean. Much of that drop, however, occurs in two hundred–plus miles of rock-studded white water that extends from today's capital, Kinshasa, to just above Matadi, and makes riverboat travel between the two impossible. In effect, most of the Congo River basin is landlocked.

4

Hired or impressed porters constituted what passed for the Congo's historic transportation system around the chokepoints of the river's lower rapids. Thanks to the labor of these wretched men, the standard nineteenth-century economic unit of measure in the Congo was the "load," a roughly thirty-kilogram (sixty-five-pound) bundle carried atop the head. Everything that could be moved was denominated in "loads," and lift was contracted for by Europeans in units of "loaded heads." Huge numbers of Congolese and other Africans were enmeshed in this business. An estimate for 1888

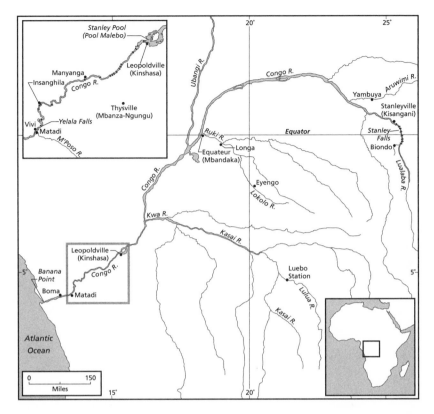

Map 1. "The Congo River, from its headwaters to the Atlantic Ocean." Only the Amazon's drainage basin is larger than the Congo's. From the highlands of equatorial Africa, the north-flowing Congo River curls in a great counterclockwise arc toward the eastern Atlantic, draining a watershed of roughly 1.5 million square miles, twice the size of the Mississippi's. This vast expanse contained in the late nineteenth century uncounted tens of millions of native people who among them spoke more than two hundred languages. The Congo is tidal for sixty miles upriver and navigable by oceangoing vessels for twice that distance, all the way to Matadi. There, or at Vivi on the opposite bank, rapids, waterfalls, and swirling currents forced the nineteenth-century traveler to leave the river and hike overland to Stanley Pool. *Map by Christopher Robinson*

counted more than 60,000 loads moved by porters between the lower and upper Congo during the year, representing almost two thousand tons of freight and personal effects.[1]

Although experiments with donkeys and mules were made, it soon became clear that moving through the cataract region was possible only on foot. No beasts of burden, other than long-suffering native porters struggling under half their own weight in loads stacked on rag cushions on their heads, could long survive the poor forage conditions and many endemic diseases of the area or negotiate as surely as men could the many rain-swollen tributaries that flowed into the river from both sides. It's possible that for a time the only draft animals anywhere in the Congo's vast drainage basin in the 1880s were three pampered mules, the personal property of the Congo Free State's first administrator-general. They were fed on grains and grasses imported from Europe.[2]

Native porters didn't dine nearly as well as did the administrator-general's mules. Edward Glave, a young Englishman whose years of experience in the Congo ended with his death there at thirty-two in May 1895, described porters from the Bakongo tribe with admiration, but without sympathy. These men were, he wrote in 1890, "slight and only poorly developed; but the fact of their carrying on their head from sixty to one hundred pounds' weight twenty miles a day, sometimes for six consecutive days, their only food being each day a little manioc root, an ear or two of maize, or a handful of peanuts pronounces them at once as men of singularly sound stamina."[3] Expedition cost estimates priced victuals for a native porter at one British shilling per day. In comparison, a white man's daily ration (his "chop," in the slang of the Congo) was budgeted at twelve times that much.

Like the lower Congo's rapids, tropical disease also slowed the Europeans' assault on the continent's riches. Foreigners who stepped ashore into the vast Petri dish that was (and still is) equatorial Africa entered a region so naturally rich in disabling and killing diseases that well into the last millennium human populations there grew more slowly than elsewhere on the globe.[4] Early-nineteenth-century British probes up West Africa's rivers, for example, typically saw between one- and two-thirds of their members fall ill and die, occasionally even more.

The "melancholy and disastrous" African expedition in 1816 of Capt. James Tuckey of the Royal Navy is a case in point. His two-ship squadron, the sloop HMS *Congo* and a reconfigured whaler, *Dorothy*, set out that year from Deptford on the River Thames in late February with fifty-four men to see if the Niger and the Congo Rivers were joined. Forced to turn back after fewer than three hundred miles of inland travel by boat and foot up the Congo, by the time the party's wan survivors raised anchor to return home that autumn thirty-five were dead, killed by yellow fever and malaria. One of them was Captain Tuckey. The fragmentary and incoherent last entries in his journal, *Narrative of an Expedition to Explore the River Zaire, Usually Called the Congo* (William B. Gilley, 1818), reveal a swift terminal descent.

Figures 1 and 2. Belgian sculptor Arthur Dupagne's vandalized and defaced statue of three exhausted Congo Free State porters is in two pieces. The larger piece, including the two more or less intact side figures on their shared base, stands alongside the nineteenth-century caravan path between Matadi and Leopoldville (just uphill from the old railroad bridge across the M'poso River, where hundreds died putting in the railroad). The truncated remains of the major figure, the center *porteur*, lie some miles away, not far from the Matadi riverfront on the grounds of the city's railroad terminal. An effort to have the two pieces reunited and the sculpture restored has failed because of central government disinterest and a lack of Bas-Congo Province government funds. Dupagne (1895–1961) spent 1927–35 in the Congo's Kasai watershed diamond fields. Between 1935 and his sudden death twenty-five years later, Dupagne sculpted some 350 bronzes, most inspired by his years in Africa.
AUTHOR'S PHOTOGRAPHS

Industrial-strength exploitation of the Congo's inanimate trade goods, initially ivory and then natural rubber, much later copper, other minerals, and hardwoods, was paced by the availability of steam propulsion: first steam boats to haul cargo along the Congo's long navigable stretches and some twenty years later a steam railroad to move it around the river's obstructing rapids. All this machinery had to be man-hauled into the interior beyond Matadi piecemeal. The requirement for portability slowed the introduction of modern technology and delayed the penetration of the continent by outsiders.

Among these outsiders was an American, Lt. Emory Herbst Taunt, U.S. Navy, whose three trips to equatorial Africa between 1885 and 1891—the third to fill the post of first resident American official at Boma on the Congo—might have made him a senior partner in the rush for plunder and much better known today than he is. That is had he not died January 18, 1891, at age thirty-nine, virtually alone, unemployed and disgraced, bankrupt and feverish at the mouth of the Congo. This book is his story, and more generally, it's the story of the United States and the Congo in the last decades of the nineteenth century.

Figure 3. "The Sectional Steamer 'Le Stanley' Leaving Vivi Beach." The effort required to bring steam power to central Africa was enormous. On June 5, 1885, Lt. Emory Taunt's small expedition hiked upriver past disassembled sections of the steamer *Stanley* being hauled around the Congo's cataracts on the way to Stanley Pool at a rate of less than half a mile per day. "Each section" of the vessel, Taunt later wrote in his report to the secretary of the navy, "was transported on a large iron-wheeled truck that required about ninety men to handle. Some fourteen months had already been occupied in the work of transportation at an immense cost to the State. . . . The advance sections of the steamer *Stanley* arrived in Leopoldville on June 24, having taken some fifteen months from Banana." *Stanley*'s sections were constructed in Alfred Yarrow's shipyard behind Folly Wall on the Isle of Dogs, the heart of early English iron shipbuilding at the great horseshoe bend in the River Thames just downstream of London. STANLEY, CONGO AND THE FOUNDING OF ITS FREE STATE

2

The U.S. Navy in West African Waters

Chief Engineer Smith . . . was on the Kearsarge when she visited the Congo River and was 60 days at a Dutch trading port on the river. He said the United States commissioner sent to investigate the Congo Country was not satisfied with it. It was not a fit place for Americans to settle in. The climate was bad, the water was miserable, and fever was plentiful. There were a number of cases of fever on the Kearsarge during her trip, but there were no deaths.

New York Times, *July 5, 1885*

5

Saturday, May 2, 1885, was a beautiful day at the mouth of the Congo River. The sky was fair, the water calm; a light sea breeze was blowing, holding the temperature in the low 80s. Lt. William Potter, USN, USS *Lancaster*'s duty officer during the forenoon watch, carefully recorded those descriptions of the weather off Banana Point in the ship's deck log, where he also noted without comment that Lt. Emory Taunt, the junior of eight lieutenants on board and coincidently one of his Naval Academy classmates, had left *Lancaster* that morning alone to proceed up the Congo River.

Standing on the Point, with all of Africa rising to the east and the ship's boat, which had delivered him and his kit to the beach, already pulling toward *Lancaster* at anchor in front of him, Lieutenant Taunt, thirty-four, would have had good reason to feel anxious. *Lancaster*'s squadron mate, USS *Kearsarge*, had steamed out of the same anchorage just before noon heading for Monrovia, Liberia, carrying the European Squadron's records, with all on board once again happy to leave the Congo, their second departure from there in five months. *Lancaster*, Taunt's familiar home at sea since December 2 (when he'd reported on board in France for duty with Rear Adm. Earl English's personal staff), was herself now preparing to get under way for a slow, two-month-long crossing of the South Atlantic to Rio de Janeiro. Half that time would be spent at anchor off the island of St. Helena, where Admiral English was to stay ashore at "Longwood," the large bungalow that some sixty years earlier had witnessed Napoleon Bonaparte's life in captivity ended by cancer. *Lancaster*'s departure just before five o'clock that afternoon would leave Taunt, he thought, the only American and one of the few white men in the vastness of equatorial Africa.[1]

In the nineteenth century several U.S. Navy officers were sent alone or nearly so into mysterious or distant places of the world, for one reason or another assigned tasks with little obvious connection to the business of their parent service. One such was Lt. William Lynch, who in 1848 led the U.S. Navy's small boat expedition down the Jordan River and onto the Dead Sea. His mission was to establish the sea level of this unique salt lake in the heart of Ottoman Syria and to collect scientific data and specimens in and around it.[2] He managed brilliantly with the loss of only one life. Lynch later unsuccessfully petitioned to be allowed to explore the mouth of the La Plata River, and after that the coast of West Africa, to seek out a homeland for former American slaves.

Another was Lt. James Gilliss, the disappointed would-be chief of the navy's new celestial observatory in Washington, who equipped with a portable, American-made refractor telescope left the capital in 1849 for Chile on a thirty-nine-month mission to observe Mars and Venus, to establish the parallax of the sun, and so to fix its distance from earth. His answer: 96,160,000 statute miles.[3]

The best-known of these and other stalwarts, thanks to Gary Kinder's *Ship of Gold in the Deep Blue Sea* (Atlantic Monthly Press, 1998), was Lt. William Herndon. He famously traveled the length of the Amazon from its headwaters in Peru to its mouth on the Atlantic in a dugout during 1851–52. Herndon's twelve-month trip downriver—in reality a covert inspection cooked up by his brother-in-law, the well-known oceanographer Lt. Matthew Fontaine Maury, USN, to see if Brazil could become a suitable bolt-hole for slave-owning American planters—became the subject of a best-selling travelogue that is still in print.[4] On September 11, 1857, Herndon, then a merchant mariner on leave from the Navy, died heroically in dress uniform on the bridge of the side-wheel steamer SS *Central America*, bound for New York from Havana and off Cape Hatteras when she foundered in a killer hurricane, drowning practically all the men on board and taking with her millions of dollars in California gold.

Although Taunt's task seemed clear—Admiral English had just detached him from the staff to conduct a one-officer "mission of exploration" as far upriver as Stanley Pool—what his selection for the unusual assignment signified was not apparent. Was it a reward for performance and an opportunity to earn additional merit in pursuit of promotion? Or, more likely given his service record since graduation from Annapolis sixteen years earlier, was it a last chance to make up for a long history of personal and professional failures and to gain redemption in the eyes of the man who until that day had commanded the small squadron bobbing a short distance offshore, and whose orders had put Lieutenant Taunt on the ground alone in Africa?

Taunt had worked for English several times before: once at the Portsmouth Navy Yard in Kittery, Maine, during 1877–78, then in Washington, D.C., at the Bureau of Equipment and Recruiting in 1879–80 (English was chief of the bureau from 1878 to 1883), and there again in 1883, just before his assignment to USS *Thetis*. Their most significant relationship, however, was not professional but personal. In 1876 Emory Taunt married Mary Jane ("Mamie") English, the eldest of then-commodore English's three daughters while English was in his first year in command at Portsmouth. Their wedding was in handsome Quarters A, the commandant's hilltop house on the grounds of the shipyard. After 1876 and for the next ten years—while his father-in-law rose in rank and gained in influence—until February 1886, when Admiral English retired, this family connection almost certainly cushioned Taunt's career from the consequences of his erratic performance and poor reputation.

Admiral English (1824–1893) served in the U.S. Navy for forty-six years, beginning with appointment as a midshipman the day after his sixteenth birthday. He was a graduate of the first, 1846, Naval Academy graduating class and saw combat three times: in the Mexican-American War on board USS *Independence* at the capture of Mazatlan; in the Second Opium War, in the sloop-of-war USS *Levant*, when he suffered a leg wound during the Battle of the Barrier Forts; and finally in the Civil War, with the East Gulf and North Atlantic Blockading Squadrons.[5] During his long career English served on eight ships and commanded six others, including USS *Delaware*, flagship of the Asiatic Squadron, and USS *Congress*, on the European Station.

The tropical vista Taunt was studying so uncertainly was famous among sailors for its lethal fevers but little else. As long ago as forty years earlier, Master's Mate John Lawrence in the sloop USS *Yorktown* had embellished his description of *Yorktown*'s approach to the African coast, "that baleful and most deleterious of all regions, that most pestilential bower from which so few white men return that are induced to visit it—or if they return—they only reappear as shadows and phantoms of their former selves," with a chilling portrait of life's last symptoms:

> The being who ventures into these insidious realms . . . after a long and heavy sleep awakes: a heavy pain has settled into his head and back, soon his pulses quicken, his pains increase, his blood acquires the heat

Figure 4. Rear Adm. Earl English, USN, and the staff of the U.S. Navy's European Squadron on board USS *Lancaster* at Gibraltar, 1885. Lieutenant Taunt stands at the far right. The other officers (*left to right*) are Lt. Nathan Sargent; Capt. Edward Potter, *Lancaster*'s commanding officer; Admiral English; and Paymaster Charles Thompson. The five are wearing the dress uniform as defined in the 1883 edition of *Navy Uniform Regulations*: "chapeaus" (cocked hats), frock coats, epaulets, and swords. The senior of USS *Lancaster*'s two surgeons on the West African cruise, Passed Asst. Surgeon Presley Rixey, USN, the other English son-in-law riding the flagship, is not pictured here. Rixey, a resident of Culpeper, Virginia, like the Englishes, married the admiral's middle daughter, Earlena, the year after Taunt and Mamie were wed. Rixey's was by far the more successful career. He spent his last years on active duty as the surgeon general of the Navy and White House physician. *NAVAL HISTORY AND HERITAGE COMMAND PHOTO NHF-8*

of molten lead—it is too much for his brain—frenzy follows, he is held in lingering torments for an indefinite season, and then, unless fortune proves unusually kind, dies a raving maniac. Too often alas this is the fate of many a noble fellow.[6]

The experience of the Royal Navy's West African Squadron's crews in these waters approaching midcentury was no less dreadful, as fully—but less poetically—described by the squadron's surgeon, Dr. Alexander Bryson, in his *Report on the Climate and Principal Diseases of the African Station* (William Clowes and Sons, 1847). Bryson's report drew on his years at sea off West Africa and considered the medical histories of sixteen deployed ships' crews over the previous twenty-three years. The West Africa antislavery patrol, he concluded, was "the most disagreeable, arduous and unhealthy service that falls to the lot of British officers and seamen."

From the data, Bryson conceded that "we know not whether the true essential cause of fever be aerial, earthy, aqueous or electrical," although "swamp emanations" and "miasmic exhalations" were suspect. He did know that "the nearer boats approached the shore the greater risk of contracting disease, this again is much increased by landing, and still more so by sleeping on shore, whether on dry or marsh ground, whether in the bush or out of it, under cover or without cover; such imprudences are generally followed by fever of a most virulent and dangerous kind."

Treatments varied. Many (for example, emetics, cathartics, blood-letting, and blistering) were positively harmful. Some ("two drachms of calomel [a mercury compound] suspended in mucilage thrown into the rectum") were both injurious and weird. Others (cold sponging) were ineffective but briefly enhanced patient comfort. Only one (sulfate of quinine in several grain doses five or six times per day for two to four weeks) was beneficial, although no one knew why. One modern count has it that the Royal Navy lost 17,000 officers and men to disease on ships assigned to the East and West African antislavery patrols in the nineteenth century, roughly equivalent to losing the entire crew of a hundred-gun ship of the line every third year while the patrols were on station.

By the mid-1880s the U.S. Navy had nearly a century's worth of experience with tropical fevers, all of it bad. The service's usual approach to outbreaks—some combination of sanitation, fumigation, ventilation, isolation, and over-winter cold-soaking of the ship's hull in especially extreme cases—was uninformed by any understanding of the disease process and generally ineffective. So too was the medical treatment of the afflicted, who recovered, languished, or died pretty much in defiance of the care provided. Consequently, visitations of malaria and yellow fever in the decades after the American Revolutionary War invariably resulted in interrupted operations and high counts of diseased and dead. Quinine, "Peruvian bark," was an important exception to the ineffectiveness of the nineteenth-century pharmacopoeia against these (and most other) diseases, but it was useful only in the prevention and treatment of malaria.

Approaching the end of the century, foreigners in equatorial Africa drew on experience and anecdote to fashion their own rituals for preserving vitality in this threatening environment. Invariably these involved drinking wine, not hastily bottled plonk but the better vintages from France and Portugal. Alcohol, ingested not applied, played a big part in every Congo traveler's health-care routine.

Once back in Europe, Lieutenant Taunt warned readers of his report on the Congo about the necessity "at all times to exercise caution to keep the system free" of malarial fevers. Overexposure to the sun, sleeping in a draft, or sleeping without a head covering he described as fatal. Preserving health required avoiding great fatigue and chills, eating "a simple, nutritious diet, with a moderate allowance of good Bordeaux or Portuguese wine," and changing underclothes nightly.

Later, Taunt's successor in his last job in Africa, Dorsey Mohun, thought that the way to combat the Congo's enervating climate was to "wear woolen undershirts and flannel overshirts; always to have a good thick coat ready to put on while on the march . . . to keep from catching cold; keep out of all drafts." To these counterintuitive fashion notes Mohun added familiar dietary and medical advice: "Eat wholesome food with very little fat to it, accompanied by a glass of good Bordeaux or Vino Tinto. . . . Keep regular hours; take quinine and iron when you feel run down; do not allow yourself to become constipated. . . . If you wish to drink spirits, do so in the evening, but not to excess, and then take only the very best you can find." Taunt had recommended drinking spirits, too, "in cases of fatigue, wet, or sickness."

Few white men could drink river water and stay healthy, but not everyone agreed that Bordeaux wine was the alternative of choice. Marcus Dorman, a big game hunter and apologist for King Leopold and the Congo Free State during the first years of the twentieth century, and author of *A Journal of a Tour in the Congo* (J. Janssens, 1905), preferred a good claret or burgundy and identified whisky as the "healthiest spirit." Dorman also believed it was "well to have some medical comforts in the shape of champagne or brandy to take after attacks of fever," a prescription Taunt, whose champagne drinking was to get him into career-ending trouble, would have endorsed. As for drugs, Dorman suggested a visitor to Africa carry iron, quinine, and arsenic, to which usual three he added phenacetin, a new analgesic in the late 1880s but familiar in the 1900s.

6

Admiral English's flagship, the steam-powered, second-rate sloop-of-war *Lancaster*, was off west-central Africa in early May 1885 with her squadron mate because former secretary of the navy William Chandler had on December 5, 1884, ordered them there, before being replaced by William Whitney on March 7, 1885, a few days after Grover Cleveland took office as the twenty-fourth president of the United States—and the first Democrat in the White House since before the Civil War.

Chandler (1835–1917), scion of a distinguished New Hampshire family, had been very briefly in the mid-1860s the Navy's first solicitor and judge advocate general, and equally briefly assistant secretary of the treasury. In April 1882 he became the thirtieth secretary of the navy, serving in President Arthur's cabinet from April 1882 to March 1885. Later he spent fourteen years representing New Hampshire in the U.S. Senate.

The most interesting thing about Chandler, however, was not his years of public service but his second wife, Lucy Lambert Hale. Chandler's first wife, Ann, daughter of his home state's governor, died in 1871. Three years later Chandler, then a newspaper publisher in the state capital, married Lucy Hale, the second daughter of Senator John Hale of New Hampshire.

A decade earlier, Lucy (1841–1915) had been John Wilkes Booth's lover and fiancée. Booth died in April 1865 at Garrett's farm with her carte-de-visite photograph among his effects . . . hers and those of four other women. Curiously, given the sweep of then–secretary of war Edwin Stanton's search for the Lincoln assassination conspirators, Lucy appears not to have been arrested following the murder, the only one of Booth's familiars not to have been detained and interrogated by investigators.[7]

"In view of the fact that an American citizen, by his discoveries in Africa, was the first to reveal the importance of the Congo Country to the commercial interests of the world," Secretary Chandler wrote in explanation to Admiral English that December, "this Government seems justified in claiming a special influence in determining questions touching all foreign arrangements for the administration of this region, and especially in regard to the rules as to its commerce." In fact, Washington claimed in Europe no right to any such outsized role in equatorial Africa, but Chandler's introduction, linking famed African explorer Henry Morton Stanley's expeditions there to special status for the United States, was drafted exclusively for English's consumption. The stage set in that way, the lame duck secretary's detailed orders to the admiral followed:

> You are therefore directed to instruct the Commanding Officer of the U.S.S. "Kearsarge" to proceed to the vicinity of the mouth of the Congo, with the view of ascertaining whether a healthful point, well situated for a commercial resort, can be found on the Lower Congo, not already

lawfully appropriated by another Power, and whether a concession can be obtained from the native authorities for the exclusive use of a limited district for a depot and factorial establishment for the benefit of American citizens in that region. It is desirable that "Kearsarge" should remain some time in the vicinity of the Congo, both for the purpose of obtaining all the hydrographic information possible, as well as to report upon the action taken along the banks of the River by the Representatives of European Powers.

In consequence of the very general interest felt in regard to the political and commercial situations along the Congo, it is believed that the position taken by our Government will be strengthened by the presence in the vicinity for a time, of the Commander in Chief of the Naval Force on the European Station. You will therefore arrange the movement of the vessels of your command as to be able to proceed in the Flagship "Lancaster" to the mouth of the Congo about the first of February, next.

While it is important that the health of officers and crews should not be unnecessarily exposed and that to protect them every necessary sanitary measure should be adopted, your attention is called to the fact that it is of the first importance that the visit of the "Kearsarge" and that of the Flagship should not be hurried ones. The "Kearsarge" should not leave the vicinity of the Congo until after your arrival in order that you may be placed in possession of all the information obtained by her Commanding Officer. Your own visit should be of sufficient length to enable you to collect all the information likely to be of use to the various branches of the Government, or of general interest to the people of the United States.

Chandler had more in mind than shopping for a foothold on the continent and collecting hydrographic data and news of European maneuvering off West Africa. "You are directed to select an officer of intelligence and tact," he added, "to proceed up the Congo River as far as 'Stanley Pool,' if practicable, for the purpose of aiding you in preparing a thorough and detailed report of your observations to the Navy Department, and it is desired that he should make a long stay in the interior if requested by the United States Commercial Agent, for which purpose he may remain after the departure of the ship or ships."[8]

Obedient to Chandler's instructions but more than a week late, USS *Lancaster* sailed from France on February 9, 1885, immediately after lengthy repairs to her steam plant's circulating pump were completed. The delayed departure exasperated the outgoing navy secretary. So, too, during

Chandler's final winter in office did everything else about his commander in Europe. In the months just before presidential administrations rolled over in Washington from Republican to Democrat, Chandler and English lobbed testy letters and cables to each other across the ocean that separated them about the former's high expectations and the latter's leaden performance.

Secretary Whitney inherited his predecessor's suspicion that *Lancaster*'s long delay in her home port prior to sailing for Africa had been to support the admiral's social schedule, not essential repairs to her machinery. The issue roiled relations between the new secretary and the new commander-designate of the South Atlantic Squadron. English's defense, that he'd been encouraged by Chandler to bring his family to Europe, which he'd done after the threat of cholera in Mediterranean France had passed; that Villefranche had been the squadron's traditional homeport under many predecessors in command (he tiresomely named them all); that repairs to the channel way of *Lancaster*'s circulating pump had been necessarily lengthy; and that, withal, the Englishes entertained no more often than weekly, didn't mollify the incumbent secretary.

With two exceptions *Lancaster*'s passage through the western Mediterranean, out the Strait of Gibraltar, and down the West African coast was uneventful. The first exception arose in Senegal, where repairs to a boiler and condenser had to be made before she could steam on. The second came in the Gulf of Guinea off Libreville, where *Lancaster* had stopped on April 23 to coal—she'd burned twenty to thirty tons each day under way heading south—and to collect mail. The next day, at sea just north of the equator, King Neptune, his consort, and the royal couple's ragged court clambered onto her deck from below to conduct the Navy's traditional line-crossing ceremony. In the midst of that messy initiation, recounted Dr. Rixey in his autobiography, former secretary Chandler materialized on board with a traveling companion, a certain Mr. Sanford, for a short visit.[9] The two had been in Libreville also. There is no record of why they'd come so far to call on the admiral or what they might have said to him.

Lancaster arrived off the mouth of the Congo River three days later, on Monday, April 27, steaming cautiously into the dark anchorage before midnight. Not far off lay her squadron mate, the third-rate sloop-of-war USS *Kearsarge*, Cdr. William R. Bridgman, USN, commanding, anchored in six or so fathoms of water above a sandy bottom, good holding ground in a place sheltered on three sides from wind and weather.

Kearsarge had spent six days off Banana Point in mid-December, the last of several West African ports of call on her way south from Lisbon, Portugal.

After picking up seventy-five tons of coal on December 3 at infamous Cape Coast Castle (an old, fortified slave dungeon on Ghana's Gold Coast and a museum today), she got to Banana on December 16, and left just six days later for Porto Grande, Cape Verde, to coal again. There Bridgeman received a cable from English to return *Kearsarge* to the mouth of the Congo "without delay." Including an intervening stop at Monrovia, "without delay" turned out to mean March 9. When *Lancaster* arrived the last Monday in April, her renowned partner had been swinging at anchor off the Congo River for seven weeks.

By May Bridgeman and his crew must have been impatient to leave West Africa. His departure report to English on his observations was unpromising. "It would be unwise in the extreme for the Government to encourage American citizens to come to this region, either to engage in business enterprise or for any purpose," he wrote. "The climate is deadly; there is no food for the white man save what he brings with him; the difficulty of establishing a new business is very great, and the chance of profit very small. There is no such wealth in the Congo Valley as has been reported, nor have I any faith in the future predicted for it by interested persons." The requested hydrographic survey never got done, either. Bridgeman claimed he lacked the time, the expertise, and the necessary steam launch, although he did correct the charted latitude and longitude of Banana Point.

Beneath the newish paint and putty, both ships were survivors of the Union navy's sudden shrinkage at the end of the Civil War, a blowout on the scale of explosive decompression, and of the austere budgets and badly managed programs that followed. By the end of 1885 the U.S. Navy had shrunk to a few more than 1,600 officers and 8,200 enlisted men, to twenty-eight deployed ships worldwide (each at sea for three years at a time), and ten shore facilities. Secretary Whitney described plaintively the shore establishment in his first annual report to Congress at the end of the year as "falling rapidly into a condition of extreme decay," exhibiting dilapidation approaching "general destruction." His appraisal of the seagoing navy was no less bleak. "It is questionable," he wrote in the same report, "whether we have a single naval vessel finished and afloat at the present time that could be trusted to encounter the ships of any important power—a single vessel that has either the necessary armor for protection, speed for escape, or weapons for defense."[10]

Such American strength at sea as there was in the 1880s had been preserved since the Civil War largely by what amounted to keel-up rebuildings of obsolete ships, often retaining little but their name. In his final, 1884, annual report to Congress, Secretary Chandler had described this as "attempting to rehabilitate at great cost worn out structures in the name of repairs."[11] One year later, Whitney provided a specific example: the screw sloop USS *Omaha*, built at the Philadelphia Navy Yard in the late 1860s and then rebuilt there in the early 1880s for $572,000 in "an act of the greatest folly." "She is a repaired wooden vessel," he explained, "with boilers, machinery, and guns all of which would have at the time been sold for what they would have brought by any other nation on earth. In the event of a war she can neither fight nor run away from any cruiser built contemporaneously by any other nation. Her rebuilding cost the full price of a modern steel ship of her size and all modern characteristics."

Kearsarge was the beneficiary of this misguided policy in 1879 at the Portsmouth Navy Yard. Built in 1861 for $286,918, by 1885 almost four times her purchase price, $1,123,416, had been spent on maintenance and overhauls. So also was *Lancaster* at the same yard one year later. The policy was forced on the Navy by a House of Representatives determined to sustain shipyard workloads and employment levels and, thanks to the absence of domestic armored plate mills and gun foundries lobbying for new business, free of any political pressures for fleet modernization.

The result was that at the beginning of 1885, twenty-three years after the historic battle of the ironclads at Hampton Roads, of the thirty-one first-, second-, and third-rate combatant ships in commission in the U.S. Navy, only three had modern iron hulls. The rest were mostly tired, wooden men-of-war.

USS *Lancaster*, decorated with a superb 3,400-pound, gilded spread-eagle figurehead and the squadron commander's two-star flag flying from her mainmast, was the larger and more imposing of the two ships off Banana Point. In compensation, *Kearsarge*, a few years younger than her consort and carrying fewer than half of *Lancaster*'s crew, had by far the more interesting history. On June 19, 1864, during a violent, hour-long duel off Cherbourg, France, while hundreds watched from the shore, shells from *Kearsarge*'s two 11-inch Dahlgren pivot guns swiftly battered and sank CSS *Alabama* in the Civil War's second-most famous naval battle and put an end to that commerce raider's assault on the Union's merchant and whaling fleets.[12] For her part, *Lancaster* (coincidently with then-lieutenant William Bridgman in her crew) had spent the entire war in the Pacific without much that was useful to do.

At the end of her West African port visits, English tried to get *Kearsarge*, in commission for the past six years, sent home. "The boiler shows marked signs of weakening," he wrote to the secretary, quoting Bridgman, "the engine is much worn and . . . the hull and spars are no longer sound." His

Figure 5. "USS *Lancaster* at Sea off Naples." Oil painting by Luigi Roberto, 1882. In 1882 *Lancaster* flew the two-star flag of Rear Adm. James Nicholson, USN, commander of the U.S. Navy's European Squadron. *Lancaster* looks handsome in this privately owned painting, but by the mid-1880s such wooden, screw sloops-of-war were obsolescent in the navies of the world. Nicholson was relieved of command by Rear Adm. Charles Baldwin, USN, in March 1883. Two months later Baldwin took USS *Lancaster* to St. Petersburg, Russia, where he represented the United States at the coronation of Tsar Alexander III. He was, in turn, replaced at the head of the three-ship squadron by Rear Admiral English in September 1884. Roberto was an Italian maritime artist who specialized at the end of the nineteenth century in portraits of ships in the Bay of Naples. *COURTESY DENNIS BRADSHAW, ALEXANDRIA, VA.*

appeal failed. Worn out and unsound, *Kearsarge* nevertheless remained deployed for another fifteen months. From Africa she returned to European waters, and then late in 1885, and under a new commanding officer, she began an extended cruise of northern European ports in company with USS *Pensacola*, the new squadron flagship.

Not so *Lancaster*. At first, the news in December 1884 that *Lancaster* was leaving the Mediterranean on a cruise to West Africa had made many of her 460-man crew, foreigners who had expected to complete their enlistments in home waters, unhappy. Their unhappiness turned to despair when the following March the ship's company learned that this was no routine deployment; instead, their ship was being transferred to join USS *Nipsic* in the Navy's small South Atlantic Squadron. English's new two-ship squadron was anemic, but its area of responsibility was vast. It encompassed not only the waters off the east coast of South America but also those that washed the coast of Africa south of Luanda and around the tip of the continent into the Indian Ocean all the way north to the equator.[13]

Admiral English suspected the squadron reassignment was a demotion, punishment for moving some women of his family to Nice, France, in December and living with them on shore while *Lancaster* was in port nearby at Villefranche-sur-Mer. The four who had wintered over in the admiral's rented villa on Avenue Verdi included English's wife, Elizabeth; two of their daughters, Mary and Frances ("Frankie"); and a grandchild, Mary and Emory Taunt's little girl, Earlena. Meanwhile, it was surmised that the officers of the flagship and staff, absent the admiral's oversight, had been "exposed to the vices of Nice and Monaco" for most of the season. Exposure they'd likely savored.

Admiral English's reassignment and *Lancaster*'s intersquadron transfer were believed by some at home—and by English, too—to have been the devious work of Rear Adm. John Walker (USNA, 1856), the powerful chief through most of the 1880s of the Bureau of Navigation in Washington. Reportedly Admiral Walker, styled as the "Grand Vizier of the American Navy" by the *New York Times*, had been offended by comments allegedly made about him by squadron junior officers during some of Elizabeth English's soirées ("high carnivals") in Nice, and the abrupt relocations were thought to have been Walker's revenge for these crimes of lèse-majesté.[14]

Walker's role in officer assignments derived from the fact that the secretary of the navy's control over officer careers, ultimately managed for him by an "Office of Detail," had been transferred in 1862 from the Navy Secretariat to the Bureau of Navigation as part of a broad reform of the department mandated by Congress.

The *Times* had a long running feud with "King John" Walker, the "autocrat of the Navy," and its reporting on *Lancaster*'s intersquadron transfer may be overdrawn or complete fiction. One month earlier the newspaper had charged that Walker had grasped firm control of the Navy two years before from a new and indolent secretary through diverting mail coming into the department from the secretariat to his bureau. Critical articles about Walker (1835–1907) continued to appear in the *Times* at least through 1894.

Whether or not Admiral English's officers had committed some breach of discipline over the year-end holidays and, if so, what it might have been wasn't certain then and isn't now. Most newspapers reported that the aggrieved party was not Admiral Walker but Secretary of the Navy Chandler, who'd been "roundly abused" from afar by *Lancaster*'s junior officers during social events on board the flagship (those same "high carnivals") for having ordered their ship to Africa. That's the gossipy story the aptly named Worcester, Massachusetts, *Daily Spy*, and the land-locked Macon, Georgia, *Daily Telegraph and Messenger*, among others, ran.

The *Philadelphia Inquirer* reported accurately in February 1885 that English had convened an investigation into allegations that USS *Lancaster*'s officers had "criticized Secretary Chandler offensively." The secretary had insisted on the investigation. He'd received a letter from an American citizen in Nice who at a party on New Year's Eve at the Grand Hotel had overheard *Lancaster*'s officers carping about their deployment orders. The ensuing interviews of the flagship's officers on February 4 "mortified" Admiral English. Every officer was required to sign a statement about what they had or had not said that evening. On February 6 Taunt signed his, denying any insubordination. For his part, Captain Potter, the ship's CO, was "deeply humiliated" that the Navy Department had "deemed it necessary to interrogate the officers of this ship in such a manner, and in consequence of such a report as that made by a self-styled American."

7

The operational reason Chandler and his successor, Whitney, had agreed to send two ships of their very small navy to equatorial Africa in early 1885 was to support a search for waterfront real estate. In his long report to the secretary of the navy on May 2, English told Whitney that all the suitable land was already occupied by European factories. Moreover, his investigation had revealed that good coal could be purchased from the Dutch, who stocked two to three thousand tons at Banana, or from the Portuguese at Luanda, not far away to the south, at reasonable prices. The *New York Herald* reported English's findings to its readers. "The Congo Country, All the Good Land Already Monopolized," read its headline on July 28, 1885, concluding, "A Poor Place for Americans . . . Not an El Dorado."

Even before USS *Lancaster*'s and USS *Kearsarge*'s 1885 African cruise the American flag and U.S. Navy jack were not unfamiliar off the West African coast. More than sixty years earlier, in 1820, the corvette USS *Cyane* (ex-HMS *Cyane*, one of USS *Constitution*'s prizes during the War of 1812) had escorted a merchant shipload of freed American slaves back to their home continent, the first installment in an experiment in repatriation that eventually saw its conclusion in the settlement of Liberia, but never fulfilled its backers' great and disparate hopes. The enormous population of slaves in the United States in the nineteenth century before the Civil War—nearly 894,000 in the 1800 census, almost 2 million in 1830, more than 4 million in 1860—guaranteed that no transatlantic resettlement scheme could be affordable or succeed in anything other than a symbolic way.[15]

Some twenty years after *Cyane* sailed for Liberia, and a year after the Webster-Ashburton Treaty of 1842 formalized American participation in the South Atlantic's international antislavery patrol, a small U.S. Navy squadron took up station off West Africa to suppress slave trading by vessels flying the American flag, and coincidently to protect American commerce in distant waters. (Thirty years was not long enough after the War of 1812 for Washington to accept Royal Navy ships stopping and inspecting American shipping at sea. The authority was granted twenty years later, in the 1862 "Treaty between the United States and Great Britain for the Suppression of the Slave Trade.") That squadron, operating awkwardly from a distant base in the Cape Verde Islands and required by treaty to carry a minimum of eighty guns, remained deployed on this mission until the start of the Civil War. Thanks largely to the determination of the Royal Navy, the long-lived ocean patrol might have been responsible for intercepting and freeing as many as 10 percent of the slaves being shipped to the New World; tragically, that still meant many hundreds of thousands of Africans slipped through the blockade to a life as property. Slavers' cunning, the small size of "U.S. Naval Forces, West Coast of Africa," as the American squadron was also known, and a lack of enthusiasm for the mission on the part of the Navy's eight (of eleven) service secretaries from southern states during those decades account in part for its relatively modest results.

Following a hiatus during and for some years after the Civil War, beginning in 1873 U.S. Navy ship visits to West Africa became almost routine. Not counting Admiral English's, there were ten such visits between 1873 and 1887 spaced at roughly eighteen-month intervals. Three of these extended for more than six months. A May 1879 visit into the mouth of the Congo by USS *Ticonderoga*, prompted by the same Henry Sanford who six years later visited *Lancaster* at sea off West Africa, saw two ship's company officers (Lieutenant Francis Drake and Paymaster William Thomson) go upriver some thirty miles to assess commercial possibilities. The obvious hostility of Dutch traders to the prospect of American competition dissuaded Commo. Robert Shufeldt, USN, the flag officer riding *Ticonderoga*, from filing a positive report despite the fact that Drake and Thomson claimed Dutch traders were realizing profits of 300–400 percent annually.

This history aside, the presence of first one and then a second U.S. Navy warship off Banana Point in early 1885 must have excited curiosity among the few European residents of the low-lying, crowded spit of land that was for a while longer the commercial heart of the world's newest country. Curiosity, too, about all the other men-of-war shuttling in and out of the anchorage, movements dutifully recorded in *Kearsarge*'s deck log as she swung idly at anchor. The mouth of the Congo became a popular port call for European navies in the mid-1880s. Writing from Berlin on November 3, 1884, Minister John Kasson reported some of the maneuvering for political advantage off West Africa to the secretary of state:

> Almost daily notices reach us either of efforts on the part of some European nation to take actual possession of unoccupied coasts or islands or sections of the interior, or of the dispatch of vessels of war to those regions for some unavowed purpose. Thus, during the last few days, we hear of the dispatch of two naval vessels by Italy, and of the immediate departure of one of the Spanish naval vessels from Cadiz; and of the reported imporation at Lisbon of a Congo native chief to claim the protection of that government against other European encroachments.

Lieutenant Taunt passed through Banana twice during 1885, while the small settlement (population roughly thirty Europeans and perhaps six hundred Africans) was enjoying the last of its glory years.[16] For a little while longer, until the lower 114 miles of the river (beyond the old slave port and soon-to-be new national capital of Boma all the way to the falls just upriver from Matadi, on the left bank) were surveyed and buoyed by a Danish team, Banana was the Free State's chief seaport on the Atlantic, its connection to Europe and the world.

Banana was also home to the headquarters of three of the six large European trading firms that did business in Congo: the Dutch-African Trading Company, Nieuwe Afrikaansche Handels Venootschap; Daumas, Béreud et Compagnie; and the Congo and Central African Company. (The last two French and English, respectively.)

The "immense depôt" of the Dutch (from a contemporary description by R. E. Dennett, writing in 1887 to members of the Manchester Geographical Society) was by far the largest property on Banana. Its counting house, storerooms, coal storage facilities, workshops, and cemetery encumbered fully half the peninsula. A high-water table, Dennett explained to his distant readers, often required a "coffin to be sunk with stones" before it could be

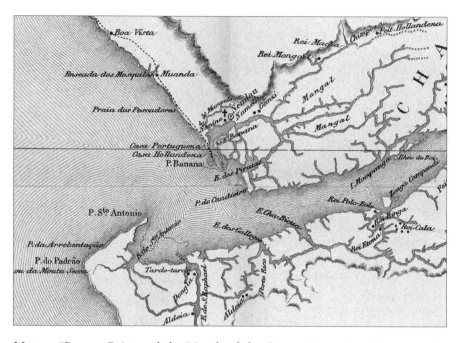

Map 2. "Banana Point and the Mouth of the Congo River, 1883." Ignoring the visible bits of what passed for European civilization at Banana Point, the vista in front of Lieutenant Taunt as he glanced up the beach had changed little during the four centuries since Diogo Cão first looked upon the same place then sailed around the corner and nosed his ship hesitantly upriver toward distant rapids to introduce Congo tribesmen to the clamorous outside world. "On the inner side of the little promontory," naturalist Sir Harry Hamilton Johnston had observed in 1894, "is a deep and capacious inlet of the Congo, where there is room for a whole navy to be moored. Here ships of the greatest size can be anchored within 50 yards of the shore." In fact, only those vessels drawing twenty-one feet or less could lay anchor, but that safe, deep-draft anchorage so close offshore made property on the spit, in Johnston's words, "as valuable as in some civilized cities." Out of sight farther east lay more than 1,400 miles of rocky escarpments, grassland, and rainforest between Banana and Stanley Falls, miles dotted with the twenty-two stations Stanley had built for Leopold II. *Detail from* Carta de Curso de Rio Zaire de Stanley-Pool ao Oceano, *1883; David Rumsey Historical Map Collection*

interred in any of the several cemeteries on the point. The peninsula stood only six feet above high water. The substantial Dutch operation shouldered the French factory of Daumas, Béreud, a cluster of Free State government buildings that included shacks housing a court and post office, and next to them the English factory, to the far (north) side of a tidal swamp and onto what remained of the point's dry land. An improvised prison, an iron hulk—the remains of an Austrian shipwreck—beached at the high-water line, completed the visible European presence on the right bank of the mouth of the Congo River.

These structures faced an anchorage thick with river traffic that hosted monthly scheduled cargo and mail service to and from England, Germany, and Portugal by steamship. By the early 1890s two Dutch and two French embarkation ports had been added to the mix, and it was possible to sail from Europe to Banana, Boma, or Matadi, depending on the carrier. Still, such was the flow of travelers moving in and out of Congo through the place that, until a second was opened with much fanfare in Boma in March 1890, Banana boasted the only hotel on the river. Banana's hotel, like much else on the sandspit Dutch owned and operated, offered accommodations for twenty. On his second trip to Africa Taunt complained to his civilian boss about the going rate for rooms at Banana, fully twice that of equivalent lodgings in Europe, he reported.

Figure 6. Banana Point from the air today. Banana has not been for many decades the busy, strategically important western gateway to equatorial Africa it once was. As Boma and Matadi flourished, Banana declined into a quiet fishing village. The peninsula and its adjacent anchorage are now home to an oilfield services company associated with the rigs offshore and to a Congolese navy base that features wretched quarters for sailors' families but little else that appears naval. Between the base and the point's southern tip lie the revetted remains and spotting towers of a long-since-abandoned twentieth-century shore battery. A few vacant picnic pavilions occupy the remaining real estate. *AUTHOR'S PHOTOGRAPH*

3

"Colonel" Willard Tisdel,
U.S. Commercial Agent

It will be impossible, except in general terms, to give a description of the country through which the Congo flows. Many travelers have as many different views, although all agree that the low land of fetid black muck and luxuriant vegetation between the sea-coast and the first high land . . . is a hotbed of fatal fevers, and that beyond Vivi for a distance of more than six hundred miles, the climate is positively dangerous. No traveler is known to have escaped the terrible fevers of this pestilential country, and lucky are they—and few these be—who live to tell the tale of their experience.

Willard P. Tisdel, "The Realm of Congo"

8

Lieutenant Taunt was the second American dispatched on an official mission up the Congo into equatorial Africa in the mid-1880s. He traveled the river in the wake of the first, "Colonel" Willard Parker Tisdel, of Painesville, Ohio, who in April 1884 was appointed by President Chester Arthur's secretary of state, Frederick Frelinghuysen, to survey the river basin and to report on the possibility of trade between the place and the United States.[1]

Tisdel's commission as commercial agent for the Congo basin was fallout from a Senate resolution on April 22 announcing American diplomatic recognition of King Leopold II's aspirations in Africa, months ahead of similar actions by Germany, Austria-Hungary, the Netherlands, the remaining Europeans, and Turkey. "The government of the United States," that resolution read, "announces its sympathy with and approval of the humane and benevolent purposes of the International Association of the Congo, administering, as it does, the interests of the states there established, and will order the officers of the United States, both on land and sea, to recognize the flag of the International Association of Congo as that of a friendly government."

Recognition was an invaluable gift to Leopold. It unilaterally granted statehood and legal status to the International Association of the Congo, which until then had been an anomaly: not a country; not a company; not, like the twenty-year-old Red Cross, a transnational institution; not much more than Leopold's personal ambition graced by an invented flag.

Washington's recognition had been prompted by the adept lobbying of "General" Henry Shelton Sanford, who between 1861 and 1869 was the U.S. minister (ambassador) to King Leopold's court and government in Brussels. Sanford's diplomatic career dated back to 1847 at St. Petersburg, where he was secretary to the American legation in the Russian capital. The next year, during the excitement of the European revolutions of 1848, he was legation secretary in Frankfurt, the capital of the German state of Hesse and a center of unification agitation. Sanford moved on in 1849 to Paris, where for the last of his four years there he served as chargé.

Sanford's appointment to the chief American foreign service position in Belgium came from President Lincoln in March 1861, the new president's first such nomination, thanks to boosting by two supporters from New York, Secretary of State William Seward and publisher Thurlow Weed. Both men were close friends of one of Sanford's maternal uncles, Philo Shelton.

Sanford served ably in Brussels during the Civil War, and managed Union intelligence operations in Europe besides. He was credited, perhaps correctly, by *the National Cyclopedia of American Biography* (James T. White and Company, 1897) with cornering for the Union during the war the European market for saltpeter at "risk of his whole fortune," and with shipping four hundred tons of it to the United States, enough to make more than a million pounds of gunpowder. The anecdote suggests meritorious patriotism and deep pockets. Not everything he did during the war years was so weighty. He was one of two American ministers in Europe, the other being George Marsh in Rome, who under instructions from Secretary of State Seward in autumn 1861 attempted to recruit the Italian patriot Giuseppe Garibaldi to the Union cause with the offer of a major general's commission. Garibaldi's conditions, including assignment to overall command of the Union army, were too onerous to accept, and nothing came of the bizarre initiative beyond embarrassment in Washington when it became public.

In 1869 Sanford was nominated by President Grant to be the American minister in Madrid, replacing former senator John Hale, Lucy's father, in the Spanish capital. Hale appears to have been Lincoln's last diplomatic appointment, an assignment made on the morning of the assassination in April 1865. The next several years saw Hale and his chief subordinate, Horatio Perry, the legation secretary, battle like scorpions in a bottle over which of the two was guilty of gross (or grosser) malfeasance in office. The nasty squabble saw both Secretary Seward and the *New York Times* take sides against Hale, who eventually resigned his post, effective July 1869.

Figure 7. Willard Parker Tisdel (1844–1911), U.S. Commercial Agent. Tisdel was an international businessman seasoned in the South American tropics, an environment in some ways analogous to equatorial Africa's. He was, moreover, fluent in four languages, including Portuguese, the Congo's first European language. When his appointment was announced in Washington on August 22, 1884, the next day's *New York Times* detailed his credentials for the post. The president, the *Times* wrote, had selected Tisdel because of "his peculiar fitness for the place." Supposedly as a reward for good service in the Congo, Tisdel was later named by President Cleveland to be minister to Ecuador, but either because he turned the nomination down (the *Pan American Union*'s take on it) or because he was denied Senate confirmation (the *Times*' opinion), he never filled the post in Quito. PHOTOGRAPH FROM THE BULLETIN OF THE PAN AMERICAN UNION, SEPTEMBER 1911, 596

For Sanford, historic, handsome Madrid would have been an upgrade from Brussels, but sadly for him, his nomination got caught up in maneuvering Senate egos, and he wasn't confirmed—not in the spring, when the subject of replacing Hale was first considered, and not later that summer, when Hale's resignation became effective. Instead, when the Senate came back in session, a onetime diplomat and hell-raising former Union major general, Daniel Sickles of New York, got the job in Madrid, with a charge to try to buy Cuba from Spain. Sickles had been offered the senior post in Mexico first, but turned it down as beneath him.[2]

The embarrassing shuffle in Washington, and perhaps the fact that he'd lost out twice—the second time in competition with a notorious character—provoked Sanford's resignation. No longer after 1869 the American minister and now self-employed, he remained in Belgium with his family, living on investments and working his contacts at court and back home.

The Madrid disappointment aside, Sanford still had weight in the American capital and a real talent for lobbying influential countrymen over elegant dinners in the service of his new best friend, Leopold. He also had enough residual heft in official Washington in December 1883 to have a self-serving paragraph of fiction about "the rich and populous Valley of the Kongo" inserted into President Arthur's State of the Union address.[3] This coup might have been, in part, fallout from a nearly three-week-long vacation President Arthur and a small party had passed in Florida that April. Secretary of the Navy Chandler, too, had been among a few, happy tourists who with the President had enjoyed Sanford's hospitality (but not his company as their absent host was in Europe) at Belair Grove and in the Sanford Hotel during the weekend of April 8–9.[4]

Arthur's ghostwritten remarks about the "Kongo" in his address reminded members of the influential New York State Chamber of Commerce (the nation's first organization of businessmen) that they'd heard something very similar about the place before, from Sanford himself in 1879. Members confessed they'd "slumbered since," but on January 10, 1885, memories jogged, the Chamber awoke to resolve that

> it is incumbent upon the Government of the United States . . . to apprise the Portuguese Government that it . . . denies the right of the latter to interfere with the free navigation of the Congo . . . and that the entry, four hundred years ago, into the mouth of the Congo by the Portuguese, not having been followed up by actual and continued occupation, can give that nation no territorial right to the river or to the countries upon its banks.

The recognition by the Government of the United States of the flag of the International African Association [*sic*], now extending over twenty-two settlements, in the heart of Africa, will be but an acknowledgement of the fact that the organization, under rights ceded to it by African chiefs of independent territories, is exercising rule and authority over a large part of Africa, in the protection of life and property, the extinguishment of the slave trade, the facilitating of commercial intercourse, and other attributes of sovereignty.

The chamber's resolutions were promptly sent to Washington. Just as their English counterparts in Manchester had four months earlier when briefed by Stanley on opportunities in equatorial Africa, New York's business elite happily plumped for a regime in the "rich and populous Valley of the Kongo" with which they thought they could do business. Secretary Frelinghuysen passed this additional ammunition over to friends in the U.S. Senate, late but still helpful in nourishing the motivation of the Congo's American enthusiasts.

Years later, as evidence of what the Congo had become under Leopold's sole proprietorship began to leak out of Africa, the wisdom of the United States' front-running role in recognition came under question, by no one more sharply than Mark Twain. Twain, in 1905 thoroughly disillusioned by American imperialism in the Philippines, looked back two decades with corrosive contempt at how, when Leopold hoisted his flag, he "'took in' a president of the United States, and got him to be the first to recognize it and salute it." Quoting Leopold's imagined, fevered confession, he had the king say, "It is a deep satisfaction for me to remember that I was a shade too smart for that nation that thinks itself so smart. Yes, I certainly did bunco a Yankee—as those people phrase it. Pirate flag? Let them call it so—perhaps it is. All the same, they were the first to salute it."[5] In the mid-1880s, however, being the first to salute the Congo's flag appeared to be a low-cost good idea, a way into a rich marketplace, but it put the United States (Twain noted) in the position of being "the only democracy in history that has lent its power and influence to the establishing of an *absolute monarchy.*"

Henry Sanford, inscrutable behind thick lenses, tall and slender, dark and bearded, later in life could have been central casting's nomination to play the manipulative monk Rasputin. He appears throughout the shared history of America and the Congo Free State, sometimes as here, in full frontal visibility, other times leaving behind only faint pug marks. Almost certainly he was the unidentified "Sanford" who was former navy secretary Chandler's companion on board *Lancaster* off Libreville as she steamed south, and equally certainly the presence of the two on the flagship had to do with Sanford's nascent business interests in the Congo and Taunt's mission to come.

During Chandler's last year in office, Sanford had several times urged the navy secretary to grant leave to Navy officers "of tried capacity and distinction" so they could become chiefs of some of King Leopold's stations on the Congo and so block the further expansion of British influence along the river. (In European capitals real or imagined Portuguese ambitions in the Congo drove policy making. In the United States the impetus was not so much fear of Portugal's designs as the nation's commercial rivalry with Great Britain, or the scary prospect of a British-Portuguese condominium in equatorial Africa that would freeze out the trade of others. Still, Portugal's "filthy, puerile and mischievous pretensions," Sanford's words, required American attention, too.) Sanford went so far as to suggest to Chandler that if congressional appropriations proved insufficient to fund a generous salary for these beached officers, private parties would be happy to supplement them.

The American grant of recognition was, however, done cautiously rather than enthusiastically, and in the face of some resistance in the House of Representatives, where it was feared such activism raised the threat of countervailing challenges to the Monroe Doctrine. Behind the oddly formulated recognition language, conceding at first not much more than willingness to render honors to the national colors, were two American foreign policy objectives: to avoid getting caught up in the conflicting Portuguese and French territorial claims in the region and to keep the Congo basin intact and "under neutral control," such that its "prospective rich trade" would be open to Americans on the same terms as enjoyed by Europeans. Secretary Frelinghuysen explained to a dubious Congress and to diplomats in the field that this stance was consistent with the traditional U.S. policy of shunning foreign entanglement. Significantly, Frelinghuysen reminded his new subordinate, Tisdel, on December 12 that his was a commercial assignment, not a diplomatic one.

Tisdel's appointment, announced to the public in late August, was welcomed by advocates of U.S. trade with Africa. "Congress surely has not taken a step too soon in authorizing the President to appoint a commissioner to the states of the Congo Association in the interest of American commerce," Frith Charlesworth, the American consul in Madeira, wrote in September 1884. "As it is now the trade of the United States is confined to an occasional sailing vessel loaded with petroleum, wheat, corn, lumber, and stores, and occasionally canned goods, salt, and dried fish. Outside of these commodities American goods that find a market in these islands and on the

Figure 8. "General" Henry Shelton Sanford (1823–1891). Sanford was born in Woodbury, Connecticut, the scion of an old Connecticut family, an early member of which had been the state's first colonial governor. In 1849 Sanford graduated with distinction from the University of Heidelberg, in the Grand Duchy of Baden, with a degree in law, but he practiced his profession only sporadically. His adult life was spent in U.S. diplomatic service in Europe or in private business at home and abroad, in which he was notably inept. Sanford dissipated a substantial inheritance during his life through unwise investment, bungled management, and poor personnel recruiting. The city of Sanford, Florida, on the site of a twenty-three-square-mile land grant he purchased in 1870, is his sole enduring success. Sanford died May 21, 1891, in Healing Springs, Virginia, of kidney disease, four months after Taunt's death on the river. *Matthew Brady photograph, Library of Congress*

African coast are first brought to England or elsewhere in Europe, largely rebranded or remarked, and put upon the market under a new name."[6] Consuls in Gaboon and Sierra Leone echoed Charlesworth's interest in expanding American trade with their markets.

The expectation was that millions of nearly naked black Africans who possessed practically nothing would in quick time become eager consumers of everything the industrialized world had on offer. A huge new market. The possibilities were intoxicating, as Henry Morton Stanley had suggested quite seriously during a speech to James Hutton, president, and the assembled members of the Manchester Chamber of Commerce in late October 1884. That talk was the first of three speeches Stanley gave in Manchester during the third week of October, a part of Leopold II's well-developed and carefully managed campaign to gain British diplomatic recognition for his property. The other two talks were delivered to the city's geographical and antislavery societies. All three were reported in *The Times* of London in its issues of October 22 and 23 in stories that were promptly quoted by the *New York Times*.

Stanley, whose knowledge of equatorial Africa after three extended expeditions there over a dozen years was accepted to be perfect, drifted off his chief subject—the abuse of Portuguese commercial aspirations in the Congo—to tantalize his friendly Chamber audience. "It was the easiest matter in the world to induce Africans to wear cotton," *The Times* reported Stanley as telling them, "but it would take them centuries to learn how to make it themselves," hence the opportunity that could become "a second India."

Stanley estimated that furnishing every inhabitant of the Congo basin— he thought there might be as many as forty million of them—with just seven outfits (two for Sunday, four for every day, and one for wear at night) and a burial shroud, and every family with a stash of cloth as trade goods, amounted to £26 million annually in sales of Manchester calico at two pennies per yard, not including, he told his rapt mill town audience, "your own superior prints, your gorgeous handkerchiefs with their variegated patterns, your checks and striped cloths, your ticking and twills."

"Your own imagination," Stanley continued, gracefully pushing aside this huge sum in pounds sterling, "will no doubt carry you to the limbo of immeasurable and incalculable millions." Members of the chamber, enthusiastic colonialists all, cooperated fully, passing a supportive resolution. Reportedly, some hungry entrepreneurs left Manchester for Africa soon after the speech, apparently without pausing long to ask from where in the impoverished continent these "incalculable millions" of pounds would be coming—given that ivory was being purchased not with money but with gin, beads, seashells, lengths of brass wire, used clothing, and other near-worthless trade goods.

Months later, the following August in London, Stanley performed a similar multiplication trick using cutlery instead of cottons, telling a traveling *New York Herald* correspondent to imagine the 5 million fathers of Congo families, another 5 million youths approaching manhood, and a further 10 million boys, every one of whom would want a cheap, cow bone–handled table knife. Twenty million knives right there and, he noted wisely, "such knives do not last forever."

Because the first Congo census was not conducted until 1924, Stanley had no scientific basis for his population estimates. Like guessing the number of jelly beans in a gallon jar, he apparently relied on nothing more precise than estimating the number of residents in an average village and then estimating the number of such villages in the Congo. The result produced numbers that ranged between 29 and something over 40 million. Multiplicand and multiplier were both suspect in Stanley's market calculations; their product drove the illusion of a huge market waiting to be tapped.

The thrilling idea that equatorial Africa represented a potential market bonanza on the scale of India found hopeful adherents everywhere. When in 1889 it came time to survey the right of way for the railroad between Matadi and Leopoldville, project board members reassured themselves and prospective investors in the enterprise that tens of millions of African natives, all born traders, were "thirsting for the goods of European manufacture, and their very fertile soil enables them to offer us in return raw materials very valuable for the industry of the old world."[7]

Any American merchant hoping to exploit this new opportunity faced daunting competition in the form of European rivals who had been in place for decades, even centuries. Banana first opened as a Dutch East India Company station in 1670, supporting company vessels sailing between the Netherlands and the spice islands of Southeast Asia. Some two hundred years later an heir, the Dutch-African Trading Company of Rotterdam, was ubiquitous along the Congo coast. Its headquarters on the southern half of Banana Point was the center node of an enterprise that, Tisdel later reported to Washington, operated fifty-two other stations spread out along more than five hundred miles of Atlantic coastline and up one hundred miles of riverfront. European competitors based off Banana included Hatton and Cookson and the Hamburg African Company (the first British and the second German), and several Portuguese trading houses with headquarters at Ambriz or a little farther south at São Paolo de Luanda, and their associated factories on the lower Congo.

The new American trade development initiative that Tisdel represented took several months to mature. It could not move forward until Congress appropriated the money to fund the diplomatic and consular service for the next fiscal year, through to June 30, 1885. That happened in July 1884, when a remarkably generous $15,000 was set aside (in two tranches) from this appropriation for "introducing and extending the commerce of the United States in the Congo Valley." Secretary Frelinghuysen issued the new commissioner his instructions on September 8, and Tisdel, then forty, sailed from New York for Congo later that month by a roundabout route that began with a stop in Brussels, where he called on King Leopold II. For the next twenty years or so official Americans and many private citizens who followed Tisdel to the Congo first made the same pilgrimage to the royal palace.

Contemplating Europe's heads of state in the last few decades of the nineteenth century—a mixed bag of autocrats and monarchs speckled with several republicans—it's possible to conclude that the most successful among them in achieving his dreams was Leopold II, the monarch of a state created as much to satisfy foreign objectives as Flemings' and Walloons' desire for independence and condominium.

In 1886 an American diplomat in Europe naively described Leopold II's motives this way: "The enlightened King of the Belgians, mourning the loss of an only heir to his throne, resolved to dedicate a royal fortune to the founding of a free and progressive state in the newly discovered center of a populous continent."[8] Looking back, the 1908 edition of *The Catholic Encyclopedia*—written just before the Congo was annexed by the Belgian government—had a less charitable vision of the king's purposes and vast powers in Africa: "Leopold II exercises over his Congolese subjects a sovereignty which makes him the most absolute monarch in the world: he governs them by his sole and uncontrolled will. He gives all important orders, constitutes the whole administration, and is the source of all authority in his African kingdom."

Tisdel's audience with Leopold in Brussels was worth the king's time. "I was received most courteously by the King of the Belgians," Tisdel later wrote. "His Majesty gave me a most interesting account of his connection with the proposed Free State, the object which he hoped to attain, and the results already accomplished, demonstrating clearly that his work was one of philanthropy."[9] Later Tisdel informed Secretary Frelinghuysen that in 1884 the king had disbursed $700,000 of his own money to operate stations in the Congo, to meet their payrolls, and to pay off local chiefs, all "expended with the unselfish purpose of doing good, without any expectation or desire for pecuniary return or profit." Tisdel's admiration for the king was very durable. More than a year later, long after his final report described to Congress a venture in Africa that could not succeed—his negative review prompted an intercontinental character assassination campaign by Leopold's minions—Tisdel was still unwilling to fault the king himself. Leopold, he believed very charitably, was being duped in Brussels by persons unknown.

Having swallowed whole the Belgian king's cover story, and under instructions from the State Department, the new American commissioner left for Berlin on October 25. There he was to sit as an observer of an international conference on West Africa hosted and chaired by His Most Serene Highness, Prince Otto Eduard Leopold von Bismarck, chancellor of the German Empire since 1871 and until 1890 Europe's dominant politician. (Bismarck's lengthy obituary in *The Times* of London the last day of June 1898 began by describing the Prussian prince as "the greatest personality in Europe . . . one of the rare men who leave indelible marks on the world's history.")

If Leopold wasn't in Indelible Bismarck's class, no one was; the Belgian king still could take his place proudly at the head of the second rank of master manipulators on the European political scene. The coming conference would see the Anglo-Portuguese Treaty of February 1884, which when ratified would have put Portugal in control of the mouth of the Congo and made Lisbon master of the gate to the river's entire watershed, become a dead letter—a diplomatic triumph that made Leopold's fantasy possible.

The initiative for this conference had been explained in a diplomatic note delivered on October 10, 1884, by German ambassadors to their host foreign ministers in Brussels, Madrid, Paris, London, Amsterdam, Lisbon, and Washington. (Austria-Hungary, Italy, Denmark, Sweden and Norway, and Turkey were invited later.) As Baron Friedrich von Alvensleben's copy of the note explained to Secretary Frelinghuysen,

> The development recently attained by the commerce of Western Africa has led the Governments of France and Germany to think that it would be for the interest of all the nations engaged in that trade to regulate . . . the conditions that might secure its development, and prevent disputes and misunderstandings. . . . It would be well to form an agreement on the following principles:
> 1. Freedom of commerce in the basin and the mouths of the Congo.
> 2. Application to the Congo and the Niger of the principles adopted by the Vienna Congress with a view to sanctioning free navigation on several international rivers. . . .

3. Definition of the formalities to be observed in order that new occupations on the coast of Africa may be considered effective.

One week later, after exchanges by cable between the secretary of state and his minister in Berlin, Frelinghuysen accepted, noting nervously to von Alvensleben his understanding that the agenda of the International African Conference was limited to these three topics, and that the conference would not resolve any territorial claims. All other invited parties accepted before the end of October. November 15 was soon set as the date of the first meeting. Several years later John Kasson, the American minister accredited to the imperial German court and residing in Berlin, described the lofty proceedings as "a meeting of the principal governments of the world for the sole purpose of promoting the peace of nations, the interests of international commerce and the progress of Christian civilization."[10] If representatives of other national delegations did not see the conference in such elevated terms, there's no reason to suspect that Minister Kasson's characterization did not genuinely reflect his perspective of the goals of their work.

9

Slow to industrialize, late to unify under Prussian leadership, and then delayed by Chancellor Bismarck's somewhat reluctant acceptance of the idea of colonialism, Imperial Germany was the last of the great European powers to join what has since been described as "the scramble for Africa," the aggressive pursuit of protected markets and cheap raw materials, and the final dismemberment of the continent. That "scramble" ran roughly two decades, the last twenty years of the nineteenth century. Appropriately, it ended in 1898 with a race, the "race to Fashoda," a British and French contest to seize Fashoda (modern Kodok, in South Sudan), a strategic crossroads on the powers' rival coast-to-coast railroad plans. In the years between the start of the scramble and the end of the race—Great Britain won, but its Capetown to Cairo railroad was never built—the remaining 90 percent of the African continent fell under direct European control. The first 10 percent, Algeria, Angola, the Cape Colony and Natal, had been snatched earlier.

Given the Germans' slow start, beginning in 1883 and during the next two years, they did well to insert themselves in the continent's remaining open spaces. Their overseas portfolio ultimately included a scattered mosaic of African and Asian properties: Southwest Africa (Namibia), Togo and Cameroon on the Gulf of Guinea, German East Africa (now Tanzania; wedged between Congo, British Kenya, and Portuguese Mozambique, the place raised British anxieties as they watched Germans maneuvering near Uganda with real alarm), plus Samoa and other small bits in the Pacific. Germany's African and Pacific colonies provided prestige but—possibly excepting tiny Togo, "the model colony"—they made little economic sense and attracted little engagement.[11]

Coming from behind and perhaps worried about being frozen out of trade with equatorial Africa, Chancellor Bismarck strove to catch up with the lead colonizers (France, Portugal, and Great Britain) by hosting this conference. His initiative guaranteed Germany a seat at the head table and substantial control over the agenda, powerful leverage for a Johnny-come-lately. Bismarck also wanted the conference to provide international legitimization of what Germany had already done. The huge (six feet four inches and husky) and hugely capable German chancellor didn't dominate the conference as he might have been expected to. His health, or his hypochondria, didn't permit that. But he did get credit for its success: an international agreement on difficult issues. The agreement took equatorial Africa off the international agenda for decades and left Leopold entirely free to follow his lights so long as he kept them concealed.

The U.S. delegation to the 1884–85 Berlin Conference included Minister Kasson and two civilian appointees as associate (nonvoting) delegates shipped in for the proceedings, the ubiquitous Henry Sanford and the hero Henry Morton Stanley.

The International Association of the Congo, born in 1878 of the short-lived, scholarly Association Internationale Africaine and later the Comité d'études du Haut-Congo, was the last of three instruments of Leopold's acquisition strategy for an African colony. All these groups of pretend international bodies were furiously manipulated by the king. Sanford was a member of the executive committee of Leopold's International Association of the Congo.

During the two months of the conference Sanford had some difficulty separating his roles as a U.S. associate delegate and as Leopold's chief American cheerleader. He spoke to delegates on the king's behalf at least once, an intervention proposing that the Congo's future European master be granted a railroad right-of-way around the river's lower cataracts to connect the upper and lower Congo regardless of which party actually held the underlying ground. Without such connectivity, the Congo's resources could not be exploited and exported on an industrial scale.[12] Immediate French opposition to his suggestion, the *Herald* reported, prompted an "indignant" response by Sanford, piously expressing "the hope that no one suspected him of being personally interested in the proposed railway."[13]

Stanley, of course, was the great explorer of equatorial Africa, the man who had famously found Dr. David Livingstone at Ujiji on Lake Tanganyika in late October or early November 1871—neither man was certain of the month, never mind the day—and who was the substance behind Secretary of the Navy Chandler's and others' occasional hints that the United States could, if it chose to, exercise a claim over central Africa on the basis of discovery by a citizen. A potential claim impaired by the fact that according to international usage, discovery had to be followed up by actual possession to make such an assertion vital—something that was not going to happen—and fatally weakened, if it ever came to it, by the inconvenient fact that at the time Stanley wasn't really an American citizen and would not be until May 1885.

Stanley might have thought he was a naturalized American on the basis of Union enlistment oaths taken during the Civil War, following his defection from a Confederate army unit after capture. If so, his status would have been ambiguous, to say the least, given that he had deserted from both the Army and the Navy. In May 1885, with the assistance of a New York City law firm, Sullivan and Cromwell, he formally applied for U.S. citizenship and received naturalization papers. The motive to regularize his status was to reassure his American publisher, Harper's, that he had standing in U.S. courts to file copyright infringement suits, thus freeing them to publish his books.[14]

It was Stanley, Kasson believed, who with "rare sagacity, intrepidity, and pluck," and "undeterred by savage nature and more savage man," had made possible the introduction of Christianity, civilization, and commerce to 40 million of "the most unknown people of earth." On the strength of his presumed citizenship and willingness to share his expertise with the assembly, and the great man's agreement to do so gratis, Kasson invited Stanley to sit with the United States delegation in Berlin. It's unlikely that anyone else among the national delegations had ever actually been to or even near the place they would soon be discussing so earnestly in Bismarck's great hall.

Later Sanford told the secretary of state that the International Association of the Congo, not seated at the conference, had been reluctant to consent to Stanley's presence there "for political considerations not needful to speak of," and that he'd been hard-pressed to gain its agreement. The "considerations" Sanford tactfully neglected to describe had to do with France's determination to freeze Stanley out of the Congo, seeing him as a

Figure 9. Henry Morton Stanley, 1885. Photograph by Messrs. Joseph Elliot and Clarence Fry. Stanley designed this hat for protection against the African sun. It also usefully added four inches or so to his height of five feet six inches. The Royal Museum of Central Africa at Tervuren, Belgium, has one such in its collection, made by A. J. White, a London hat and cap maker. Stanley's first two expeditions into equatorial Africa, the hunt for Livingstone and later the long trek east to west across the continent's waist, brought him the rapt admiration of the English-speaking world. From then to his death he was inextricably connected to equatorial Africa. Among the three European powers interested in the region, Portugal, France, and Belgium (in the person of its king), only the last was hiring, and King Leopold courted Stanley aggressively, using Sanford as the chief go-between. As soon as Stanley was persuaded that Great Britain had no interest in a new colony in central Africa, his connection to Leopold's ambitions became inevitable. Established in London in 1863, Elliot and Fry offered high-quality portrait photography to prominent men and women in three studios about the capital and sold photographic plates and paper and related materials and services to the trade. In 1887, not long after this portrait was shot, the partnership was dissolved when Elliot bought out Fry. AUTOBIOGRAPHY OF SIR HENRY MORTON STANLEY, *348*

Figures 10 and 11. Henry Morton Stanley statue by Arthur Dupagne. This vandalized sculpture lies on the grounds of the national museum on Kinshasa's Mount Ngaliema. Before 1971 the intact statue stood on the slope, gesturing grandly toward the pool in the river that bore Stanley's name through the colonial era. A British initiative in 2010 to have Dupagne's statue of Stanley repaired and re-erected to mark the DRC's fiftieth anniversary of independence quickly fell through. That ruined plans to have a duplicate cast and placed in his home town in Wales on the centenary of his death. Instead, admirers commissioned a life-sized original, by Welsh sculptor Nick Elphick. It was unveiled by author Tim Jeal in March 2011. *AUTHOR'S PHOTOGRAPHS*

stalking horse for Anglo-Portuguese mischief at the mouth of the Congo, and with Leopold's desire to keep the French mollified.

Tisdel arrived in Berlin on October 25 and left there on November 10, having passed the intervening two weeks on the margins of Prince Bismarck's conference, where Kasson at first had approved of what he saw in his Congo-bound countryman. "Tisdel is here," Kasson wrote Sanford several days later, "and he is an excellent man for his place." Ten days or so earlier, October 17, Sanford had written the secretary of state a similar, strong review of the new man. "I have seen Mr. Tisdel and I am very much pleased with him and he made at Brussels a very good impression. The King said to me but yesterday that the selection was a most gratifying one." Soon these endorsements would appear premature.

After more than three months of intense deliberations during plenary meetings held several times a week, the conference published its product, the "General Act of the Berlin Conference on West Africa," on February 26, 1885. The act's text encompassed thirty-seven paragraph-long articles under eight chapter headings, all in the language of the best nineteenth-century European diplomatic practice, addressing the agenda originally announced in Bismarck's invitation.

Arguably the most significant article was in Chapter VI, "Declaration Relative to the Essential Conditions to Be Observed in Order that New Occupations on the Coasts of the African Continent May Be Held to Be Effective." Article 34 in that chapter established how further land grabs in equatorial Africa were to be regularized. "Any Power which henceforth takes possession of a tract of land on the coasts of the African continent outside of its present possessions," it said, "or which, being hitherto without such possessions, shall acquire them, as well as the Power which assumes a Protectorate there, shall accompany the respective act with a notification thereof, addressing the other Signatory Powers of the present Act, in order to enable them, of need be, to make good any claims of their own." This was interpreted to mean that territorial claims had to be substantiated by uncontested possession, an effective governing presence on the ground.

Despite the boost to the Berlin proceedings given at the outset by American diplomatic recognition, the United States' active role in them, and Minister John Kasson's signature on the General Act, the Senate never ratified the treaty. Never even considered it officially. President Grover Cleveland (inaugurated on March 4, a week after the conference adjourned) withdrew the treaty from consideration generally because neither he nor his new secretary of state, Thomas Bayard, supported the activist foreign policies of their Republican predecessors.[15] (In the same spirit, the new

Democratic administration also withdrew from Senate consideration the 1884 Frelinghuysen-Zavala Nicaragua Canal Treaty, which would have given the United States rights to construct an inter-ocean canal, railway, and telegraph along a zone two and a half miles wide through Nicaragua on payment of $4 million.)

Cleveland's specific objection to the Congo pact, he explained December 8, 1885, to Congress in his first State of the Union message, was that U.S. delegates to the Berlin Conference had attended on the understanding that their part was "merely deliberative, without imparting to the results any binding character. . . . This reserve was due to the indisposition of this Government to share in any disposal by an international congress of jurisdictional questions in remote foreign territories":

> Notwithstanding the reservation under which the delegates of the United States attended, their signatures were attached to the General Act in the same manner as those of the plenipotentiaries of other governments, *thus making the United States appear, without reservation or qualification, as signatories to a joint international agreement imposing on the signers the conservation of the territorial integrity of distant regions* where we have no established interests or control.
>
> This Government does not, however, regard its reservation of liberty of action in the premises at all impaired; and holding that an engagement to share *in the obligation of enforcing neutrality in the remote valley of the Congo would be an alliance whose responsibilities* we are not in a position to assume, I abstain from asking the sanction of the Senate to that general act.

In February 1886 Kasson, now no longer a State Department employee, publicly objected to this embarrassing renunciation and to the charge that he'd gone beyond his brief, but the lack of ratification made his signature meaningless. Years later, the fact that the United States had not been a formal signatory to the act became an excuse for government inaction on reform, with the argument that the United States had no legal standing to get involved.

Unsaid in the act was that at the conference's margins delegates seemingly had also resolved the competing claims of France and Portugal to territory in the Congo River drainage basin, a result that Tisdel had described the previous June to Secretary of State Bayard as having secured for the two "all that they wished for and much more than they had expected . . . the richest, best and most productive of all the vast territory which came within the scope of discussion."[16]

Like Tisdel, the national delegates to the conference apparently also believed in King Leopold's charitable purposes in the Congo, or affected to. By the time the conference ended, and following the Americans' lead, all participants but the Turks granted Leopold's vision—then embodied in no more than a slender string of what amounted to scout camps along the river—the dignity of their diplomatic recognition. (Istanbul got into line at midyear.) The result was that just under 1 million or so square miles of the continent fell to Leopold II himself.

In the end, each of Europe's great powers preferred to see the Congo in the presumably weak grasp of the king of the Belgians than in the hands of a stronger rival, and Leopold's cunning grant to the French of a right of first refusal to the property should he walk away sidelined at least temporarily the only great power with an ambition in the region as all-consuming as his and with a man on the ground, Pierre de Brazza, capable of pursuing it. Better yet, Leopold and not they would pay to open this presumably vast new market to great power trade on a basis that would privilege no single entrant.

Any seer, or a cynical observer with normal perception, could have predicted the future: By 1889 the cost of exploiting his enormous new property consumed much of Leopold's personal wealth, driving him first to renounce in 1890 promises of duty-free trade and then, in 1892, to sharply restrict trade by outsiders. In that same year his agents levied a brutally enforced "labor tax" on the king's suffering African subjects, a tax soon indistinguishable from the slavery Leopold had sworn to suppress. While skeptics had doubted the Africans could be "induced" to labor for white men, they hadn't given enough consideration to the possibility that they could be compelled to.

10

Commissioner Tisdel's charter, as Secretary Frelinghuysen described it to him September 8, 1884, was very broad. He was to inquire into and to report on international politics, local government, geography, river and land transportation, and agriculture, essentially anything that bore even tangentially on commerce. Lest he become too academic in his researches, Frelinghuysen focused Tisdel on the bottom line. "While it is important that accurate information . . . should be obtained," the secretary instructed his new hire, "the effort should be made to find out without delay what articles the inhabitants of the Congo Valley are in need of, or what American manufactures or products would there find a market." To heighten his sense of urgency, Tisdel had been told to proceed to Africa "at the earliest practicable moment . . . by the most available route," then to begin his investigation at the mouth of the Congo, and to proceed as high up the river "as you may find it advisable without exceeding the appropriation made by Congress."

At first, before he saw Africa, Tisdel was very much in the pocket of the American Congo lobby, and he wanted Sanford et al. to know it. His two weeks in Berlin were enough to persuade Tisdel, he wrote Sanford, that the American delegation could "dictate the policy of the Conference in the interest of the Association." "I shall hope to hear soon," he continued, "that the Powers have followed the example of the U.S. in recognizing the Free States." Several days later another letter suggested something more accommodating. "I will be glad if you will send me a rough memorandum of what you think should appear in my report," he invited Sanford, "and I will enlarge upon it and send it back. . . . This will be *strictly confidential* and your notes returned to you, if you wish." His extraordinary offer to let an interested private citizen, Sanford, ghostwrite the first draft of his first report to Congress was repeated for emphasis a few days later. Much later Tisdel would forget these unseemly offers and publicly recall his brave and entirely imaginary resistance to Sanford's early seduction.

British and Dutch ship schedule complications, aggravated by Portuguese quarantine restrictions, had the effect of holding Tisdel in Europe for weeks after he left the bleachers overlooking Bismarck's conference. He finally arrived at Banana Point from Berlin via Lisbon sometime in January 1885, after two brief port calls at Portuguese islands in the Bight of Benin, Prince's Isle (Ilha do Principe), and St. Thomas (São Tomé).

Tisdel's first month in West Africa was a revelation. The contrast between his expectations on arrival and reality on the ground was stunning, a difference that at first Tisdel attributed to management failures in Europe. "There is something radically wrong in Brussels," he wrote to Sanford the last day of January 1885 from Vivi, "and you should go to the bottom of every transaction, if you value your own interests & those of the king. I am dumbfounded with the conditions of things out here, and shall have much to tell you." That bombshell in the mail to Europe, Tisdel left the next day with a caravan for Stanley Pool, expecting to reach it near the middle of February.

Like Taunt's would be, Tisdel's trek from Vivi was nominally a one-man expedition into the interior. In his case that one man was accompanied by fifty-six Loango porters (from what is part of Angola today, each of whom struggled under a seventy pound load of "provisions, medicines, luggage, tents, cooking-utensils," and trade goods), twelve armed Houssas from Lagos, four Zanzibari servants, a cook from the Gold Coast, and a Kabinda interpreter—a procession of seventy-five and an indication of how difficult and expensive even simple things, namely, moving a single white man and his life support a few hundred miles, were to do in this remote place.

Sunday, March 15, Tisdel was back downriver. That night he visited with Captain Bridgman on board USS *Kearsarge* anchored off Banana. He was on board again the next day, this time with Governor General Francis de Winton, who received "the usual honors," and on Wednesday, too. Tisdel's skepticism about the Congo's commercial prospects powerfully colored Bridgman's negative report to his superiors.

March 20, Friday, Tisdel was at Boma, where he spent part of the day writing his last letter to Admiral English. The next day he left for Europe in the Portuguese mail steamer, "having traveled by special caravan," as he reported in April to the secretary of state, "to the interior of Africa as far as Stanley Pool . . . calling at Kinchassa, De Brazzaville, and other points." April 22 he arrived in Hanover, Germany, surprising Sanford by his early reappearance in Europe. Nearly three of his four weeks at sea had been spent ill in his cabin, and some days would pass on the ground in Hamburg before Tisdel felt well enough to travel farther.

Tisdel's first report, the one dated November 23, 1884, and written in London to Frelinghuysen long before he'd set foot on Africa, had been optimistic, full of the happy expectations that were the typical product of the uninformed and inexperienced contemplating imaginary riches. Congo was, he'd written then based entirely on secondhand information filtered through selfish interests, "more than 1,000,000 square miles of great fertility . . . with boundless resources"; it would attract "multitudes" of bona fide settlers from all countries; its fifty million natives "find civilization dawning upon them, and they welcome it with a cordiality hitherto unknown in heathen lands"; and most compellingly, "these millions of people inhabiting the interior of Africa, will, under the inspiring influence of civilization, become purchasers of every kind of provisions, manufactured goods, agricultural implements, &c." Exactly the kind of heady reporting that would enhance investors' confidence in Europe and America and aid in personnel recruiting. In view of what preceded this report and what was to come, it's easy to conclude that at first Tisdel was playing the dummy for Sanford the ventriloquist. A role for which he'd volunteered, twice.

Five months later, Tisdel's travels on the continent finished, everything was different: The country was not only being mismanaged from afar but also, he concluded, its territory was so naturally hostile to white men as to be unlivable. In three letters written from Hanover to Sanford at his country estate in Flanders—the first dated April 26, 1885, just four days after he returned to Europe—Tisdel now spoke on the basis of personal knowledge, fleshing out his first impressions of the lower Congo that had prompted the short, "dumbfounded" warning in January with the discovery that colonization of the middle Congo was impossible.

Tisdel's first post-expedition letter to Sanford asked, "Will I find you in Brussels or Gingelom? I have much to say to you, and much which I wish you to say to me before I make my report." He followed that query immediately by a roster of nineteen dead and dying white men left behind in Africa or being evacuated to Europe, annotated with "There is not a Dr. any where above Vivi, and *no* medical comforts." "I could not go far beyond the Pool because the Association had no means of transportation. *Not even a whaleboat*. . . . Much more I can say which will interest you (perhaps) when I see you."

"I am exceedingly anxious to talk with you before I communicate to or with the Department," Tisdel wrote to Sanford three days later. One subject of their talk was certain to be internal transportation. As Tisdel described them to Sanford, the association's logistics on the river were in crisis: full warehouses downriver, thousands of loads interminably awaiting transportation upriver, losses in transit of 25 to 30 percent, and more news that was as bad.

On Friday, the first of May and the day before Taunt's great African adventure began at Banana, Tisdel accepted Sanford's invitation to breakfast (at noon) for the following Wednesday but declined dinner that same night: "If I were to meet the gentlemen who you gather about you, naturally the questions would flow in about the Congo. *This I wish to avoid.*"

"Did it ever strike you," Tisdel then asked almost impertinently in this last of the immediate post-expedition letters in the Sanford Archive, "that there is no food in the country for oxen, and that every pound of corn (and they must have solid food) must be brought from Europe? Do you know that in the six years that the Association has been at work in the Congo, that they have never been able to raise one particle of food? Letters are published every little while telling about the fertility of the soil, and about the things they can grow, etc, etc. *Yet they never have grown anything.* Only in small patches in sheltered areas are the natives able to grow the pea-nuts and the mandioca upon which they live." And here, the final bad news for Sanford, whose terrible investments in Florida and elsewhere were making a new, very lucrative project in Africa essential. "Surely you will have to abandon the up-river stations. Already men have deserted, and made their way to Stanley Pool in canoes, and told terrible tales of suffering. . . . Talk about the suffering for food up-country; why, within 75 miles of Vivi men are nearly starved."

Commissioner Tisdel's post-expedition reports, the first one dated April 25, 1885, and written in Lisbon and the second dated June 29 and written in Washington, were duly submitted to Secretary Bayard. The dismal assessments they contained seriously threatened Leopold's and Sanford's heady plans. Later dissenters had it that Tisdel's judgments and reports about what he saw were inadequate because he'd failed to go far enough upriver to conduct a thorough survey. It was a seemingly fair critique. Tisdel claimed in self-defense that there was no transportation available to move him beyond Stanley Pool. Regardless, long before Tisdel's final reports were delivered, even before he went on the river, momentum in Washington and Brussels was growing behind a plan to ask the same questions of someone else.

Tisdel's final report to Congress covered his travels in February and March from Vivi to Stanley Pool and back. There might be a market for "canned goods, common cutlery, ready-made wooden houses, lumber, medicines, beads, and 'Yankee notions,'" he wrote at the end of June, but Americans looking to establish themselves on the lower Congo below Vivi needed to be well capitalized and have sure access to transportation in and out. They also needed to anticipate no return on investment for at least a year. Worse yet, "this country is densely populated, yet it is next to impossible to induce the natives to gather the valuable products which nature produces. With the exception of the Loango and Kabinda tribes, they are a wild, savage and cruel people. They do not like the white man; and while they are glad to have his cloth and gin, they would much prefer never to see a white man within their domain. . . . The men lounge about drinking, gossiping, fighting, or hunting, as it may suit their tastes." The prevalence of alcohol abuse cannot have surprised anyone, given that fully 40 percent of the basin's total imports was in the form of cheap gin, distilled in Holland exclusively to be used in trade with the natives.

Colonel Tisdel's last words on the Congo and his mission to Henry Sanford—hardly his last words on the subject—were written in Washington on November 17, 1885, the month after Tisdel, his wife, and their sixteen-year-old daughter left Hanover for the United States. Citing their "differences of opinion upon the Congo matter," Tisdel explained that he did not think Sanford had cared to see him again since their meeting in early May. "I have resigned my position as Agent of the U.S.," he wrote, "but not until I received letters from nearly every white man in the Congo confirming all which I had written. These letters are from Col. De Winton, Major

Parminter, Dr. Leslie, and others, and are in the hands of Secretary Bayard, who has given me a letter, approving my course and thanking me for the services provided, etc., etc.":

> I wish to have nothing further to do with the matter and certainly shall not unless attacked from Brussels, where, I may say, I have been very badly treated because I dared to tell the truth about Congo as far as I saw it. I know well what has been said and done there against me. . . .
>
> I have none but the kindest feelings for His Majesty, the King, who has been, and is still being, duped by *some one*.[17]
>
> The officer who is [?] in the Congo is Lieutenant Taunt of the Navy, under orders from Rear Admiral English. I hope he will go to the Falls. Thus far his reports confirm all that I have said and show a terrible state of affairs there. . . .
>
> I shall have nothing further to say about the matter, but if attacked, will defend myself.

In a fit of candor, de Winton (he left his post as administrator general in 1886) and his subordinates might have endorsed Tisdel's negative views as he claimed, but when this letter was written in November, Taunt had been off the river for only a few weeks and his report to Secretary Whitney was still seven months from completion. Anything Tisdel inferred about it was premature.

Later, Tisdel's conclusions were repeated for public consumption in the February 1890 issue of the *Century Illustrated Monthly Magazine*. "It is claimed by travelers," he wrote without naming any claimants, "that the interior of the Congo Free State offers great inducements to the trader, and even to one disposed to become an actual settler. Upon this point I cannot coincide with anyone who recommends the Congo country as a desirable place for residence."[18] Not just undesirable for settlement. His observations about the place, its people, and prospects were all uniformly negative, and those judgments expressed first in private, then officially, and finally in public put him across the breakers with powerful men who anticipated acquiring fantastic wealth from the Congo. By shopping his opinion around like that, Tisdel was provoking one of the great figures of the century, one who had an enormous readership and audience, and a symbiotic relationship with the English language press, to battle.

II

Tisdel's judgment was an insult to Stanley, long since double-hatted as equatorial Africa's proprietary explorer and its self-appointed chief marketing officer. Stanley had very reluctantly adapted to the idea that Great Britain had "black subjects enough" and no interest in colonizing the Congo, but he bridled at suggestions from any source that the place was not the prospective bonanza that he claimed it to be.

During the summer of 1885, and for the next several seasons, Tisdel's and Stanley's rival assessments of the Congo's prospects and both men's ungenteel attacks on one another filled columns in the *New York Herald*. Their fight was a spectacle that, thanks to the newspaper, avid readers could watch from ringside, fascinated by counterpunching paragraphs. For the *Herald* and its flamboyant publisher, James Gordon Bennett Jr., Henry Morton Stanley continued to manufacture content; he was the gift that kept on giving.

Tisdel quoted a German scholar, Dr. Eduard Pechuel-Loesche, a naturalist and watercolor painter, to substantiate his critique. Pechuel-Loesche (1840–1913), who had on Leopold's invitation trekked up and down the north bank of the river as far as Stanley Pool about the time that Tisdel's caravan moved along its south side, wasn't completely unknown in the United States. But he was close to it. Tisdel introduced his eyewitness to *Herald* readers as "a learned scientist without a superior in Germany; [and wrongly as] the head of the celebrated university at Jena."

In 1885–86 Pechuel-Loesche's second foray in the Congo resulted in two pamphlets and several letters to the Committee of the International Association of the Congo and to a popular German newspaper, *Gartenlaube* (Gazebo). In them he generally echoed Tisdel's conclusions: "A settlement on these unhealthy tracts [land near Stanley Pool] will never have a shadow of success" one of his booklets predicted, "the colonists die off like sheep; there is no commerce worth speaking of, for there are no merchantable goods in sufficient quantities and hence the railroad projected from the coast north of the Congo will never pay."[19]

Stanley, who needed no foreign allies to bolster his credibility, reacted reflexively to these challenges to his status. In letters written to the *Herald* November 29 and December 13, Stanley backhanded Pechuel-Loesche as condemned by nature to be "a callow dilettante," who together with Tisdel should be for his flaws "forever disqualified from expressing an opinion about Africa and the Congo." In July 1882, however, when the two men had first met at Vivi, Stanley had been pleased to learn that the German had been selected by his sponsor committee as his successor in the event that he were disabled. A month later Pechuel-Loesche was at Manyanga, in charge of negotiating with its six chiefs the cession of tribal lands and rights to the Comité d'études in exchange for "superior stuffs" and other consideration. In 1882 Stanley admired Pechuel-Loesche's "African experience and scientific acquirements."[20] The harsh judgment he announced three years later was invented to reflect a new situation.

Stanley's rebuttal of Tisdel came to its climax in the *Herald* on January 24, 1886, where Stanley described Tisdel's report to Secretary Bayard. "It is such a tissue of 'untruths,' or exaggerations if you please, that it would have been utterly unworthy of my notice were it not for the fact that the man poses before the American public as an immaculate and truthful reporter—solely 'for the benefit of American merchants,' and has publicly challenged me to contradict him." Stanley then went on to claim that he had found more than fifty errors in Tisdel's twelve-and-a-half-page report to the secretary. Here followed page-long columns of paragraphs under six subheadings (among them "freight and food supply" and "the death toll") correcting forty of them, "which are either the result of ignorance or caused by an unworthy motive of some kind." That motive, Stanley hinted later, had something to do with Tisdel being too close to the despised Portuguese.

Tisdel's report, Stanley said, was "interesting for its sublime audacity, for its rich and copious abuse of men and ideas, through which such an anomaly as a free commercial State in Africa was created. . . . I could write a great deal more," Stanley wrote to Bennett for the delectation of the *Herald*'s readers,

> I could send you letters from the Congo describing the ridiculous pose of the commercial agent during his too brief stay at Stanley Pool; of the lavish salutes of artillery fired in his honor; of the big words he used; of the many assurances he gave everybody there that he would be my ruin, and that he would make a big sensation on his return; of his disinclination to leave Berlin until the United States Minister politely hinted that it was time to depart on his commercial mission from [*sic*] the Congo; of his harried departure from Stanley Pool after only two days' stay there, and of many other interesting and instructive things.

Remarkably, Tisdel kept his feet in the face of this blast. In spring 1886 from distant "Buenos Ayres," six months after he told Sanford he wanted to have no more to do with the Congo and about the time that Emory Taunt was politicking hard to be selected to lead Sanford's new Congo enterprise while on leave from the Navy, Tisdel returned fire. He sent Secretary of State Bayard a letter meant further to discredit Stanley and to destroy Sanford, and a copy to the *Herald*, which promptly published it in the issue of May 31. "I might have been blessed with the smiles and approval of [Stanley and his associates] had I but allowed Mr. Stanley to relieve me from the trouble of preparing my reports," he told Bayard,

> Indeed, I fear I neglected a fine opportunity, for when I arrived in Brussels I was invited to Château Gingelom, the residence of the ex–United States Minister Henry S. Sanford, where was unfolded before me the scheme of the 'Great Semi-Political Commercial Trading Company of the Congo' (capital to be raised in England), with the intimation that my fortune would be assured if I should make a prudent and practicable report in harmony with the proposed scheme. When it was known I had neglected so fine an opportunity, and had made my reports on the basis of unadorned facts and unvarnished truth, I at once inherited the hatred, malice and vituperation of Mr. Sanford and Mr. Stanley and press, cable, telegraph and platform were used against me.

True enough as far as it went, but Tisdel was careful to conceal from Bayard the extent to which, at first, he'd auditioned to become Sanford's willing co-conspirator. Instead, he suggested an investigation of Washington's recognition of the Congo and its participation in the Berlin Conference, and the role played in all this by Sanford, who had told Tisdel "time and again that he wrote the clause about the Congo which appeared in President Arthur's message; that he supplied all the information to the Department of State about the Congo; that he passed the bill in Congress which gave recognition to a State having no existence; and that he brought the call for the Berlin Conference."

At the end of May 1886, nearly a year into their nasty fight on its pages—the paper called it "a somewhat ireful controversy"—the *Herald* reminded readers what had started it all: the two men's "difference of opinion as to the value of the Congo region from a purely commercial point of view . . . Mr. Stanley believing it to be a possible bonanza and Mr. Tisdel regarding it as worthless."

12

In letters from the State Department and Navy Department, which provided him with copies of Admiral English's orders, Tisdel had learned early in 1885 that the Navy was planning to send an officer up the Congo River. For a while he thought the officer selected was to travel with him upriver. When it became clear that was not going to happen, Tisdel wrote to Admiral English, first from Vivi on January 31 and then from Boma on March 20. The first letter possibly intercepted English in Libreville, the second before English left Banana in May. Or perhaps not; they might have failed to catch him both times.

"Except from a scientific point of view," Tisdel wrote to Admiral English in January,

> I cannot see what is to be gained by sending an officer or officers to the interior, and, if it is for scientific purposes that the detail is made no possible good can come from it without a special and large caravan, which should be fitted out at the expense of the United States Government and under the direction of [the governor general of the Congo Free State]. ... Such a caravan would require at least four months to march to and from the Pool.
>
> Unless you consider that your instructions are imperative upon the subject, I would recommend that the proposed expedition to the Pool be abandoned and that you confine your operations to the Lower Congo.

Tisdel's second letter to English was even more direct. "I recommend your early departure," he told the admiral abruptly five weeks before *Kearsarge* dropped anchor at Banana. "First, because from a sanitary point of view it is absolutely dangerous for you to remain here, the climate in this season being particularly bad. Second, having finished my mission the object of you coming here cannot be realized." He then shared with English a prescient assessment of the Free State's prospects, one that he later delivered to Secretary of State Bayard:

> The reported wealth of the up country has, in my opinion, been greatly exaggerated, and admitting for a moment that all the glowing reports of good climate, fertility of soil, wealth of mineral deposits, and inexhaustible stores of ivory are true, it would still be an undesirable and unprofitable country for the white man to make his home, or to embark in any business enterprise.

Between Vivi and Stanley Pool I saw on all sides misery, want, sickness, and death amongst the employees of the Association. The country does not and cannot produce for the white man to eat, and barely produces enough for the natives.

In the lowlands along the coast, within a 60-mile limit inland, the country is rich and the established trading companies have been moderately successful; but now the business is overdone, and I fear that the excitement caused by the reports which have been laid before the Berlin Conference may lead to much suffering on the part of would-be traders and missionaries, who are rushing into a country and climate for which they are wholly unsuited, and from which no good results can possibly come.

English's orders gave him no latitude. He couldn't heed Tisdel's recommendations. *Lancaster* must show the flag, his flag, during an unhurried port visit, and a squadron officer was going to be put ashore with instructions to proceed far upriver.

Whatever could be said about Emory Taunt's intelligence and tact, he was otherwise no Willard Tisdel. Although he could boast some weeks on the ground in Colombian jungles in connection with an early Navy survey for a trans-isthmus canal route, he had no business experience anywhere. Taking time out from his brawl with Stanley, Tisdel must have been offended eventually to learn that his work was going to be fact checked by a sailor.

4

Lieutenant Emory Taunt, U.S. Navy

Rear Admiral English and Commander Bridgman have both recently visited the mouth of the Congo River, and, from the accounts they give of the country, it is a most excellent place for Americans to keep away from. They say that it produces only enough for the natives, and, as the wants of African natives are limited to as many bananas as they can possibly swallow and a piece of cotton cloth a yard and a half long, a vivid idea may thereby be obtained of the capabilities of the Congo Valley. In the interior it is said to be better, but most of those who have tried the coast are willing to take the word of anybody for what may be in the interior. A sample of the coast climate and fever goes a long way towards dampening curiosity.

St. Louis Post Dispatch, *August 10, 1885*

13

Little in Emory Taunt's career in the U.S. Navy suggested that he would be a good choice for this extraordinary mission. Granted, several of his commanding officers had judged him to be a very capable mariner. Their assessments of his seamanship were likely reinforced in 1883 by the publication in Washington, D.C., of Taunt's encyclopedic *Young Sailor's Assistant in Practical Seamanship*. The book's title page noted in small capital letters that topics covered included "the rules of the road, instructions for resuscitating the apparently drowned, etc., etc., salutes and etiquette on board a man-of-war; the general service code, and homographic code of signals; the cautionary weather signals; with color plates of flags of all nations, naval signal flags, Very's lights, and the international code of signals." In short, everything the novice watch stander at sea needed to know.

The illustrated 460-page manual, containing a wheel chart (a "volvelle") illustrating boxing the compass with a rotating ship cutout, was quickly accepted as an official text for the instruction of naval apprentices. This imprimatur came from the naval bureau, commanded by his father-in-law, that oversaw naval cadet recruiting and training. Despite this achievement, several explicitly adverse evaluations by his commanding officers afloat, a general court-martial conviction in 1873 (even then not a career-enhancing

event) on a charge of absence without leave, and almost two decades of service reputation were arguments against Lieutenant Taunt's dispatch on any
unsupervised, solitary assignment.

That reputation began to be assembled in late July 1865 with Taunt's
arrival at the U.S. Naval Academy in Newport, Rhode Island, with the incom-
ing class of 1869. (In September the school returned from four years in its
Civil War refuge on the New England coast to its original home in Maryland
at the Severn River's mouth on the Chesapeake Bay.) He was born in New
York in April 1851, but on application to the academy fourteen years later
Taunt, then barely five feet three inches and weighing only 115 pounds, was
living with his parents in Pittsburgh, Pennsylvania. He could have been even
less substantial and still been admitted to the Naval Academy as a young
teen. The medical standard excluded applicants who were "manifestly undersized" for their age, meaning only that a child his age had to stand at least
four feet ten inches high, weigh 106 pounds, and exhibit "cerebral, osseous
and muscular development" proportionate to his size.

Taunt's father, James Frederick (usually "J. Frederick"), born in Rhode
Island in 1831, wasn't one of the fourteen Taunts who served in the Union
army. Later in life, and perhaps even during the Civil War, Frederick Taunt
was a churchman. A deacon until his ordination in Meriden, Connecticut,
December 18, 1877, the Reverend Taunt seems to have moved with Marie,
his French (possibly French Canadian) wife and Emory Taunt's mother,
between parishes in New York and in neighboring Pennsylvania and New
Jersey before and after he became a priest. In 1878 the peripatetic Reverend
Taunt was called from Groton, Connecticut, to the rectorship of thriving
Zion Episcopal Church in Greene, one of the townships of southern New
York State's Chenango County. For five years beginning in 1888, and span-
ning the final crises in his son's life, Taunt senior was the rector at Trinity
Episcopal Church, on Seymour Street in Syracuse, New York, where he lived
with Marie.[1]

During four years at Annapolis Taunt generally was in the bottom third
of his class in order of merit, although his conduct grades were somewhat
better. In his final year Taunt stood 43 of 78 in conduct, nearly breaking
into the upper half of his contemporaries, despite getting twenty demerits on
February 10, 1869, for "causing liquor to be introduced into" quarters and
drinking it. (Tobacco was also strictly forbidden on the academy's campus.)
It's tempting to read into this offense a portent of later career ruin, but that's
attributing too much to a violation that wasn't uncommon in the 1860s.

Cadet Midn. Emory Taunt graduated sixtieth in his seventy-eight-
man class. Weak grades and conduct demerits aside, he'd made it through

Annapolis on schedule. He left the academy in late May 1869 for duty in USS *Sabine* and an obligatory year at sea before becoming eligible for commissioning as an ensign. In July 1870 Taunt made ensign. He was promoted twice more, to master in 1872 and to lieutenant in 1876.

Taunt's unimpressive academic performance as a second classman might have been affected by "intermittent fever," malaria, the cause of a request to the secretary of the navy for convalescent leave away from Annapolis during December 1867–January 1868. "Having been suffering for the last five weeks," he wrote Secretary Gideon Welles on December 7, "with intermittent fever; and believing that a change of climate is essential to my recovery; I most respectfully request a leave of absence of thirty (30) days, on account of ill health." Taunt's request was approved, as was his doctor's subsequent request for an extension until January 20, but he apparently spent his leave in Washington, D.C., not in 1867 a healthier place than was Annapolis.

Fatal disease, especially malaria, cholera, and tuberculosis, powerfully shaped the history of the nineteenth century in a way that we moderns— despite the impact of AIDS—don't fully credit. When Taunt became feverish at Annapolis he joined the recently murdered Lincoln and four earlier presidents who are believed also to have suffered from malaria. At least one later president, Teddy Roosevelt, did, too, contracted while a "Rough Rider" in Cuba. So did countless other eighteenth- and nineteenth-century Americans in more humble stations. (Henry Morton Stanley got his first attack of malaria not as a reporter in East Africa in the early 1870s during his search for Livingstone but as a shop clerk in Cypress Bend, Arkansas, in 1860.)[2]

In the late nineteenth century, malaria was endemic along the American Atlantic seaboard south of New England to Florida and between the Alleghenies and the Rockies from the Rio Grande to the Dakotas. At the time, many medical practitioners still believed that it was somehow caused by "the decomposition of vegetable substance," and while swampy ground and bad air were thought to be associated with the disease, no one had yet made a connection between marshland and bogs and mosquitoes.

The state of medical knowledge about malaria approaching the end of the nineteenth century is best reflected by Dr. William Osler's enormously influential (and enormously long) medical textbook, *The Principles and Practice of Medicine* (D. Appleton, 1892).[3] Against the two chief unknowns of the disease (what made some place malarial or not and the life cycle of the blood parasite that caused malaria and how it entered or left the body) was one certainty: quinine worked. As to malarial places, Osler wrote, "In short it is impossible to ascertain from the nature of the soil and climate in any given place whether it is malarial or not. . . . The only means of deciding this point is by noticing the effect of residence in such a place on the human subject, preferably one of the Caucasian race" (114). Nothing as simple as "the decomposition of vegetable substance."

Taunt's "intermittent fever" at Annapolis likely was *Plasmodium vivax*, a form of the disease then fairly common in the low-lying or swampy areas of eastern Pennsylvania, Maryland, and Virginia, and one that would have produced recurrent attacks every two days for several weeks while the parasite was stepping through its life cycle.

By the late 1860s quinine, from the pulverized bark of the cinchona tree, had been used in the prevention and treatment of malaria for some 250 years since it was first adopted by Jesuit missionaries in South America as a cure, an application they learned from natives of today's Peru and Bolivia. In *The Greatest Benefit to Mankind* (W. W. Norton, 1997) author Roy Porter suggested that quinine was "arguably the first effective specific drug" in medical history, meaning that all the other early drugs relied entirely on the placebo effect.

To preserve health during six months in the Congo basin, Taunt wrote that he dosed himself daily with either quinine or arsenic, increasing the dose of quinine—according to Osler, ten grains per day was the recommended amount—when he somehow determined that he'd been "more than usually exposed to malarial influences." In either case Taunt mixed the dose of one or the other powder into a glass of wine to mask quinine's bitter or arsenic's metallic taste. (Arsenic, a favorite of poisoners during many centuries, and famous since the fifteenth as the preferred fatal chemical of Caesar and Lucrezia Borgia, was an important drug of the nineteenth century. It was often used in patent medicine health tonics and prescribed together with iron in cases of "malarial anemia" through to the end of the 1800s. Where Taunt got the idea to take it as a prophylactic isn't known.)

On his return from Africa, Taunt reported to the secretary of the navy "the malarial fevers on the Congo are of two forms, the remittent and the bilious-remittent fevers":

> The latter is the most fatal type, few white men surviving the second attack. In the bilious remittent many of the symptoms of yellow fever are met with, such and vomiting blood, yellow skin and eyeballs, bloody urine, &c., but it is not at all contagious. Another fatal type of fever is a form of low continuous fever that gradually but surely exhausts the strength of the patient and saps the life out of him. The malarial poison also works off from the system in ulcers, xemia, and anemia.

Entirely forgetting his medical history as a midshipman at Annapolis, Taunt later boasted of his durable constitution and described himself proudly, and as it would develop inaccurately, as the one white man in five naturally resistant to the enervating fevers of Africa. His collapse in late 1885 ("a bilious attack and liver complications") on board a Dutch steamer from Banana one week out of Madeira after months of "perfect health" on the ground Taunt dismissed as the result of "fatty food on board and a sudden change in the weather in the northeast trades," not as a symptom of something he might have caught on the river. Whatever it was, a slow, weeks-long recovery on Madeira followed.

14

Taunt's Navy career flashed through its apogee during 1883–85, a peak marked at first by the publication of his *Young Sailor's Assistant in Practical Seamanship* and then by commendable, back-to-back assignments at sea in 1884–85. The first was when he was embarked as the second lieutenant in USS *Thetis* while she was the flagship of the Navy's successful mission to rescue the survivors of a calamitous U.S. Army expedition in the Canadian Arctic. The second was his remarkable solo trip up the Congo River from its mouth on the Atlantic to distant Stanley Falls and back. These two triumphs became the entire summary of his Navy career when in 1891 the *New York Times* looked back on his life, thereby omitting a great deal that was unflattering. The brief obituary concluded generously by describing the deceased as having been "one of the brightest young officers of the navy." The *Times'* evaluation aside, Taunt's service in Navy uniform before 1884 had not been a brilliant success.

Capt. Christopher Rodgers, USN, commanding USS *Franklin* in the Mediterranean in 1869–70, remembered Midshipman Taunt as a man who gave a pledge not to drink and broke it. "I had preferred charges against him for drunkenness," Rodgers wrote to the lieutenant examining board in 1876, "but as I was at that time detached from the Franklin I consented to withdraw them, he taking a pledge and his messmates undertaking to see that he kept it." Rodgers noted that Taunt "would be professionally qualified for promotion only if he were sober" and went on to describe his subordinate's service reputation in a single word—"bad." Capt. James Mullany, of USS *Richmond*, agreed, recalling that "at the time he served with me his reputation for sobriety was not good."

While Taunt was a junior commissioned officer, the serious matter of his uncontrolled drinking was also observed by Capt. George Belknap, USN, commanding officer of USS *Tuscarora*, who wrote that Ensign Taunt "was given to habits of intemperance aboard Tuscarora which gave me a great deal of trouble." Belknap, like Rodgers and Mullany, believed that although Taunt was "mentally and professionally" qualified for promotion, he was not qualified "morally."

Prompted by these reports, every promotion examination raised the same embarrassing issue. Taunt's "far above average" grades in ordnance and seamanship were insufficient to get him advanced to lieutenant in October 1876, as were the previous eighteen months of unblemished service at sea. The promotion board agreed to Taunt's elevation only after receipt of his written pledge to "abstain from the use of intoxicating liquors during his naval career."

That promotion came, curiously, despite a court-martial conviction in November 1873 that punctuated the end of Taunt's seventeen months in *Tuscarora* under Belknap's command, the "great deal of trouble" cited above. Taunt was charged with disobeying orders and neglect of duty as well as with a weeks-long absence without leave extending through September and into October.

The court, convened by Secretary of the Navy George Robeson as prescribed by "the Act of Congress of 17 July 1862 for the better government of the Navy," met at the Mare Island Navy Yard on November 19. Taunt, serving as his own counsel, pled "not guilty" to all charges and specifications. After five days of proceedings and sworn testimony by several prosecution witnesses and one defense witness, the members of the court found the first charge and its associated specifications "not proven" but adjudged him "guilty" of the second charge and its two specifications. He was sentenced to six months' suspension on half-leave pay. Taunt served that suspension in Buffalo, New York, his family's home city, during the first half of 1874.

Sixteen years out of the Naval Academy and after nine years in grade as a lieutenant, by the time Taunt sailed to Africa in *Lancaster* he was an old salt. He'd served at sea with squadrons in the Mediterranean (in *Sabine*, *Franklin*, *Guerriere*, and *Richmond*), threaded the Strait of Magellan, and sailed in the Pacific (in *Tuscarora*), the South Atlantic (in *Brooklyn*), on the West Indies Station (in *Shawmut*), and most notably up and down the icy Davis Strait in USS *Thetis* during the Lady Franklin Bay rescue expedition.

Time ashore had included some weeks in the jungle in early 1873 at the head of a working party from USS *Tuscarora* supporting one of the Navy's Panama Canal surveys and several years at the Portsmouth Navy Yard.[4] From January through May 1873, USS *Tuscarora* was assigned to Cdr.

Thomas Selfridge's survey of the Isthmus of Darien. Taunt was a member of her crew between May 1872 and September 1873 and spent weeks on shore between January and May 1873 near Chiri-Chiri Bay leading a working party of sailors under conditions that Henry Cummings, the ship's writer, described in 1874 as dangerous and miserable. The route surveyed by Selfridge, through the jungle sixteen miles to the Atrato River and then down the river to the Atlantic, proved impassable.

The years at the shipyard in Kittery, Maine (across the bay from Portsmouth), might have been the most important of his career: Portsmouth is where he met the Englishes, married Mamie, and so gained a sea daddy who insofar as he was able appears to have coddled his new son-in-law's Navy career. Now followed two assignments working for his father-in-law in Washington interrupted by duty in USS *Portsmouth*, a tired former sloop-of-war converted into a training ship for naval apprentices. The first assignment was in 1879–80, when the 1880 census says the Taunts lived with her parents in Washington, and the second was in 1883–84.

15

Taunt got credit, too much credit, for his part in the 1884 rescue of survivors of the U.S. Army Signal Corps' disastrous expedition to the Canadian Arctic. It was more a matter of his being in the right place at the right time, an accident, than noteworthy performance on his part.[5]

Despite substantial skepticism in Washington, most notably on the part of Robert Todd Lincoln, President Garfield's and later President Arthur's secretary of war, in 1881 Congress had agreed that the United States should join ten European participants in a cooperative, international effort to collect scientific data in the Arctic—a constellation of fourteen temporary camps ringing the Arctic and supporting a population of more than seven hundred men representing all eleven countries.

That March Congress funded the establishment and operation of two American scientific stations, one to be at Point Barrow, Alaska, the second "on or near the shores of Lady Franklin Bay," at roughly 82° north latitude, 65° west longitude. The project fell to the Army's Signal Corps, perhaps because no other Washington agency craved the mission as much or lobbied for it as hard as did the Corps' new chief signal officer, Brig. Gen. William Hazen. Hazen selected Lt. Adolphus Washington Greely, thirty-seven, a career Army officer, model anal retentive personality, and enthusiastic volunteer to be commander of the American station on Lady Franklin Bay.

The agreed master plan was simple. Greely's encampment in the eastern Arctic was to be established in June 1881 and then visited by resupply vessels in the summer of 1882 and again in mid-1883. Unless one visited his camp by early summer 1883, Greely was to withdraw his men south along the coast in their small boats that September, carrying with them the amassed scientific records for which they had traded two years of their lives. On one side or another of the entrance to Smith's Sound the expedition would meet up with its saviors from the second resupply ship, and then—somehow—all would proceed home.

The first annual resupply mission left St. John's, Newfoundland, in steamship *Neptune* July 8, 1882, but because of ice never got past 79° 20' north, thus falling short of Greely's campsite by an unbridgeable 150-plus miles. A year passed, and in June 29, 1883, the all-important second resupply mission sailed from St. John's in SS *Proteus*. "It is my painful duty to report," Hazen's handpicked expedition commander wrote ten weeks later, "the total failure of the expedition. The *Proteus* was crushed in pack ice in latitude 78,52, long. 74, 25, and sunk on the afternoon of the 23rd July. My party and crew of ship all saved . . . all well." The blithe "all well" encompassed only the twenty-two former crewmembers and U.S. Army soldiers in *Proteus*. The men with Greely on the ice at Lady Franklin Bay had not been heard from since *Proteus* had deposited them on the beach two years ago.

Roughly two weeks after *Proteus* sank, Greely, ignorant of everything beyond the horizon, left camp with his men in the expedition's small boats as planned, carrying rations for forty days, their scientific instruments, and the precious records. On October 21, after first abandoning its boats and then drifting about atop an ice floe for the previous month, the party managed to make camp on Cape Sabine (not a cape but a small island), more than two hundred very hard miles below the former base. Here Greely's men were entirely alone, facing winter at 78° 43' north dreadfully ill equipped and unprotected. The next eight months saw predictable horrors.

In Washington it was clear that Greely had to be recovered as soon as shipping could move next year through Baffin Bay into Smith Sound and, with luck, up the Kane Sea if necessary. On December 17 President Arthur established a joint Army-Navy board to recommend to Secretary Lincoln and Secretary Chandler "the steps . . . to be taken for the equipment and transportation of the relief expedition, and to suggest such plans for its control and conduct, and for the organization of its personnel, as may seem to them best adapted to accomplish its purpose."

The board's recommendations proposed the purchase and dispatch of two specially outfitted Scottish whalers or Newfoundland sealers on the mission, to be accompanied by a Navy ship. Not until February 13, 1884, did a fractious Congress approve a resolution funding the rescue, finally freeing the executive departments to proceed. A few days later Secretary Chandler assigned Cdr. Winfield Schley, USN, forty-five, to take command of the Greely Relief Expedition. Commander Schley's orders gave him great discretion in the configuration and equipment of the ships, the stocks they would carry, and the selection of their officers and crews, all of whom were to be from the U.S. Navy. The second of the three lieutenants Schley chose for his squadron's flagship was Lt. Emory H. Taunt, USN, nine years Schley's junior at the Naval Academy.

Ship selection and procurement had begun before the enabling legislation was passed and even before Schley was appointed. Steamer *Bear*, out of Greenock, Scotland, a ten-year-old sister ship to SS *Proteus*, was purchased for $100,000. She was soon joined by *Thetis*, of Dundee, purchased for some $40,000 or so more than *Bear*. The last of the three ships selected turned out to be HMS *Alert*, a choice eased by the fact that *Alert* came gratis from the British Admiralty, a loan in appreciation for American assistance in the recovery of HMS *Resolute*, abandoned in the Arctic in 1855, found, and returned to Great Britain in 1866. All three were especially hardened for Arctic service.

Schley's plan, passed to the secretary of the navy March 17, was that his ships would sail in the spring individually when ready for sea, head for St. John's to coal and then join up at Upernavik, Greenland, and sail in convoy to Littleton Island and begin the search. Impelled on their way by powerful pushes from Secretary Chandler, all the ships left to go north early, fully loaded, handsomely stocked, and manned entirely by volunteers.

This high-level support was one of the reasons for the success that followed. Secretary Chandler was determined to use the rescue of the Greely expedition as the vehicle for restoring the Navy to favorable congressional and public regard. The second reason flowed naturally from the first. Chandler's Navy spent money on the relief mission freely, $762,996 by the time the last bill was paid, nearly 5 percent of the service's annual budget. Nothing was too good or too much for Schley et al. Near-nothing had been good enough for Greely once he was out of sight.

The ships of the relief squadron proceeded generally as planned. On Sunday, June 22, a four-man search party from USS *Thetis* led by Lieutenant Taunt found a cairn on Brevoort Island containing letters from Greely. The last was dated the previous October; it revealed that his expedition was on Cape Sabine, two miles to the north with forty days of rations—eight months ago. On a neighboring islet another cache was found containing the original records of the expedition. All that remained was to find the men.

Figure 12. The Greely expedition abandoned its base camp in full strength in late August 1883 as planned, after nearly two years in the Canadian Arctic. The survivors were rescued by the Navy almost exactly ten months later. Here the officers of the U.S. Navy's rescue squadron stand proudly behind the six survivors of Lieutenant Greely's expedition. Greely is seated on the deck, center. Schley stands to his immediate left, right hand on Greely's shoulder and left hand in his pocket. A bearded Lieutenant Taunt is behind the rail on the poop deck at the extreme right, looking left. *Thetis'* third lieutenant, Lt. Samuel Lemly, USN, is one of two officers standing on the uppermost step between the main and poop decks. Lemly's right hand rests on the railing. This photograph was taken in Upernavik, Greenland, on July 2 or 3, 1884. The ship is probably Commodore Schley's flagship, USS *Thetis*. *NAVAL HISTORY AND HERITAGE COMMAND PHOTO NHHC 2875*

July 17, 1884, Commander Schley sent Secretary Chandler a telegram from St. John's: "Thetis, Bear, and Loch Gerry [a chartered collier] arrived to-day from West Greenland, all well, separated in a gale from Alert yesterday 150 miles north. At 9 p.m., June 22d, five miles west of Cape Sabine in Smith Sound, Thetis and Bear rescued alive Lieutenant A. W. Greely, Sergeant Brainard, Sergeant Fredericks, Sergeant Long, Hospital Steward Bierderbick, Sergeant Elison, and Private Connell, the only survivors of the Lady Franklin Bay expedition." With that the waiting world knew the ordeal was finally over.

Schley's return in midsummer 1884 from the Arctic with Greely and the other survivors on board was a weeks-long triumph. His small squadron stopped first at the Portsmouth Navy Yard, then at New York City, and later in other East Coast ports, a floating parade deliberately extended and stage managed by Secretary Chandler and the Navy for the maximum effect on Congress and the public. The celebration's climax came the night of August 8 in New York, where President Arthur personally welcomed with fulsome praise the returning rescuers and their dazed charges in a speech supporting Navy modernization and expansion.

Four months later, December 1, President Arthur's first State of the Union message—the same address in which he reported "pursuant to the advice of the Senate at its last session, I recognized the flag of the Internal Association of the Kongo as that of a friendly government"—put the new president on record as endorsing the Naval Advisory Board's recommendations for ship construction. Evidently persuaded, the following March Congress funded the acquisition of the cruisers *Charleston* and *Newark* and the gunboats *Yorktown* and *Petrel*, byproducts of the rosy afterglow of Schley's success at Cape Sabine.[6]

Mission accomplished to enthusiastic public and official acclamation, Schley went to Washington to take charge of the Navy's Bureau of Equipment and Recruiting, relieving Rear Admiral English and freeing the admiral to take command of the European Squadron at Villefranche-sur-Mer, France. At about the same time Lieutenant Taunt detached from USS *Thetis*, joined USS *Lancaster*, and slid smoothly from Schley's command back to English's.

Schley and most of his rescue expedition's officers did well professionally. He was promoted to commodore while in charge of equipment procurement and enlisted recruiting, and eventually to admiral in 1899 (despite some sharp criticism from brother officers of his performance in command of the American squadron at the Battle of Santiago de Cuba the year before). Among his twenty subordinate officers in *Thetis* and *Bear* in 1884, five also rose to become admirals. Most of the other fifteen went on to distinguished careers, in part because Schley had been generous with his praise of the officers and men who, under his command, had rescued what was left of Greely's expedition.

"To whom it may concern," he wrote,

Lieut. E. H. Taunt USN served under my command in the Greely Relief Expedition sent out in 1884 to rescue or to ascertain the fate of Lieut. A. W. Greely and twenty five of his command of the Lady Franklin Bay Expedition to the Arctic Regions. During this exacting service I found Lieut. Taunt a most competent and efficient officer.

His habits came daily under my observation and were regarded as exceptionally good. I would have trusted him on any service however delicate or perilous with confidence. His official integrity and competency impressed me as of the highest order. His character during this association was always that of a steady, reliable man, and his behavior always gentlemanly.

W. S. Schley
Captain, USN, Chief of Bureau
of Equipment and Recruiting
Navy Dept.

Such praise from Schley was powerful stuff, strong enough, Taunt must have hoped, to put a shine on a service record otherwise marked by poor performance and marred with critical appraisals.

16

Sometime early afternoon of his first day on the ground in Africa, Lieutenant Taunt boarded *Ville d'Anvers*, one of the Congo Free State's small, flush-deck steamboats, at Banana Point and departed for the port of Boma and Vivi Station beyond. Most of what any white man in 1885 knew about equatorial Africa came from Henry Morton Stanley's books about his epic expeditions. The center of the continent was not impenetrable or arid. The Congo River, despite what Livingstone had hoped, did not flow into the Nile. Nor did it join the Niger, the passionate belief of the Admiralty's Sir John Barrow notwithstanding. Instead, its river system washed a huge and apparently fertile land peopled by millions of Africans. Taunt might have prepared himself for this mission if he'd anticipated it, assuming that Admiral English shared that part of Secretary Chandler's orders with his son-in-law before they sailed from Gibraltar, but it's likely he knew little more about what to expect upriver than what he'd overheard during Administrator General de Winton's official call on the admiral on board the flagship.

That call, on April 30, was marked by a ceremonial twenty-one guns fired as his boat approached the flagship, a salute to the gold-starred, sky-blue flag of the Congo Free State. Later in the day the administrator general's departure from the ship was observed by *Lancaster* with a further seventeen guns, acknowledging its guest's personal status as the chief of state. These salutes were the first international honors granted to the Congo's colors.

Figure 13. "The 30-ton Paddlewheel Steamer *Ville d'Anvers.*" *Ville d'Anvers* appears here during an unknown event fully dressed under colorful flags, with what seems to be a small party of merrymakers under canvas on deck forward of the stack. She was the first of three small steamboats in which Taunt hitchhiked during his trip up- and downriver in 1885. Built for the lower river, *Ville d'Anvers* drew more water than did the upriver boats. She was wrecked just below Boma on a partially submerged rock that same July, sinking so fast that her passengers, including the administrator general, were lucky to escape drowning. Her loss halved the Free State's steamer fleet on the lower Congo. STANLEY, CONGO AND THE FOUNDING OF ITS FREE STATE 2:226

Banana to Boma took half a day steaming against the current, so getting under way around noon on Saturday, May 2, would have seen *Ville d'Anvers*' passengers arrive at their first stop before dark the same day. Everyone spent the night at Boma.

Taunt's two passes through this small town in 1885, the first heading upriver in May and the second heading down in October, were several years too early to see Boma in its prime (and a decade or two too late to see it as one of the world's largest slave markets). In May 1886, one year after Taunt first visited the place, the state capital relocated to Boma from Vivi because of that station's dangerous river approach and the exhausting climb from the waterfront landing to the high plateau on which Vivi stood. After the move was completed Boma was home to the administrator general,

Figures 14 and 15. Government House and the Roman Catholic cathedral in Boma. Boma's status as chief city of the Congo Free State beginning in mid-1886 was soon confirmed by the erection of Government House and of a compact Roman Catholic cathedral, the snug seat of the Congo bishopric. Both structures were assembled from prefabricated metal panels imported from Europe. (As built, Government House's second story had no wings and its verandah was open.) In 1926 the colony's capital was removed to Leopoldville, now Kinshasa. Today Boma's derelict nineteenth-century Government House is home to several encamped tenants, while its tiny first cathedral stands vacant and locked just yards down slope from the seat of the modern Diocese of Boma, the brick Cathedral of Our Lady of the Assumption. *AUTHOR'S PHOTOGRAPHS*

the offices of the other chief officials of local government, the site of the Congo's first Roman Catholic cathedral, and the headquarters and boot camp of the national army, the Force Publique.

Taunt left Boma early Sunday morning for Vivi, where he arrived on Monday, May 4. He disembarked around noon, the plucky *Ville d'Anvers* having earlier safely passed through swirling water and powerful currents flowing down from nearby Yelala Falls, which invariably made the last mile of the approach to the station thrilling.[7] He was met and entertained there by Count de Pourtales, the station's chief. The count's slight command high atop the north bank of the river was a cluster of stick-built, prefabricated wooden buildings sharing a flat space half the size of a football field with the optimistic beginnings of a small banana plantation. The four larger structures were residences for white men; the several smaller ones were storehouses. Among them for a few months longer stood the Free State's capitol, a former hospital from which no patient was said ever to have emerged alive.

Between May 6 and May 13 Taunt readied himself at Vivi for the upcoming trek around the rapids cross-country to Stanley Pool, assisted in his preparations by Major William Parminter, one of the Free State's four division chiefs and its acting administrator general. Pourtales and Parminter must have been the unnamed Tisdel critics to whom Taunt referred in his report to Secretary Whitney. On its first page he informed the secretary that he "had heard many criticisms concerning the report of the United States agent, Mr. Tisdel, to the effect that he had not seen the Congo Valley . . . &c. I therefore felt it my duty," Taunt added, "to go into the interior as far as practicable and gain all the information possible of the valley of the Congo." Taunt said nothing of Tisdel's self-defense, that there had been no boat available months ago to carry him beyond Stanley Pool.

By Wednesday, May 13, when Taunt's caravan was finally ready to leave Vivi for Stanley Pool, what had been naively imagined in Washington as a one-officer expedition had swelled into a procession. It included fifty native porters carrying more than a ton and a half of Taunt's personal effects, his "chop," bottled drinks, and camp equipment, all parceled out into individual loads; a Zanzibari interpreter and a Kabinda cook, both men unnamed; and the first of several government minders and guides, Alfred Parminter, the major's nephew.

Two days later, nearly two weeks after he had been detached from USS *Lancaster*, Lieutenant Taunt and company struck out purposefully from an overnight camp at M'Poso Station, on the south (left) bank of the Congo almost directly across from Vivi, heading upriver around the falls toward

Stanley Pool.[8] Their hike through "mountainous, rocky, barren country" took Taunt's caravan eastward along a string of places whose names sound like the vocabulary for speaking in tongues: M'Pallabolla, M'bauza Matake, Lukungo, Manyanga. Joseph Conrad, who hiked along the same track four years later, described the experience: "Paths, paths, everywhere; a stamped-in network of paths spreading over the empty land through long grass, through burnt grass, through thickets, down and up chilly ravines, up and down stony hills ablaze with heat; and a solitude, a solitude, nobody, not a hut. The population had cleared out a long time ago." In 1885 the track was marginally less desolate than in 1889. The next few years, however, would see the last of the trackside native villages disappear into the interior.

In South Manyanga Station at the end of the month Parminter fell ill with "bilious fever" and was replaced by Charles Bateman, chief of Lutété Station, some eighty miles farther upriver. At Lutété, conveniently now at his home station, Bateman collapsed on June 2. "Bilious fever" again. His place in the line of march was promptly filled by Stanhope, Bateman's assistant. Such health problems, Taunt observed blandly, were typical in cataract country. His report quoted statistics on missionary mortality that counted thirteen of twenty-six English Baptist missionaries dead. American Baptists, curiously, seemed to be hardier. Only sixteen of forty-five had died at their post.

In the chapter of his report on missions, Taunt opined that "missionaries should under no circumstances go to the Congo, except they go as members of one of the missions already established, or with the means and authority to establish a new mission that can look for *permanent support* to some sect or society at home. . . . It is useless to send missionaries to the Congo unless they are supplied with ample means for establishment and for *permanent support*; should [religious societies] neglect this provision, they are sending their people to *certain death*." Taunt's sermon was prompted by the fate of six men sent to Congo by the Reverend A. B. Simpson's Faith Cure Tabernacle, on Twenty-third Street in New York City, who left their mother church for Africa with only $500 between them. One promptly died; four others had their passages home charitably paid by Baptists; the sixth joined another mission.

Midday on Sunday, June 7, twenty-three days and 236 hard miles out of M'Poso, Taunt arrived at Leopoldville, atop the heights facing French Brazzaville across the river's exit from Stanley Pool and just above the long reach of white water through the Crystal Mountains Stanley had christened "Livingstone Falls." ("Livingstone" as a name for the whole Congo River never managed to catch on.) Counting six days' delay at stations en route, his small caravan had averaged a little better than ten miles a day, at the high end of the usual six to ten miles per day averaged by caravans trudging through central Africa.

Taunt's arrival beneath a fluttering thirty-eight-star United States flag on the heights at Leopoldville Station was marked by military ceremony. Tisdel had been greeted by gun salutes, and it's certain that Taunt was, too. The show was made possible because Leopoldville, three years old and the seat of the third of the four administrative divisions of the Congo Free State, was home to a small detachment of Houssa tribesmen, from Lagos on the Slave Coast (now Nigeria). Armed Houssas, here under the command of the English division chief, Captain Seymour Saulez, were the state's usual enforcers of order and discipline. When not so occupied, they were available to provide such pomp as was appropriate for foreign visitors straying past. When Houssas were not available, stations were impossible to defend and a shortage of these mercenaries occasionally forced the abandonment of operational bases either because of native or Arab slaver pressure.

Saulez was an old hand at the station. He took command in early 1882, promising Stanley "that he would distinguish his governorship by the industrious improvement of Leopoldville." Stanley's natural inclination had been to staff his expeditions with Britons, which until Leopold needed the French more than he feared them fit with the king's requirements, too. At first Congo Free State station chiefs represented a mixed bag of nationalities, including, surprisingly, a disproportionate number of Swedish army officers. Constant "bickerings and jealousies" tearing at this small, international community had, Taunt would report, led to a decision "to officer the State with Belgians, retaining only such of the other nationalities as have proved themselves especially adapted for the work."

Taunt's promised ride for the 1,100 miles to Stanley Falls from Leopoldville was to have been in the government steam cutter *Royal*, but he arrived to find her urgently preparing to move upriver, loading men, two Krupp artillery guns, war rockets, and other materiel to reinforce Stanley Falls Station against an anticipated attack by Arab slavers from the east.

Royal, a 30-foot lifeboat built by J. Samuel White's, of Cowes on the Isle of Wight, together with the larger paddle steamer *En Avant* (Forward), was one of the five steamers Stanley had brought with him upriver when he was first setting out Leopold's stations on the Congo in 1879. She was a gift to the expedition from King Leopold, hence the name. Her relatively deep draft, three feet six inches, guaranteed frequent groundings.

Alternative transportation, *Henry Reed*, a sternwheeler belonging to the American Baptist Missionary Union, was offered, but she didn't depart until

Figure 16. The steam launch *A.I.A.* today. Nothing remains of the first steamer fleet on the Congo River, the five powered boats shipped in June 1879 from Antwerp to Banana on board the Belgian transport SS *Barga* for Stanley's use. The last remnants of any of his riverboats are the rusting, skeletal remains of the steam launch *A.I.A.*, exposed to weather on a wheeled cart in the Groupe Chanimetal shipyard, on the grounds of the old port very near where she first went into the water. She's probably best known for her role as part of Stanley's river flotilla during his abortive mission in 1888 to rescue Emin Pasha. *AUTHOR'S PHOTOGRAPH*

July 3, a few days after the heavily laden *Royal* finally got under way on her military mission. Taunt used the intervening nearly month-long delay to putter around enormous Stanley Pool, sightseeing in *Peace*, a twin screw–propelled launch belonging to the survivors among the English Baptists of the Livingstone Inland Mission, at Leopoldville. Like everything else the missionaries had, *Peace* (launched June the year before) and *Henry Reed* (in the water two months later) had been hauled up in pieces from the lower river by porters, something under a thousand or so loads for each boat.

The overriding engineering design objectives for all the river steamers on the Congo, shallow draft and very light weight component construction, pressed the state of the boat builder's art very hard. Achievement guaranteed that the assembled boat steaming in a demanding environment would be ornery and delicate, a combination that must have made operations

Figures 17 and 18. The upper Congo River steamers *Peace* and *Henry Reed*. Steamer *Peace*, of the English Baptist Missionary Society, shown here "wooding up," was designed and built in 1881 by Thornycroft and Company at their works on the Thames at Church Wharf in Chiswick, England. The specification called for a steamboat 70 feet long and 10 1/2 feet wide, drawing eighteen inches of water when loaded with six tons of cargo, and capable of twelve miles per hour under way on both engines, fired by a single boiler. The process from establishing the requirement to launching the boat took four years. Compared to Sanford's first steamboat

exquisitely frustrating. Henry Morton Stanley, who for a time in the spring of 1887 commandeered and then commanded the Congo's entire fleet of river-worthy boats, was contemptuous of them all, but especially of *Peace*.

Peace's 16-inch propellers turned at a maximum of 460 rpm in tunnels that rose to five inches above water level but remained full of water while under way. The shrouded props got fouled repeatedly. Steaming, her boiler couldn't hold working pressure, and she required stops for lubrication every half an hour. Stanley described *Peace* as "asthmatic," "spasmodic," "good-for-nothing," and a "poor, miserable thing." The other steamers were only slightly less cranky.

The factor pacing Taunt's progress upriver from the Pool turned out to be the availability of fuel for *Henry Reed*'s engine. Steamers on the lower Congo burned imported coal, but those on the upper river had to be fueled by dead wood chopped into short lengths. Cutting wood in the dark during overnight stops wasn't easy, but man-hauling coal for miles uphill past the

Florida, everything about *Peace*'s construction, shipment, transportation upriver to Stanley Pool, assembly, and trials on the river in 1884 went remarkably smoothly, notwithstanding the death of three engineers practically on arrival in country. Very nearly the same size as *Peace,* the American Baptist Missionary Union's steamer *Henry Reed* was also built on the Thames, but by Forrestt and Son. *Henry Reed* arrived disassembled at Stanley Pool in April 1881 and was finally afloat on the water late November. Brown, Story of Africa 3:120, from photos by Reverend Darby and Reverend Billington, in Bentley, Pioneering on the Congo 2:13

rapids was more than anyone was willing to take on. Every night the launch tied up and put a party of twenty Loango woodcutters ashore to collect it. The river had recently flooded its banks, and they were hard pressed to find enough dry wood to keep the fire hot and steam up in the boiler. "The question of fuel is already becoming serious," Taunt wrote describing yet another of the vulnerabilities of the state's upriver logistic system:

> While there is plenty of live timber, the dead dry trees necessary to make steam are fast disappearing. There were days during my trip that we were not able to steam more than one hour on account of the difficulty in obtaining fuel. If railway communication is established between the sea and Stanley Pool, coal will, of course, solve the fuel question. . . . As it is now the wood-cutters must be paid and fed, and the necessary saws, axes, &c. provided. But in the meantime, unless depots for wood are made by killing a number of trees between the Pool and Stanley Falls,

the supply of dry fuel will be exhausted in a year's time and the steamers obliged to lay up.

The availability of firewood was not a new worry for steamboat crews in the mid-1880s. English Baptist missionaries Henry Crudgington and William Bentley had hiked up the Congo River to Stanley Pool in January and February 1881 at the head of a train of twenty porters, a trek described in the first volume of Bentley's *Pioneering on the Congo* (Religious Tract Society, 1900).[9] Once settled in the country, like other white men they moved largely by boat. "On a steamer wood is the daily anxiety," the Reverend Bentley wrote in his memoir, "from four o'clock in the afternoon the banks are eagerly scanned for a large dead tree. . . . The tree being felled . . . several cross-cut saws are brought, and the tree is cut into sections of about two feet. The sections are brought to the bank, and riven with large axes and steel wedges. . . . It may be two or three o'clock in the morning before it is all cut up, riven into suitable chunks for the furnace, and stowed on the steamer."[10] In common with real crews, fictitious boat crews worried about firewood stocks, too. In *Heart of Darkness*, Joseph Conrad has Marlow telling his shipmates on the Thames about the challenges of Congo riverboat command; among them was constantly keeping a lookout for dead wood that could be cut up in the night for next day's steaming.

Sometimes restricted by wood shortages to as little as an hour a day under way, *Henry Reed* slowly passed Kwamouth Station (above the southern bank at the mouth of the Kwa-Kasai, later this tributary's watershed would become prime elephant hunting grounds), then one after the other Bolobo ("the healthiest spot on the Congo"), Lukelela, and Equator Stations, to reach Bangala Station at the entrance, Taunt noted, to cannibal country on July 30. The next day—and several days behind *Royal*—*Henry Reed* again got under way, still flying an American flag but now festooned with wire guards, fine mesh screens hinged to drop down when necessary to protect the steersman and engineer, and fine enough to stop even small poisoned arrows. Between Bangala and Stanley Falls lay five hundred miles of river lined with "suspicious, savage, and hostile" natives living on its banks.

Their hostility should not have surprised Taunt. Riverfront villages were the natural prey of Europeans moving upriver from the Atlantic or Arabs moving down from the Indian Ocean, with the result that native warriors were in semipermanent combat against foreign passersby. Taunt arrived at M'Pesa just behind the *Royal*, which had paused on her trip upriver long enough to burn the village and kill some of its warriors. In a few days *Henry*

Reed was to pass the mouth of the Aruwimi River, where only a few months earlier the despised slaver "Tippoo Tib" had been by to burn villages, take slaves, and steal ivory. "Tippoo Tib" (1837?–1905), of mixed African and Arabian descent, was the ruthless and powerful chief of the Arab traders and slavers based at Kasongo. Beginning in the 1870s his raiding parties swept downriver from beyond Stanley Falls and terrorized the natives of the upper Congo.[11]

August 13 at Monongeri, a week beyond M'Pesa, things got very hot for Taunt and his shipmates. "I had heard that Stanley and Lieutenant Van Gile had both been obliged to burn villages here [along the narrow Monongeri Channel of the river]," he wrote, not explaining this obligation, "but I never imagined we would meet with the reception we did":

> At 2.30 p.m. we ran up opposite the large village of Monongeri. To our surprise we were greeted with yells, war-drums, war-horns, &c. The men were armed to the teeth with knives, spears, and poisoned arrows, and, to all appearances, were frantic with rage. I took my guns out and placed them in full sight, but at this they only increased their uproar.
>
> Finding that we were steaming on, some of the men, absolutely devoid of fear, rushed waist-deep into the water to throw their spears, and as we passed the town, others launched their canoes to follow, many running along the banks. . . .
>
> After passing the last town I calculated that we were followed by two to three hundred men, some in canoes, and the others running along the banks. To add to my anxiety, I found that we were running short of wood, and I knew that if we were obliged to anchor in the channel it would be a hard fight all night and a harder one in the morning when we attempted to land for wood. . . . Shortly after 8 p.m., to our surprise, we were again greeted with the yells and war-horns, and I found that we were surrounded by from ten to twenty war canoes filled with men. It was some time before we drove them off.

Thursday, August 15, *Royal* with thirty men on board and her whale boat in tow joined *Henry Reed*. She had dropped down from Stanley Falls Station to provide armed support for the missionary steamer's final dash to her destination. The scenery to either side on these last five days of heading upriver looked everywhere the same: "From the [Aruwimi] to Stanley Falls the natives were living in canoes; the villages on both banks had been burned by the Arabs in the spring, and in only a few instances had the people commenced rebuilding."

Next Tuesday afternoon Taunt in *Henry Reed* finally steamed up to Bouki Island and Stanley Falls Station, but not before twice hitting rocks on the approach to the landing. Running onto rocks in the river was an occupational hazard. The next year, after *Henry Reed* was turned over to the state, she was again holed on some rocks. After repairs, the boat returned to Stanley Falls Station, to be kept there to support exploration. Heading upstream into the river's powerful current (but assisted by strong tailwinds in the narrows between Stanley Pool and Kwamouth), Taunt had traveled over one thousand miles in forty-eight days, just over twenty miles per day. About double the speed of a fast-moving expedition on foot.

Taunt stepped ashore at Stanley Falls Station, the far eastern and furthest upriver outpost of Leopold's African empire, into a war zone. The station was pressed into a no-man's-land between hundreds of Tippoo Tib's "Arabs" with modern arms camped not far upriver, and uncounted thousands of enraged natives with primitive weapons living in the great valley below the last cataract. In this miserable, indefensible place, the mission of its 3 resident white men and 35 Houssa troops (of the 150 on state rolls) seemed to be simply to survive. In August, while Taunt was there, they were doing so exclusively on a diet of fish. The last of their canned, imported provisions had been consumed two months earlier.

Pushed along by the Congo's current, six to eight knots in places, and enthusiasm to put Stanley Falls Station behind him after five days ashore, Taunt's trip downriver was much faster than the trip up. As if it were propelled by the same favorable current, Taunt's written report to the secretary of the navy raced through the details of his return trip. Out of Stanley Falls the morning of August 25, *Henry Reed* steamed past Bangala, Equator (delayed five days for boiler repair), Lukelela (now abandoned), Bolobo (a "nasty, lumpy sea" roiling the adjacent twelve-mile-wide reach of the river delayed departure for a day and a half), by Kwamouth, down the river's narrow canyon and finally across Stanley Pool and, on September 12, back to Leopoldville, where Taunt found the steamer *Stanley* assembled, finally in the water, and now ready for her maiden voyage. He'd done the two-thousand-mile-plus round trip, Leopoldville to Leopoldville, in seventy-two days.

On foot again, Taunt walked out of Leopoldville heading for the Atlantic at the head of a caravan of twenty-five Zanzibari porters on Friday, September 18. On familiar ground, he reached Lutété (now home only to the English Baptist Mission; the state had closed its station there between his visits because of garrison shortages) on the twenty-third, Lukungo (division headquarters and site of the American Baptist Mission) on the twenty-fifth, and M'Poso on October 4. On Friday, October 9, Taunt left Vivi for the hike to Banana and not too long after arrival there he sailed for Europe and an audience with King Leopold II.

Because *Lancaster*'s cruise schedule had not permitted Leopold to tenderize Taunt ahead of time, the call on the king amounted to an exit debriefing, an opportunity for the monarch to massage his American visitor before any report got written. Their audience over, on January 2, 1886, Taunt passed through Montreux, Switzerland, heading south for Nice and his squadron, there to resume for a short while his career as a Navy officer on sea duty.

Taunt had been in the Congo Free State for just over five months, a month longer than had Willard Tisdel. His probe upriver proved to be a life-changing experience. Beginning then, Taunt searched for a way to convert his knowledge of the Congo River into a successful, new career.

17

"Portuguese wine or Bordeaux is supplied, one bottle being allowed each man each day. Brandy and champagne is supplied in moderate quantities, the latter especially being considered invaluable in severe fever cases." That information about the state's alcohol ration for white men in the Congo might have interested the vintners, if there were any, among the readers of Taunt's report in the Senate. Senators from agricultural states—and in 1887 all thirty-eight states were—would have been interested but not surprised to learn that horses, mules, and donkeys imported to work in the cataract area could not eat "wire grass," and most died a few months after being put ashore. Still other senators might have might been fascinated by instruction in the Congo basin's topography and its network of rivers; in the Free State's political structure and system of government; in its steamer fleet and what constituted good ship design for the river; in the appearance, character, and morals of natives, foreign troops, and laborers; in slavery and cannibalism ("of this I have had *positive proof*," he wrote on page 26, sounding as if he'd dined with them); and in the trial-by-ordeal jurisprudence of the Baskunga tribe of the lower Congo Valley ("a weak, indolent, superstitious race"). After Taunt had described his movement upriver and downriver, the remaining thirty-two of his report's forty-two pages addressed special subjects. But the reason that Taunt and Tisdel before him had been sent upriver was to scope the commercial opportunities this new country might offer to American farmers, manufacturers, and traders, and that's what senators wanted to read about.

Like Tisdel, Taunt saw no prospect that an American start-up on the lower Congo could compete successfully with the Europeans already there. The construction of a railroad around the downriver cluster of rapids could open up new opportunities, however. A railroad, most thought, was the essential solution to the problem of Congo's uncooperative geography: the fact that the great basin was land-locked unless an economical way could be found to replace "loaded heads" and to move cargo in bulk around the lower rapids.

As submitted by Secretary of the Navy Whitney to Congress on February 1, 1887, Taunt's report also included samples of trade articles and currency as well as six "documents": *Henry Reed*'s deck log, a map of European holdings on the Congo, a copy of the International Association of the Congo's agents' regulations, rules and regulations for the Houssa armed guards, "practical hints for travelers in the tropics," and notes on African fevers and on dysentery.

His assessment—made public because, prompted by Sanford, Senator George Edmunds of Vermont arranged for the Senate Committee on Foreign Relations to call for it—gave hope to Congo enthusiasts, who needed new money and new people to make their fantasies of wealth possible, and to those others, potential investors and volunteers, who could make these fantasies vital.

Those same enthusiasts could not have been pleased by press coverage in the United States that had suggested something different. The September 5, 1885, edition of the *Cincinnati Commercial Tribune* quoted (and perhaps misquoted) Taunt as saying, "This is a beastly country. White men can not live here, and for my part I can see nothing to draw them here, especially into the interior. . . . Stanley Pool is certain the best post I have struck thus far, and that is bad enough. I shall be heartily glad when I can leave this fever-ridden hole."

18

Taunt returned to the United States from his first trip to the Congo with an assortment of African specimens and artifacts, including weapons, instruments, jewelry and decorative items, furnishings, and even a "fly flapper" and "hairs from a rhinoceros's tail." Forty of these items (and a dozen others he turned over in June 1888) were delivered to the National Museum, then occupying much of the Smithsonian Institution's "castle" on the capital's Mall, in October 1886 and remain in the Smithsonian's African collection today.

The collection of specimens and artifacts to which Taunt contributed was the progeny of another, much larger contribution in 1842 by a naval officer to the National Museum's forerunner, the National Institute for the Promotion of Science. That officer, "Commodore" Charles Wilkes, USN, who like many men in this story affected a rank or title that was not his, returned that June after four years at sea in command of the U.S. Exploring Expedition, a circumnavigation of the world in squadron strength that maritime historian Nathaniel Philbrick called in 2003 "one of the largest, most sophisticated scientific and surveying enterprises the world had ever seen."[12] And so it was; never mind that the Ex. Ex.'s return was marred by open warfare between most of its officers and the commander they loathed, and highlighted by the sensational courts-martial of Wilkes and four of his junior officers that followed. Once unloaded from the flagship, USS *Vincennes*, and delivered into the Great Hall of the new Patent Office Building, the enormous size of his expedition's scientific collection became apparent. Thousands of tools, implements, weapons, instruments, and items of apparel and decoration. Many hundreds of plants, birds, mammals, fish, seeds, shells, and fossils. A library of journals. The immense cache forced the construction of a dedicated museum building, finally putting to work the $508,000 inheritance from James Smithson, who in 1829 died and left the money to the United States (a country he'd never visited) for the "increase and diffusion of knowledge."[13]

The first items in the National Museum's African collection from a Navy officer came not from Taunt but probably from Commo. Matthew Calbraith Perry, USN, who years before he famously "opened" Japan had commanded the antislavery patrol off West Africa in 1842–45. He returned home from the assignment with souvenirs from Liberia that, by a roundabout route, ended up in the Smithsonian in 1867. That collection grew very slowly, amounting in 1920 to only several thousand items, a rate of increase that suggests how relatively few Americans found themselves for any reason in Africa below the Sahara in the nineteenth century. In 1921 a gift to the museum from Herbert Ward—an employee of Taunt's during his upcoming incarnation in the Congo—of some 2,700 items from equatorial Africa effectively doubled the museum's holdings.

Taunt's initial gift in 1886 marked the start of a relationship with the Smithsonian that continued nearly to the end of his life. At first, he looked to the museum for employment, after that for endorsement, and finally for training in an apparently sincere effort to continue to contribute to its collections from his last post on the Congo.

19

So who was right about the Congo's prospects, Tisdel or Taunt? September 21, 1886, the *New York Times* published a long column by David Ker titled "No Trade on the Congo," datelined Huard Point, lower Congo. In it Ker voted for Tisdel. He spoke with some authority, or at least he affected some.

David Ker was a frequent contributor to *Harper's New Monthly Magazine*. From 1885 through 1892 he served as *Harper's* utility columnist, writing more than thirty pieces on unrelated subjects in those seven years with a fluid style that required nothing more of his readers than free-form curiosity and a little endurance. Ker's "Africa's Awakening" appeared in *Harper's* March 1886 issue. In it he surveyed the continent in twelve pages and concluded, yes, it was rising, a process he thought might be accelerated if the White Nile River and the Congo River conveniently connected somewhere, thus permitting commerce to move easily between West Africa and the eastern Mediterranean.[14] Sadly, as John Speke and Henry Morton Stanley had confirmed during the past twenty years or so and as Ker should have known, they did not. That same year Ker published *Lost Among White Africans: A Boy's Adventure on the Upper Congo* (Cassell, 1886), proving he was capable of intentionally writing fiction about Africa, too.

"I dare say you've read what the last two men who have been out here— Tisdel, Taunt—say about the Congo," Ker wrote in the *Times*, quoting an unnamed "head of a large trading house" on the river. All Ker's interlocutors quoted in the piece might have been imaginary, but perhaps they were not. "Well, they've both given their own personal impressions of it, and I have no doubt that they've both written in good faith; but still, if you were to ask me which of the two has come nearest to the real state of affairs on the Congo, I should certainly vote for Tisdel," the trader is supposed to have said. Others Ker allegedly spoke to—the purser of an English steamer, an English station chief, a Free State official, a "veteran trader"—would vote that way, too. So one-sided was the commentary that Ker suggested he should write a sequel to "Africa's Awakening" called "Africa Gone to Sleep Again."

Never mind what a *New York Times* columnist might happen to write, Henry Shelton Sanford, living in scenic Flanders at the time beyond his means, knew what side he was on in the debate about Africa's promise. Taunt's.

5

The Sanford Exploring Expedition

Your own discretion and good judgment must guide you in all matters not especially provided for in these examples.
Trusting a kind providence will protect you and your colleagues in the important work you have contracted to do.
I am,
Truly yours on behalf of the [proprietors of the] Sanford Exploring Expedition

H. S. Sanford, from Brussels, to Emory Taunt, June 22, 1886

20

"Although General Henry Sanford is little known to his compatriots," Catherine Anne Cline wrote forty years ago, looking for an arresting topic sentence for an article in the *Catholic Historical Review*, "he probably had a greater influence on world events than any other American of his day."[1] Considering the constellation of Sanford's Civil War contemporaries, first among them Abraham Lincoln, Cline overshot badly. Still, Sanford would have been flattered even by her more modest assessment, which followed: "If one accepts the view that the establishment of the Congo Free State did much to stimulate the scramble for Africa and to establish the lines of the partition, and if, as it is generally agreed, American recognition was a crucial factor in its establishment, then Sanford, the former United States minister to Belgium who engineered that recognition emerges as a figure of considerable importance." Given Sanford's seminal role in early American diplomatic relations with the Congo, "considerable" is certainly fair.

Inheritance in hand in 1841—a product of the success of his late father, Nehemiah, manufacturing iron tacks and brads in Derby, Connecticut—Sanford's reverse Midas touch led him into western and southern land speculations and investments in patents and start-up railroads and mines that almost invariably lost money through the next forty years. By the mid-1880s, years of living large on two continents, coupled to poor business sense and episodes of what could be confused with bad luck (among them a great freeze in central Florida in early January 1866 that killed his citrus groves), had slowly eroded Henry Sanford's substantial fortune.

The Sanfords, husband, wife, and surviving six children (Leopold, their second son, died at age five in 1885, leaving behind a brother and five sisters) were still living well in the 1880s, but sometimes on the float and with borrowed money.[2] Republican Americans, meaning those instinctively disdainful of continental royalty and aristocrats, who knew Sanford accused him of aping the expensive tastes of European elites. Even Sanford's mother, Nancy Bateman, was put off by his showy style.

This criticism was given substance by the Sanfords' elegantly appointed legation apartments in the Belgian capital, while he served there as minister, and more so by "Gingelom," the family's baronial estate in southern Flanders, recently privately restored. Chateau Gingelom in the 1880s was a marvel: three-story interconnected building blocks of lovely russet brick, capped by spires and towers stretching into the sky above. Complete with eight servants and a cluster of outbuildings, the family seat practically oozed aristocratic pretensions. In 1888, forced to economize, the Sanfords relocated to Chateau Maillard, a substantial but somewhat less grand property in Meldert, Belgium, west of Gingelom and closer to Brussels. It's a school today.

Behind the handsome walls, however, all was not well. Husband and wife—she nearly a generation younger than he—fought about money and other things. The Sanfords' sole common perspective seems to have been their views about young Henry Junior ("Harry"), their eldest child and heir. His parents both believed that their surviving son was a wastrel, who approaching his twenties was already running up allowance-busting cigar, wine, and club bills for his parents to pay.

Harry, born in 1865 midway through his father's diplomatic assignment in Belgium and a year after his parents married, was a disappointment almost from the beginning. Sent off at eleven to boarding school in England in 1876 and then to Harvard in 1884, he matured from an indifferent secondary school scholar into an often invisible collegiate one. Harry's Harvard professors wrote his parents regularly from Cambridge to report his absences from class. Attendance, in those days, was required. He never graduated.[3]

The low point in family relationships came in January 1891, when Harry, now twenty-five, wrote from Belair a long, bitter letter to his mother, following one from his father on December 10 that had disowned him and hers to him a week later, in which he recalled it was "seven years since I have had one kind word from you . . . and . . . six since you told me you did not love me." There wasn't time for their relationship to recover. Henry Shelton Sanford, twenty-six, died of tuberculosis in New York that October, a few months after his father's death. He's buried together with both parents and three sisters in the family plot at the Long Hill Burial Ground in Shelton, Connecticut.

21

Something—naiveté, optimism, or neediness—blinded Sanford to Leopold's true character, to the implications of what Leopold was planning for equatorial Africa. Henry Morton Stanley, raised an orphan and educated in a poorhouse, was more clear-eyed. "My Dear General," he wrote to Sanford on March 4, 1885 (several weeks before Tisdel completed his mission and two months before Taunt first stepped ashore at Banana Point),

> But seriously I tell you this—I found at Brussels the same disposition of miswisdom, the same put off of the evil, the same enormous voracity to swallow a million of square miles, with a gullet that will not take in a herring. Grandeur of ideas—yes, but the means poor and scant, so that all will be endangered by an extravagance of ideas which lead to bankruptcy and slovenliness. . . . Don't try to do more than your purse will warrant. Read this note to Mrs. Sanford—she will, as a housewife, understand thoroughly what I mean, and you surely as a real estate owner will recognize the truth of it.

Stanley meant by this to warn Sanford from being taken in by Leopold's grand visions or adopting them for his own. But Sanford seems to have learned little from his own real estate speculations, plantations in South Carolina and Louisiana, and some 23,000 undeveloped acres in central Florida.

In view of Henry Sanford's years of pro bono service to the first King Leopold and then to the second, much of it after 1876 having to do with Africa, he expected to be named Leopold II's viceroy for central Africa when, in July 1885, the Belgian parliament approved the king's new role and the new African state was officially created. Such a post would have been fitting reward for Sanford's essential services to his patron: recruiting the irreplaceable Stanley into Leopold's service, regularizing the Congo's international status through obtaining American recognition, and massaging delegates to the Berlin Conference to the point that the Congo fell softly into the king's hands. By any measure, however, elevating such a self-indulgent man, one disinterested in detail and prone to management by remote control, would have been a disastrous misstep for the canny king.

Leopold didn't need a chief executive in Brussels. He did need a surrogate in Africa. How the high-living Sanfords—his wife, Gertrude Ellen, had tastes every bit as elevated as his; she wasn't prepared to live in the United States, much less in Africa—might have adjusted to life in tiny, hot and wet, rustic Boma will never be known. That job offer never came from the king.

Leopold II selected Henry Morton Stanley—in his element in just such conditions—as the Congo's interim chief executive. In April 1884 Stanley was replaced by Sir Francis de Winton, an Englishman, who made way in July 1886 not for Sanford, but for Camille Janssens, a Belgian (whose great, squared-off beard made him a reasonable body double for the king). Janssens' appointment as administrator general—he served for six years—was a hint of things to come. Over time Leopold II filled most senior administration positions in the colony with malleable subjects from home, in part to strengthen his personal control and in part to mollify the French, who watching from over the fence of their own Congo colony were always suspicious of Britons in executive positions abroad or at home.

In the same way that the king put Stanley aside when his usefulness as the property's explorer, builder, and first chief was done, he also sidelined Sanford, but Sanford's shelving came with a sweetener: what Sanford took to be a promise of a royally supported franchise to trade in ivory on the upper Congo. The franchise became the "Sanford Exploring Expedition," a name that, in common with everything else in Leopold's property, sounded much more elevated than it was.

Years later, in *The Crime of the Congo* (Hutchinson, 1909), Arthur Conan Doyle connected the dots between the diplomatic recognition that Sanford had maneuvered through the U.S. Senate and his reward, on the way distinguishing Sanford's effort spreading Leopold's dollars around Washington from work done there by "honest publicists." "America hastened before the rest of the world in 1884 to recognize this new state," Conan Doyle wrote, "and her recognition caused the rest of the world to follow suit. But since then she has done nothing to control what she has created. American citizens have suffered as much as British, and American commerce has met with the same impediments, in spite of the shrewd attempt of King Leopold to bribe American complicity by allowing some of her citizens to form a Concessionaire Company and so to share in the unholy spoils."[4] Conan Doyle was not referring in this instance explicitly to Sanford and the S.E.E., but he could have been.

22

"Lieutenant Emory H. Taunt of the United States Navy, the bearer of this note, has been far up the 'Congo,' much further than Mr. Tisdel went I am told, and can perhaps interest you with some of his personal experiences, observations, and opinions. I have, therefore, asked him to take this introduction to you." So wrote Benjamin Franklin Stevens on December 28, 1885, to his old friend Henry Sanford.[5] By the end of 1885 Sanford certainly knew of Taunt's expedition upriver earlier in the year—most people interested in the Congo in the English-speaking world knew about it—but Benjamin Stevens' letter brought the entrepreneur and Navy officer face to face sometime during the first half of 1886 for the first time.

Stevens was an American archivist, librarian, bookseller, and literary agent from Vermont who lived in London for much of his adult life. His part-time job between 1866 and his death in 1902 was as the U.S. government "despatch" agent in the British capital. Stevens was responsible for receiving and forwarding official mail through his office on London's Trafalgar Square to State Department addresses in that city and to Navy ships throughout the Atlantic. He is best known today for having in the 1880s sifted through the national archives of Great Britain and France for original documents relating to the colonization of North America and to the American revolution, and publishing his findings.[6]

Stevens knew the Sanfords well: The Sanford archive contains more than 150 letters from him to "the General" spanning more than thirty years of correspondence beginning in 1853. Stevens seems to have known the Englishes also. His several letters to Sanford while Taunt's personal tragedy played out in the spring and summer of 1887 express sympathy for Mary Taunt and "the Admiral," then suffering from some undescribed ailment complicated by his senior son-in-law's trespasses and humiliation.

Stevens' letter of introduction triggered a fateful four-year relationship between the former American diplomat–cum–international businessman on the make and the U.S. Navy officer. For Sanford the timing of Stevens' letter was perfect. Beginning that same December and well into the following year, he and eleven associates—nine wealthy Belgians from Brussels, a Paris lawyer, and briefly, while he lived, an American textile executive (nine men and two women)—organized a joint stock company to do business in the Congo under the beneficent patronage, they thought, of the king. The investors put $60,000 into the venture, and several among them lent it another $50,000. Money in hand, the Sanford Exploring Expedition was soon operating. Sanford held twenty of the fifty-nine shares and four of the governing board's fifteen votes. No one else had more than two votes, and most held only one.

Right away the company had need of a man with Taunt's experience in equatorial Africa. Not until such a manager was in place could it begin to install its own agents, construct depots, assemble boats, and move goods up and down the river in commercial volumes. Only then could the company join in the rich business of trading trinkets for tusks.

23

Whatever Stevens might have intended by his introductory letter to his friend, Taunt's first meeting with Sanford evidently and unsurprisingly went well. Roughly two years later, after everything had imploded, the *New York Herald* generously described the dark-haired, blue-eyed Taunt as a "handsome man, below medium height, but of powerful physique. His manners are easy and pleasant." These "easy and pleasant manners" must have lubricated a first conversation that smoothly morphed into a job interview, if it hadn't started out as one. In early 1886 Taunt was already maneuvering in Washington in search of a way to capitalize on the past year's Congo experience, and the call on Sanford was a heaven-sent opportunity—heaven here in the unlikely form of the bearded and balding Benjamin Stevens, age fifty-three.

To Sanford, Lieutenant Taunt would have presented a model of vigor, competence, and experience: a man who had sailed the seven seas during more than a decade as an officer on board American warships, camped in the jungle on the Isthmus of Darien for weeks in charge of a U.S. Navy shore party, married an admiral's daughter, helped rescue desperate Arctic explorers, and trekked "alone" deep into equatorial Africa's interior as few white men and no other native-born American had done and emerged months later—remarkably—with his health apparently intact and voicing an optimistic assessment of international trade prospects on the upper river. In view of the essential role steamboats had to play in Congo logistics, Taunt's prior service on the water and presumed familiarity with ship design and modern marine propulsion were bonus qualifications that Sanford would have valued.

June 11, 1886, Taunt told Sanford that his application for a year's leave from the Navy had been approved. On June 22 Sanford appointed Taunt "Cheif" [*sic*] of the Sanford Exploring Expedition. The appointment came in a three-page letter detailing his duties in general. (Specifics about business

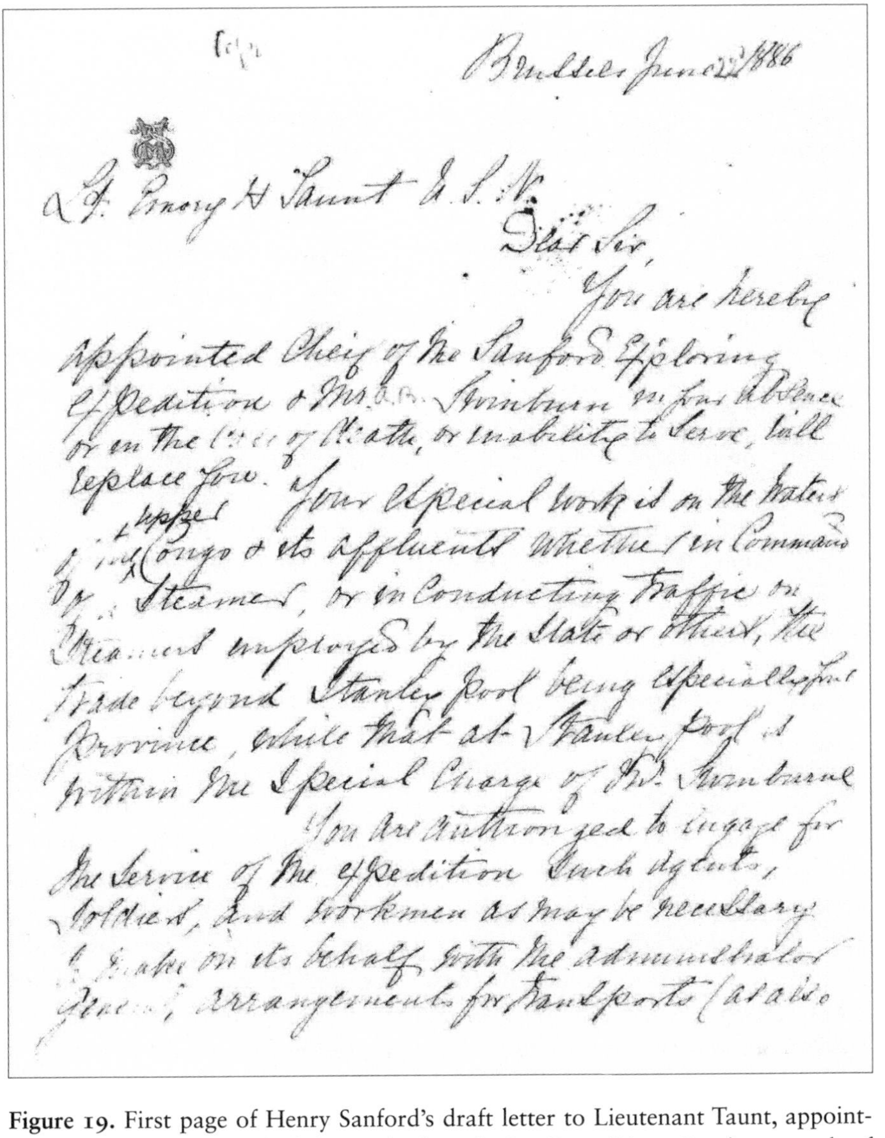

Brussels June 22d 1886

Lt. Emory H Taunt U.S.N.

Dear Sir,

You are hereby appointed Chief of the Sanford Exploring Expedition & Mr. A. B. Swinburne in your absence or in the case of death, or inability to serve, will replace you. Your special work is on the waters of the upper Congo & its affluents whether in command of steamer, or in conducting traffic on steamers employed by the State or others, the trade beyond Stanley Pool being specially your province, while that at Stanley Pool is within the special charge of Mr. Swinburne.

You are authorized to engage for the service of the Expedition such agents, soldiers, and workmen as may be necessary & make on its behalf with the administrator general, arrangements for transports (as also

Figure 19. First page of Henry Sanford's draft letter to Lieutenant Taunt, appointing him to become chief of the Sanford Exploring Expedition. On the strength of this commission, from now on Taunt signed his correspondence to both his masters in Europe and to others as "commanding" the expedition, a form that revealed the new entrepreneur had not yet entirely put aside the status, perspectives, and leadership style of a Navy officer. *H. S. Sanford Papers, Sanford Museum, Sanford, Fla.*

practices were addressed separately.) Mercifully only its last paragraph, quoted in the epigram above, was in Sanford's execrable script, possibly the product of his weak vision.

A week after he got the job, Taunt was still building his case for employment, sending to Sanford a letter from Commodore Schley, then in Washington atop the Bureau of Equipment and Recruiting, written June 14 and meant to be helpful. It contained a discordant note. "Under my command in the Greely Relief Expedition," Schley wrote in response to a solicitation from Taunt dated the last day of May, "I always found you to be prudent, zealous, careful, and possessed of rare good judgment. I regard you as fully competent and well fitted to command the expedition you speak of in exploring Central Africa. But at the same time would most earnestly urge you to relinquish the undertaking if not already too fully committed to it—while fully appreciating and commending your drive to make a name for yourself and add to the reputation of the service—I cannot help thinking that you may be making a great mistake in trying to do it in that part of the world." Precisely what lay behind Schley's anticipation of calamity is a mystery, but given the history of crew health on ship patrols in West African waters, every senior American naval officer would have looked on service in the interior with trepidation.

If members of the S.E.E.'s board of directors needed more evidence of Taunt's suitability to lead their venture than Schley's ambivalent endorsement, Taunt told Sanford, "my record of 21 years of Navy service [counting four at Annapolis] stands apiece, for anyone's inspection in the Navy Dept, and can always be reached." Pure bravado: Taunt knew that his papers in Washington wouldn't survive even superficial examination. They included the record of his trial by general court-martial at the Mare Island Navy Yard in 1873 and the minutes of the two naval examining boards that in June 1874 and October 1876 evaluated his fitness for promotion to master and to lieutenant, with their damning comments signed by former commanding officers. The collected documents would have revealed an otherwise capable officer prone to episodes of heavy drinking followed by sudden, extended disappearances.

Their business deal was described in a contract Taunt signed with Baron Louis Weber de Treuenfels, Austria-Hungary's consul in Antwerp, a principal in Messrs. Ed. Weber and Company and an investor in the S.E.E. Next to Sanford, Baron Weber was the biggest player in the S.E.E. He had two votes on the board of directors and acted as the company's comptroller. He shared the role of European agent with the French investor's law firm, Levita et Compagnie, whose principal, Jules Levita, had been a Sanford familiar for more than twenty years. Baron Weber and Monsieur le Jurisconsulte Levita pocketed a percentage on everything the S.E.E. bought and sold, and so did Stevens for transactions on the company's behalf he did in England.

Negotiations over his contract (and also those of the Expedition's second and third employees, Anthony Swinburne and Edward Glave) took up the last few days of June 1886, almost until Taunt and Swinburne sailed from Plymouth on July 3 for Banana Point to begin work. The two left England for Africa with hand baggage only. Taunt would soon regret that all of their other personal effects, "chop," tents, and camp equipment, were more than a month behind them with Glave on board SS *Portugal*. In October Taunt was matter of fact about it: They had sped out to the Congo a month too soon, he wrote, and unprepared.

24

Little exploring and no serious science ever got done by the Sanford Exploring Expedition, although very early on Lieutenant Taunt twice asked Sanford for instruments to permit the calculation of the latitude and longitude of important places (a sextant or quadrant, an artificial horizon, "a chronometer watch," and a copy of Bowditch's *Practical Navigator*) "to keep up . . . the *Exploring* part of the Expedition."[7] Such work, he wrote on July 7 in Madeira on the way from England to take up his position, "will give us a status in the 'Movement Geographique' all of which will come back to the Congo and reassure the traders—and in the future history of the Congo the Sanford Exploring Expedition will hold a well-earned record."[8]

That said, Taunt didn't forget for long that the S.E.E.'s objective was not to earn the admiration of Belgian colonization enthusiasts but to rather quickly make Henry Sanford and his fellow investors rich under cover of a high-sounding name. In his long September 24 report to Sanford, Taunt responded to his employer's lack of enthusiasm and, sounding as crass as Gordon Gekko announcing that "greed is good," reassured Sanford that he understood his core purpose:

> Give yourself no uneasiness about the scientific part of the Expedition—I came out here *solely and entirely* to make money. . . . The instruments are for use as a secondary matter and only to give coloring to the Exploring part of the Expedition. You can rest assured that all the science in Africa would not have tempted me back to the hardships of this life away from

my profession and from my family, if I had not thought there was plenty of money in it. Therefore you can rest easy, in the belief that I am just as anxious to get the ivory, and make the money, as any stockholder in the Company. Were it not so, I would not take my life in my hands and come here. I have a competency in my profession but, unfortunately, I am one of that class that wants more—and if there is more to be had out here D.V. [God willing] I mean to get it.

Taunt's arrival with Swinburne at Banana Point near the end of July was a surprise to everyone on shore. No one in Brussels had alerted local officials the two were coming to the country to establish a new trading company, ostensibly with Leopold II's blessings.

A few weeks after first stepping ashore, Taunt suddenly decamped for the island of São Tomé.[9] "I was taken with a bad bilious attack in Banana," he explained breezily to Sanford on August 22, "and was obliged to clear out fearing worse complications. . . . Don't give yourself any anxiety on my account, I am all right now and no doubt but that I will be all the better for this turn. . . . Please be careful that news of my having been 'seedy' does not get to Mrs. Taunt's ears. She would only worry needlessly." He sailed the next day to return to his post. Beginning with this one, such sudden evacuations became a recurrent event during Taunt's few years in the Congo. The next came the following March.

Pay for a U.S. Navy lieutenant with five years or more service in grade and on duty at sea was $2,600 per year. The same lieutenant on shore awaiting orders received $1,800, while one on extended leave—Taunt's status while he worked for Sanford—still continued to collect $900, near the annual pay for a "workman of average capacity." Taunt was fortunate to be able to draw this amount from the Navy while he worked and waited for the big payoff expected to follow an S.E.E. success in the Congo. His contract with Baron Weber gave him four of the thirty-five common shares in the venture (there were also twenty-four preferred shares, all held by investors) but no salary. Later Taunt negotiated with Weber an advance on the expected profits (he called it "a mortgage on my shares") and solicited another half-share when he learned that Swinburne's deal with the company gave him four, too.

What looks like a bold leap into the unknown over a very small net by a man with family responsibilities was probably more calculated than it appears. Under orders, Rear Admiral English gave up command of the South Atlantic Squadron at the end of November 1885. He reached sixty-two, mandatory retirement age, three months later. With English's transfer to the retired list on February 18, 1886, the admiral's son-in-law lost his sea daddy, the man who had protected his Navy career from self-inflicted wounds. Taunt seems to have decided then to explore his options as a civilian.

Apparently he did so without English's blessing. "I am convinced from letters I have received that he is opposed to my going," Taunt told Sanford several days before he'd sailed for Africa, "that however is a matter for me to decide and I have made my decision. It can be questioned by no one but the Secretary of the Navy and he has endorsed it by granting me a year's leave of absence." (With 1,549 officers listed in the register and a Navy comprising some three dozen ships and fewer than a dozen shore stations, Secretary Whitney was probably happy to let one of 250 lieutenants drift loose over the horizon.)

What Mary Taunt thought about her husband's decision to take leave and disappear for twelve months into a jungle is unknown, but the letters reporting her father's opposition to Taunt's initiative must have come from her.

But more than just a year's leave from the Navy was afoot. On November 28, after less than six months in his new role as a businessman in Africa, Taunt told Sanford that he would soon apply for an additional eighteen months leave. "I wish you would pave the way for [the request]. Say write Walker next May," he suggested, referring to the powerful, long-service chief of the Bureau of Navigation. That application for a leave of absence left Boma on February 15, 1887, to Walker via Sanford, so that the latter could attach an endorsement. "I must have a reply by July 1st next. It is most important that I get *some* extension. Please attend to it at once," Taunt urged. (On April 12, 1887, Sanford was able to write Taunt that the Navy had granted the request and even agreed to a further extension should one be desired in the future, confirmation that lieutenants were in long supply.)

At the same time, Taunt had another iron in the fire. "In case I am to get the appointment from [Secretary of State Thomas] Bayard don't send the application in," he added. The appointment he sought was to a new post that he and Sanford were incubating with friends in Congress, an assignment as the United States' first resident representative in the Congo.

25

Sanford's appointing letter had instructed Taunt, "Your especial work is on the waters of the Upper Congo and its affluents [tributaries] whether in command of a steamer or in conducting traffic on steamers employed by the state or others, the trade beyond Stanley Pool being especially your province." The supervision of company trade at a site on the Pool was carved out by Sanford for Anthony Swinburne.

That focus defined, the appointment letter went on to authorize Taunt to hire "such agents, soldiers, and workmen as may be necessary" and to arrange with Congo Free State officers for transportation and other services, and for men to run the river stations. Under usual circumstances, he was not to commit to expenditures of more than five hundred pounds sterling without authorization from the headquarters office.

Two important instructions lay embedded among the letter's several other paragraphs addressing administrative details:

> You will be especially careful to avoid all cases of collision with the natives & to use your arms only in cases of legitimate self-defense—we wish to be at peace and on good terms with all.
>
> Remembering how much we owe to & how much we depend upon the Government of the Independent States of the Congo for favor and facilities accorded to us & for how much we are indebted to the King for his special interest, it behooves you & your associates to keep on good terms with the officers of the state, & it will be especially agreeable to know that yr. relations with the Administrator General & the officers on the Lower Congo are cordial.

So Sanford's guidance to his "cheif" on scene was clear: no warfare with the natives, and none with Leopold II's appointees either. With respect to the latter, Sanford wrote, "Your own tact and good sense will know how to avoid difficulties in this connection."

As it happened, Taunt's relations with the Congo's native peoples were oppressive (in the usual style of white colonizers) but, with one exception, peaceful. That exception came in early September, when Taunt volunteered some men to join in a Free State raid on a native village. Although the chief and ten villagers were killed, "the fight was a complete 'fizzle,'" he told Sanford. Still, he suggested, "You must make as much capital out of it as you can, and impress upon H.M. [His Majesty, King Leopold II] the fact that we will aid them on all occasions." Good relations with the officers of the Free State, however, and especially with Lt. Louis Valcke, the state's resident interior minister and under Janssens the man who had "sole and entire charge of the transport from Banana to Stanley Falls," soon proved to be impossible.

Valcke (1857–1940), a Belgian army engineer officer, came to the Congo in mid-1880 with the leading edge of what would eventually become a Congo civil service no longer drawn generally from Europe but one manned largely by his countrymen. Now promoted, working for his king, and holding the portfolio that controlled the economic life of the new colony, Valcke's parochial interests practically guaranteed that a relationship with the new trading company could never be amicable.

"The French House are much more active than the Dutch," Taunt wrote in complaint to Sanford in early September, six weeks or so after he first arrived and began to see the lay of the land, "and it is with Valcke's assistance that they are pushing as hard as they do." That assessment was repeated in a note in mid-September. "You must know that he is false, a scoundrel who has sold himself to the French House and we can look for no help from him." And several weeks later, "tied down here with his wife," Taunt sniffed, "[Valcke] is unable to properly attend to his duties. Either that or he is inefficient. . . . He told me yesterday that if he gave three hours per day to the State he considered that quite sufficient." Later it developed that the French were unhappy with Valcke, too. "The French House threatens to sue for 50,000 Frs damages for breach of contract. Valcke has not been able to deliver their loads as he contracted to do."

The problem wasn't just Valcke. As Roger Casement, one of Taunt's employees, later recognized, there was nothing like a true transportation system in the Congo in the 1880s:

> The State Transport—like that of the trading houses—depends entirely upon the willingness of the natives, and that may be stimulated or depressed by a good whiteman or a bad, by suitable cloth or otherwise by a super abundance of "Malafu" [fermented sugar cane juice] or a paucity of sunshine, in fact, by a hundred petty circumstances—and I think here in this very fact, the general disinclination of all the Congo natives to anything like disciplined labour or to encounter present hardships for some ulterior benefit—lies the great obstacle at present to the proper development of the country in the interest of trade.[10]

From Madeira, and still three weeks from arrival at Banana Point to take up his new job, Taunt had teased Sanford with the hope that their first ivory shipment could be sent home on the steamer scheduled to depart the Congo November 16, "or perhaps . . . before that." With the wisdom gained during his first month on the ground, the goal changed to shipping one hundred ivory tusks out before the end of the year. And a few weeks later, still wiser, the date slipped again. "I am in hopes," he told Sanford on September 24, "that a fair shipment of ivory may be made by the first part of January

1887, notwithstanding the many obstacles we have met with. I am anxious to show ivory in Europe. . . . You can rest assured that the first part of the year will see a lot of ivory sent to Europe."

Looking back on his first weeks on the ground "commanding the Sanford Exploring Expedition" Taunt affected optimism. "We have had pushbacks and disappointments, but once we get started, fairly, success is certain," he predicted. "In Europe *you must have patience.* We are doing all we can do—and we are bound to come out ahead." Subsequent progress reports repeated the same optimistic message. One mailed from Boma months later began with a catalogue of failures, small disasters, and the usual complaints about people and conditions and then concluded with a non sequitur: "But please give yourself no uneasiness. All is going well. And *will go well.*"

The expectation that Leopold would keep his promises explains Sanford's language in Taunt's instructions. It explains, as well, Taunt's naiveté when, on July 28, 1886, he first approached Janssens, the new administrator general, at Banana with a five-page wish list containing requests for support numbered "a." through "q."[11] He must have been thrilled when, at meeting's end, Janssens had acceded to almost all of them (most having to do with access to riverfront land for stations) and only declined two outright. He would not permit Taunt to recruit armed men from among the Free State's soldiers, saying he had none to spare; nor would he permit Taunt to buy ivory on credit. The most significant request Taunt made was to be furnished with four hundred porters per month, and one thousand during the months of September, October, and November, which Janssens granted "if possible." The fact that this wildly unrealistic provision of human transport would not be possible was one of several lapses that ensured Taunt's and Sanford's future failure. Taunt left that meeting with high hopes, imagining that the aid and hospitality of the state had just been guaranteed by its chief executive. Throughout all the turbulence that followed he credited Janssens with being honorable and supportive.

26

Recruiting the men who were to live at the company's river stations and to do its trading and then managing their work under arduous conditions were among Taunt's most important new duties, duties complicated by the fact that no subordinate remained in Taunt's confidence or retained his respect for very long after he was hired. In the scope of a single, short paragraph to Sanford, he charted one such decline from appreciation ([William] "Parminter is able, quick and industrious"), through admiration ("a sweeter man does not live on the Congo"), down to contempt ("He is not honest. . . . I do not think a more thorough blackguard, at heart, walks the earth in the garb of a gentleman").[12] In a bonus appraisal Taunt dismissed Parminter's nephew, Alfred, as "simply a worthless boy," indolent and lazy.

In response, no employee remained loyal to his new boss for long. With one exception—the engineer, who was to assemble the steamboats and ensure their successful operation; he had to know something about practical steam propulsion—no particular skill set was required of these men other than an ability to stay reasonably healthy in the Congo basin's famously hostile environment and not to go mad from frustration, isolation, and insect bites. Prior experience in equatorial Africa was proof of both gifts.

The candidate population from which Taunt could choose his staff was limited to alumni of Stanley's expeditions still in Africa or back at home, to the international officers of Leopold's royal property in Africa looking for a career and leadership change, and to private traders working in factories along the river for one of the established European trading houses. He had no difficulty in signing up his team, almost exclusively from among Stanley's acolytes who had lost their jobs in Congo as part of the king's program to replace other foreigners with Belgians. (Before which Stanley had padded the rolls with Britons. When 1884 began, over forty of the state's employees, more than one-third, were British. A year or so earlier only three had been citizens of the United Kingdom.) "Don't send agents from Europe," he instructed Sanford after he arrived. "I can get fifty out here."

Experience and availability aside, another qualification of these men, most of whom Taunt first met during his 1885 Navy expedition upriver, was that they spoke English. Notwithstanding that it was his mother's native language, Taunt's French had not survived the years since graduation from the Naval Academy.[13]

After six months on the ground, Taunt had S.E.E. stations almost fully operational at Matadi, Stanley Pool, Equator, and Luebo, and more planned. At peak strength in 1886–87, the Sanford Exploring Expedition's roster approached a dozen white men in addition to Taunt.

Anthony Swinburne was first among them. Taunt's appointing letter from Sanford identified Swinburne as his substitute in case of Taunt's "absence, or in the case of death, or inability to serve." In 1886–87 Swinburne had years more experience in Africa than did Taunt, and even absent Taunt's alcoholism, Swinburne would arguably have been a better choice to lead the S.E.E. than was the American naval officer.[14] Swinburne thought so, too. The two men made a very uneasy team. Taunt characterized him as "simply harm-less," saying the man had "absolutely no force, and no head to work."

On September 29, 1887, Swinburne wrote Sanford to defend himself from Taunt's parting accusation that he'd built a home for his African fam-ily with company money. The accusation was a lie, he said, but the family, described euphemistically by Swinburne as "a necessary African adjunct," was real. "Every penny that the said family costs me I religiously pay." Taunt, on the other hand, had not been so scrupulous, Swinburne wrote. "You no doubt will be astonished to hear that Lieutenant Taunt (a married) [*sic*] had also a female companion while here, which he did his best to keep secret, but as you say the Congo lights or shadows are no longer hidden under a bushel, consequently every one knew all about it, and thought the more of it because he tried so hard to conceal it." Belgian officers, for that matter, often had two such "so called" families, Swinburne told Sanford, "one in one sta-tion and one in another. . . . The fact being known from Brussels to Stanley Falls, perhaps farther."

"Africa is not my home," he explained, "but wherever I am, I try to be comfortable, and my last thought would be to cast a slur on your unsul-lied name. If you have the slightest idea that the fact of my having a little daughter does, kindly let me know and I shall be only too happy, much as I should wish to remain, to resign my position and all claims on the Sanford Expedition." Sanford was in no position to call Swinburne's bluff and tell the man to go. The "African adjunct" stayed. Taunt wouldn't let go of the transgression. Fifteen months later he told Sanford that Swinburne had "become so utterly debased by his subjection to that black thing that he is to be pitied."

Author Tim Jeal called Edward Glave, an Englishman from Yorkshire, Stanley's "honorary son," another of the young men with whom Stanley developed a powerful, personal bond. Stanley's effusive expressions of grief in a letter after Glave suddenly died of fever at Matadi May 12, 1895, days before he was to sail for home, confirmed that description of their special relationship.

Glave had built Lukolela Station on the upper Congo for Stanley in late 1883 and stayed there and elsewhere along the river during the next three years while the Congo Free State was created around him. He'd hosted Taunt as the latter passed through the station in mid-July 1885 heading for Stanley Falls. A year later in London Glave joined the S.E.E., at the same time Swinburne did.

Whatever it was that Stanley saw in Glave, Taunt, uncharacteristically, saw it, too. He was the only one of the S.E.E. employees who remained throughout high in Taunt's estimation. "Glave is *honorable, true, honest* and a very hard worker," Taunt enthused. "He has not a lazy bone in his body. I have seen him with his coat off doing the work that properly belonged to the blacks, but in order to have it done well, Glave did it himself. He was not paid enough with us and I sincerely hope you will insist on giving him a good salary. He is a treasure in any position."

Glave, who identified himself as "one of Stanley's pioneer officers," spent the last twenty-three months of his life exposing slavery in Africa on assignment for the *Century Magazine*, a handsome monthly published in New York City between 1881 and 1930. Beginning with Glave's first *Century* piece, "The Congo River of Today," printed in the magazine's February 1890 issue, his byline appeared on articles about Africa seven more times in the next seven years. The last five, starting with one in May 1895 that reported his discovery of the tree beneath which Livingstone's heart was buried, were published posthumously.

Even more than the S.E.E.'s other employees, Major William Parminter, late of Baker's squadron of the Frontier Light Horse Regiment in the Transvaal, would have been unimpressed with Taunt's slender African c.v. Parminter was the one who a year ago in May had assembled the caravan that introduced Taunt to conditions on the river. Unlike Taunt's, Parminter's credentials as a man with real Congo experience were impeccable: when he left Africa to deal with problems at home after his first tour Stanley described him as "the most superior chief at Vivi we have had yet."

Parminter didn't like Taunt any more than Swinburne did. When he and Taunt crossed paths at the Hotel St. Antoine in Antwerp at the end of June 1887, Taunt on the way home in disgrace, he on the way back to the Congo, Parminter was quick to report to Sanford that Taunt had not ceased drinking. "This morning [June 26] he asked early for a bottle of Champagne but did not get it as the manager assures me he has stopped all liquors for him," Parminter wrote in a short note on this single subject. "I only hope if his money comes tomorrow that he may not relapse again completely." Given how quickly he moved to report the lapse of his former boss, the wish sounds insincere.

Later, Taunt had his revenge. In an exchange of letters with Sanford during December 1887, with Taunt now basking in the warm afterglow of his recent appointment as the new U.S. commercial agent at Boma, he roasted the major: "He is scheming, treacherous, and *not honest*. I never heard one of his own countrymen have a good word to say of him."

Herbert Ward arrived in the Congo in 1884, fresh from months on the other side of the world in the jungles of New Guinea, and like all the others by 1886 knew more about equatorial Africa than did Taunt. "He will prove a most useful Agent," Taunt exulted in September.

Two months later Taunt's opinion of Ward was less enthusiastic: "I have the same opinion of Ward that I have always held," he told Sanford confidentially, changing his original story. "I cannot trust him. . . . He talks well, has a good appearance and until you find him out no one could be better but he is *not truthful.*" Still, "if he is willing to come out for a fair salary take him for he is a valuable man but he must always have someone to keep an eye on him, *and he is not indispensable.*"

Ward was hired for $170 per year and sent to Manyanga Station, but he lasted with the S.E.E. only until Stanley's expedition to rescue Emin Pasha left the Pool with *Florida* for upriver in May 1887. Ward joined Stanley to become an officer in his ill-fated "rear guard," the contingent that for months stayed behind at Stanley's base camp on the Aruwimi futilely waiting for porters and died there in great numbers.[15] When it broke, publicity about the debacle nearly destroyed Stanley's reputation in Great Britain.[16]

William Davy, a New Zealander recently off the British India Company's screw steamer *Duke of Buccleuch* and Glave's brother-in-law, was nominated to the S.E.E. for the post of engineer by *Florida*'s builders. Davy was present on the river during all of the steamboat's notorious growing pains (and responsible for some of them), but his greatest service to the company probably came in September 1888 when he was deposed about the condition of *Florida*'s hull when she returned from Yambuya after two months on the river with Stanley. "She has been roughly used," Davy swore, estimating that the abuse suffered had reduced the small vessel's useful life by three years. "It appears . . . that the hull of 'Florida' has never had half a chance," Forrestt and Son explained to Sanford on November 24, 1887. "She seems to have been used as a lighter by Mr. Stanley before her intercostal girders were put in. This of itself—if any amount of cargo was put into her, of which there seems no doubt—was sufficient to strain and materially alter the shape of the hull. She appears to have received much damage on her return, and absolute holes were knocked into her. This circumstance alone, was quite enough to greatly disappoint Mr. Davy, before he was able to begin with the erection of the engines & boiler."

Charles Bateman, an Englishman, built Luebo Station, on a tributary of the Kasai, in November 1885 for the Congo Free State.[17] He then ran the station until December 1886, when his contract with the state expired and he left Africa because of ill health. The S.E.E. took over Luebo that January, with Taunt gloating to Sanford that their new property was important as the

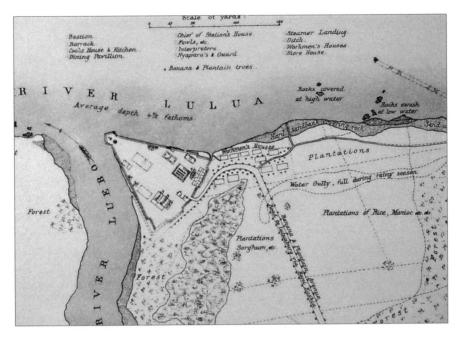

Map 3. "Plan of Luebo Station, on the point at the mouth of Luebo River on the Lulua." Luebo Station was fully one hundred miles south of the Lulua's junction with the much larger Kasai River and more than three hundred miles east of where the Kasai becomes the Kwa and joins the Congo River at Kwamouth. The station's location deep in the Kasai's basin indicated the already vast scope of ivory and rubber collection operations in the mid-1880s. Luebo's layout, a mix of housing and warehouse space inside of a three-acre compound and cultivated plots outside of it, was typical of stations on the Congo River system in the late nineteenth century. BATEMAN, FIRST ASCENT OF THE KASAI, 65

"center of the rubber wealth" and because it was just one day's march from the largest ivory market in the Kasai's watershed.

Taunt went on to boast that he'd recruited "a most able substitute" for Bateman as station chief at Luebo, a young Belgian, Amédée Legat. For political reasons Taunt had wanted some "good Belgian blood" in the Expedition, despite his view that in general "Belgians are jealous to the very last degree . . . [and] are not competent to hold responsible positions and work as we want the work done." The solution was to "nurse them up a bit" and then "give them minor positions and make them think they are doing it all." Taunt was very pleased with his new hire, telling Sanford "this young man is shrewd, speaks Portuguese fluently and I am firmly convinced that he will turn out all we can wish."

Taunt's best-known employee was Roger Casement, who first arrived in the Congo in 1884 as an employee of the *Association International du Congo*. He resigned the following year when the Congo Free State was officially established and later joined the S.E.E., where he was put in charge of Matadi Station. At first Taunt judged Casement to be "an upright, honorable gentleman," but soon he soured on him, too. The two got into a spat over subsistence pay that degenerated into an exchange of threats and invitations to resign. Later, passing through Matadi, Taunt found the station in confusion—the few loads delivered there spread out in a disorderly jumble—and promptly relieved Casement, sending him to assist Ward to herd *Florida*'s engine parts upriver and taking over Matadi himself.

In February 1888, with Taunt gone and the Expedition now under Swinburne's leadership, Casement made good on his threat to resign and joined the ongoing railroad survey. He explained his departure somewhat mysteriously in a letter to Sanford in late August, a year and a half after Taunt was fired: "I regret that circumstances have so arranged matters that I am no longer a member of your Expedition—but the fact of my being so was brought about against my wishes although at the end I quitted the Expedition willingly. However, I do not wish to reopen that question now— for, unfortunately, it involves personalities." Casement's employment with the survey was relatively short lived. He went from there to managing logistics on the lower Congo for the Société Anonyme Belge and later, famously, into the British consular service.

Consul Casement's historic 1904 report to Parliament on atrocities in the Congo followed a three-month investigation during the previous summer that was prompted by the uproar created by publication of observations of reformers, most notably those of journalist Edmund Morel. Casement's report was the first official description of Leopold's abusive rule over his private African property. Its publication triggered the creation of the Congo Reform Association and contributed to the ensuing global humanitarian outcry that ultimately delivered the Congo from the king to the Belgian government in 1908.

In 1911 at age forty-seven, after years of distinguished service as a consul in Africa and South America—there his report in 1906 had also exposed the horrific abuse of natives in the Amazon rainforest—Casement was knighted by King George V. Five years later, during World War I, he was tried, convicted, and executed for treason, sabotage, and espionage, charges arising from his attempt to foment armed revolution in Ireland with German assistance.[18]

During the last week of 1888, while Taunt made his preparations to return to the Congo in his new role of government commercial agent, he shared with his former employer his assessments of the S.E.E. team in the Congo post-Taunt. Those judgments had sharpened during the months Taunt impatiently stalked Washington hoping for "a position of dignity and trust" in the Congo.

It's hard to imagine how such a dispirited, antagonistic team pulled it off, but in two years (much of the time after Taunt's departure) the Sanford Exploring Expedition managed to export to Europe 35,000 pounds of elephant ivory and 61,000 pounds of natural rubber.[19] Not nearly enough to make the business profitable, but an impressive amount nonetheless and an indication of the riches that could be wrested from Leopold's private property if one were rapacious enough.

27

The Sanford Exploring Expedition faced significant front-end costs for many months before any ivory sales in Europe could be expected to start moving the enterprise out of the red and into the black. Sanford's business plan and Taunt's operating concept were to minimize initial costs and to accelerate the start of an ivory revenue stream by piggy-backing on the Free State's existing trade infrastructure and sharing some of its people while the Expedition's own capabilities came on line. Only with generous outside help, for example, could that first, hoped-for early shipment of one hundred elephant tusks to Europe have been possible. Sanford thought his deal with the king included extraordinary cooperation, that the king owed this to him, and Taunt believed Janssens had willingly agreed to such help to the extent that Free State resources in the Congo allowed it. As it happened, both men were wrong.

The problem was that Leopold II saw his property in the Congo—saw life—as a zero-sum game: Everything someone else extracted from his personal fief and sold was riches out of the king-sovereign's own pocket. The promises he made to Sanford, which Sanford thought ensured his business' success, could not be redeemed, even if for a short while Leopold pretended to believe them. It would slowly be revealed, very slowly to Sanford, that the Sanford Exploring Expedition was built upon a fantasy. Reality on the ground guaranteed competition and increasing strains between the king's men and Sanford's.

Worse yet, two of the Expedition's major cost drivers, the steamboats *Florida* and *New York*, proved to be sumps into which money disappeared almost without a ripple. The S.E.E. needed its own riverboats inland of

Stanley Pool, as nothing else could move enough loads fast enough along the upper river to produce profits, but both vessels proved to be costly problems. *Florida* finally went into regular service on the Congo in November 1887, a schedule that by itself denied any possible Taunt claim of special expertise where boats were concerned. However, seamanship had nothing to do with her plight. *Florida* was a failure of logistics and the victim of what amounted to a kidnapping.

Florida was designed and constructed by Forrestt and Son, a century-old London shipbuilding company whose engraved letterhead displayed eleven tiny images of medals won at international conventions by its steam-powered sternwheelers and whose customer list boasted the Admiralty, the War Department, and the Royal National Lifeboat Institution. Near the end of June 1886, just before Taunt left for Africa, Forrestt and Son's Britannia Yard, on the River Thames' Isle of Dogs, began work on *Florida*'s iron. A short seven weeks later the boat's kit of components was finished and ready to be shipped.

On September 17, 1886, *Florida*'s crated parts arrived at Boma on board Walford and Company's Atlantic steamer *Brabo* from Antwerp, together with a small boat and other S.E.E. freight.[20] From Boma the crates were to be transshipped to Matadi and then man-hauled around the rapids all the way to Stanley Pool, where *Florida* was to be assembled and launched. Taunt thought the little steamboat would be ready for service the next February.

"A fatal mistake was made in packing the loads in such large packages," Taunt wrote to Sanford on September 26. "I cannot understand it, for my instructions to Mr. Forrestt on this point were most explicit. In Africa," he continued, "all bulk is moved by hand, and it will be one of the impossibilities to land some of the large cases at Matadi where everything is landed in a canoe—some of these cases weighing 1500 to 2000 lbs. But I shall make the best of it and open the larger cases . . . before landing."

"Forrestt, by making a shaft weighing 1100 pounds has given us a hard nut to crack," he complained. "And there was no necessity for this. Henry Reed's only weighed 200 lbs. Had Forrestt told me he could not make a shaft of 200 lbs weight I should have ordered a twin screw boat." The proud, old company (established in 1788) was deeply embarrassed by the S.E.E.'s outspoken unhappiness with its product and barraged Sanford with long letters through late 1886 and early 1887 defending its design and materials choices as being the result of the press of time, all approved in advance by Expedition representatives. "With regard to making the six heavy pieces lighter," one letter said, "we explained to Mr. Swinburne most fully and carefully that these could be done so if time was allowed but in order to do it,

special compressed steel would have to be made and used for the purpose ...
and therefore it would be impossible for us to give delivery under 18 weeks.
He decided that he would rather have the quick delivery ... than the delay
in construction."

Taunt had hoped to have all of *Florida*'s pieces in Matadi by October 1,
1886, when possible hitchhiking them there in *Heron*, another steamer. In
fact, the last of *Florida*'s crates did not get to Matadi until two weeks after
that, where once sorted and laid out in construction order, they waited for
overland transportation to Stanley Pool. By the end of November *Florida*'s
construction slip was all ready for her on the Pool, but heavy rains and
flooded streams closed the road to the station, stranding a large caravan
hauling her first crates just hours away.[21] Looking ahead to the end of the
rainy season (and the start of the "short drys" in December, when porters
would be able to move more easily) Taunt now wrote Sanford that it would
be the last of February or the first of March 1887 before the steamer was
ready for engine trials.

In January 1887 Davy, the engineer, had *Florida*'s hull pieced together
but not yet assembled. "For some unaccountable reason"—reading this
Sanford must have again writhed in exasperation—the rivets and tools to fit
the rivets had not been delivered with the hull plates. They and other heavy
loads of ship parts still rested at Matadi. In six months Valcke had moved
fewer than eight thousand pounds of S.E.E. freight through the state system. Taunt planned to head to Boma to conciliate Valcke. "He is a man that
requires a great deal of smoothing down," Taunt observed.

Still, things looked pretty good in Africa as 1887 began, or so Mary
Taunt believed. At the time she, baby Earlena, and a kitten were living in
Washington at 1206 P Street, next door to Senator George Vest, Democrat
of Missouri, early in the second of his four terms in Congress. On January
19 she sent Sanford a cheery note reporting that she'd heard from her dear
husband the day after Christmas, who "wrote that he felt very encouraged
at the way things were turning out and hoped to do a great deal once he
got his steamer on the river." That said, Mary got down to business. "He
surely has had a good many trials to endure," she wrote loyally, "and there
is hardly a man living who could have accomplished so much in so short a
time with such odds against him. He surely should be well rewarded." Mary
would hold off lobbying friends in Congress during the short session, she
volunteered, until Sanford was present in Washington to advise her.

28

Her star-crossed history with the Expedition aside, steamboat *Florida* had bit parts in two other dramas: Stanley's last cross-country mission in Africa and (about which more later) Joseph Conrad's near-deadly twenty-six weeks on the Congo while he auditioned for riverboat command.

In 1887 Stanley was dispatched to the Sudan on a mission to rescue the governor of Egypt's Equatoria Province, Emin Pasha, from a fundamentalist mystic who styled himself the "Mahdi," the Deliverer, and had taken over the rest of the Sudan. Events would later prove that Emin (despite his Turkish name and title a Silesian by birth named Eduard Schnitzer) didn't want rescue any more than Livingstone had sought discovery, but propelled by a near-complete misunderstanding in London of the situation on the ground in Africa and fears about German motives in East Africa, and by Stanley's sense of self, he headed out, pushed along by privately raised funds and enthusiasms.

After steaming around Africa from Zanzibar, the nearly thousand-man-strong expedition arrived at Banana in mid-March. Next to come was a long boat ride around the bend in the Congo to the Aruwimi River and a landing one hundred miles upstream where all were to go ashore for the final trek through hundreds of miles of jungle to Emin Pasha's redoubt. Stanley's force, its officers, armed men, and porters, together with many hangers-on, was like a swarm of locusts. Anyplace it alit was soon stripped of all food-stuffs; hence the pressure to keep the expedition moving was enormous.

Arriving in force at the Pool, Stanley discovered that despite Leopold's promises of transport, among the Free State's fleet of steamers on the upper Congo only *Stanley* was seaworthy and self-propelled. As explained later to the American minister in Brussels, "when on its arrival at Stanley Pool the expedition found . . . a grave famine. . . . The provisions there scarcely sufficed for the ordinary needs of the population, and the only means of saving a disaster to the numerous caravan of Mr. Stanley—nearly a thousand men—was to put him in the way of continuing sooner on his journey. In the presence of this situation, Mr. Stanley was obliged to endeavor to procure all the means of transport then available at the Pool."[22]

Translation: Compelled to move on, Stanley got grabby. He commandeered steamboats *Peace* and *Henry Reed* from the missionary societies that owned them, intending that each would tow expedition cargo hulks. Unlike the missionaries, who protested the seizures at the time, Swinburne volunteered to lend *Florida* to Stanley. Towed behind the government's paddlewheel steamer named after the great man, even minus her engine *Florida* could contribute to moving some of Stanley's Emin Pasha rescue expedition toward its goal.

Stanley's rescue convoy finally left Leopoldville for upriver Sunday, May 1, with *Florida* under tow, grossly overloaded with eighteen-plus tons of men, equipment, and stores. Six weeks later, June 15, the fleet reached Yambuya, the expedition's base camp nearly one hundred miles up the Aruwimi River from its mouth on the Congo. There the badly abused *Florida* turned about after unloading to head downriver. She reappeared up at the foot of Stanley Pool on July 3.

Swinburne shared his evaluation of *Florida* with Weber in a letter dated October 2, months after her return from Yambuya and now, finally, operating under her own power. "I must tell you frankly," he wrote, "I am disgusted with the *Florida*, she is a real brute in every sense of the word. . . . I condemn the sternwheel and shall never advise another to be sent out. They are clumsy, slow, bad to steer, and the consumption of fuel is simply awful."

Anticipating success in the future, Taunt had sent Weber two specifications for the Expedition's second steamer, later to be called *New York*. One was in the form of ten short paragraphs reflecting lessons he was learning at great cost from his experience with *Florida*. The first lesson was portability: No section of the new boat, he wrote, including boiler or engine parts, was to weigh over 120 pounds, and as many of the constituent packages as possible were to weigh half that or less. "*This limit of weights to be strictly adhered to,*" he emphasized.

If built as first specified, *New York* would be a 36-foot launch with a 7-foot beam, roofed and curtained so that her interior could be sealed against rain and the cargo protected, with cushions in the stern to serve as beds. She was to draw no more than sixteen inches of water, fewer if possible, carrying a one-ton load. A later specification called for a 50-foot boat, with proportional increases in beam and capacity but the same draft.

A ton of freight, roughly thirty porter loads, wasn't much. What Taunt really was asking for was less a small freighter than a tugboat, one capable of towing several loaded lighters behind her on the river. "In order to compensate for the small carrying capacity," Forrestt and Son should be instructed, he wrote, to "give as much power as possible for towing purposes." Towing bollards were to be installed port and starboard, fore and aft. "If a boat like the above is too expensive reduce the size and give us towing power."

New York's machinery was to be "made as simple and durable as possible." The boiler was to be designed to burn wood. "If we can get the draught of water required," she was to be propelled by a screw of "tough bronze

Figures 20 and 21. "Launching the Steamboat *Florida*" and "*Florida* Tied Up Outboard of *Stanley* on the Riverbank at Yambuya Six Weeks Later." In exchange for extending *Florida*'s construction slip to reach the river and assisting in her launch, Swinburne offered the boat to Stanley, saying that until her machinery and shaft were delivered, not expected until the end of July 1887, the completed hull was of no use to

metal" (with a spare screw provided by the builder). If not, then *New York* would be pushed along by a flailing paddlewheel on her stern, just like *Stanley* and *Florida*.

For years Sanford had attempted to run his business interests in the United States from afar in Europe, with predictable problems. He tried that in the Congo, too. In September 1886, for example, while steamboat *Florida* lay disassembled in newly delivered stacks of crates on the riverbank at Boma with no date afloat in sight, Sanford was already pushing a second steamer onto the start-up expedition, and more trade goods, too. The pressure forced an exasperated Taunt to write from on scene, "When more material is wanted you will be quickly notified and in ample time to get it out here for us—but this expedition cannot be managed from Europe—No more than the State Dept. could have controlled your movements during the war—Or the War Dept. have fought the battles of the war."

Taunt didn't want a second steamer heading for the Congo anytime soon: "Let me impress upon you the fact that *we don't want another*

anybody else. On Saturday morning, April 30, 1887, two hundred natives pulled *Florida* out of her slip and into the river on a roadbed of rollers and then floated her to alongside *Stanley*, tied up at the Dutch landing for loading. The two became part of a motley fleet of eight watercraft, three under power (the others were *Peace* and *Henry Reed*) and five under tow. H. M. STANLEY, IN DARKEST AFRICA *(1890), 96 AND 113*

steamer now. Make all your estimates, have your plans ready, &c. so that when needed it can be built at short notice. But when the time comes for us to employ another steamer I will let you know." Taunt didn't want any more trade goods just yet, either. Thanks to Sanford's incessant pushing, *New York* was ordered from the builder much too soon and never contributed to the business during its brief corporate life.

29

On Monday, April 11, 1887, Taunt materialized in center city Liverpool, where he stayed overnight at the North Western Hotel, planning to leave by train on Tuesday for London. He had just arrived in England from the Congo on board the British and African Steam Navigation Company's SS *Lualaba*.[23] Neither Sanford nor Weber had expected to see Taunt in Europe that spring. Not until a cable in late March from him passing through Accra, on the Gold Coast (Ghana today), announced to Benjamin Stevens that he was already on the way to London did anyone know he was coming.

As he would prove next year in Manhattan, Taunt had a taste for elegant urban hotels. The nearly new North Western (built in 1879; it's a university dormitory today), facing Liverpool's iconic St. George's Hall and conveniently next to the London and North Western Railroad's Lime Street Station and its trains to the capital, was one of the city's largest and handsomest commercial structures: a block-long building containing 330 rooms on five floors, punctuated by a slate-roofed tower at each of the four corners and two more spanning the entrance. He'd checked in without European clothes, thinking to get those in London at his next stop, the Caledonian Hotel on Adelphi Terrace. Moving about in worn and stained expedition garb, Taunt likely attracted sidelong glances from better dressed guests at both places.

His chatty, seven-page letter to Sanford didn't contain much to explain his sudden appearance in England.[24] (Perhaps one written to the general the previous Saturday on board the steamer did, but it's been lost.) He did write on the 11th in one place, "I have picked up wonderfully in the cool weather," and in another, "Don't let anyone know that I have been ill as I don't want it to get to America. I am north on business," but the rest was generally about Expedition matters and specifically about the challenges posed by Stanley's Emin Pasha Rescue Expedition, now in full strength (and overgrazing local food stocks) and nearing the end of its march overland from Matadi to Leopoldville.

"I find that Stanley takes the Congo route," Taunt wrote Sanford (the alternative was a channel crossing to the mainland of Africa from Zanzibar, followed by a very long overland hike). "I cannot see what Janssens can be thinking of. Stanley will devastate the country as far as food is concerned, and they will not recover in three year's time. He will certainly want our Steamer but this I earnestly protest against. *We Cannot* spare it as we must visit Luebo in July with stores &c., &c. Write explicit instructions to Swinburne at once. For he cannot be trusted where Stanley is concerned." And then, changing subjects, "I once more beg that you will leave no stone unturned about my extension. *I must* get more leave, for Swinburne will never answer to run matters. *It is not in him.*"

Taunt's narrative line, that he had left the Congo because of failing health and came to England and its more temperate weather to do company business while he recovered, was fiction. He had not so much left the Congo with *Lualaba* in March as he'd abandoned it, after an extended drinking spree at the hotel on Banana Point. News of that spree, and a substantiating bar bill, reached Sanford days ahead of Taunt's deceptive letter.

The report of Taunt's drunken excesses at Banana prompted a despairing letter from Sanford in Brussels, written while Taunt was on the train to London. It exists only as a draft in correspondence files. "I will not comment on this ugly business," Sanford wrote, "so seriously compromising yourself as well as the interests confided to you. [Later the "ugly business" was described as Taunt's "unhappy weakness."] As for your return after all that has occurred," Sanford continued, "I don't see how the Webers can feel authorized to trust you again. Your business contract was with them. There were greater moral obligations to me, who am held not blameless for recommending you to this trust and my friends subscriptions to the charge of one so reckless. . . . You now have to report to Antwerp and give an account of your stewardship."

On April 25 Benjamin Stevens wrote Sanford his reaction to the news: "I cannot tell you how sorry I am for poor Taunt. How much more for his poor wife who still believes in him and loyally sticks up for him. . . . Please let me know if Taunt has gone home and if you have written to his wife. She is very anxious her Father, the Admiral, should not know anything of the short comings. I so pity her more than words can tell in this further lamentable disappointment." Stevens then helpfully mentioned the names of three Royal Navy officers who knew their counterparts in the U.S. Navy well and could be relied on to recommend good replacements for Taunt from the American Navy, where there were, Stevens reassured Sanford, "very few officers in the service now with the weaknesses that have troubled you so much recently."

Two days later Stevens backed away from the responsibility of having introduced one man to the other. "You told me some months ago that you appointed him to command the expedition on my introduction," Stevens wrote to Sanford on the twenty-seventh. "I answered to the effect that I thought you attached too much importance to my letter [of introduction]."

With that disclaimer in the record, the rest of Stevens' letter counseled Sanford about how he might wish to manage his alcoholic subordinate, should he wish to return Taunt to duty. "I have no doubt Taunt is as full of ability, courage and pluck as is possible," Stevens continued. "The chances are he will not put one [drunken] bout quite on top of another. It is possible he may go several months without another under average circumstances." The suggestion was that Sanford get Taunt to sign an oath promising good behavior. (Curiously, Sanford once took such approach with his son, who signed a formal contract full of legal jargon swearing reform and then, in his father's eyes, reneged on it.)

Baron Weber wasn't looking for any stratagems to keep his fallen employee in place. Soon after Taunt's binge and collapse at Banana Point,

Weber described Taunt as "a lost man" to Sanford. "I always and every time I saw him here [in Antwerp] suspected him to be under the influence of liquors," he wrote, and went on about Taunt's "drinking Cognac all day long" until the hotel cut him off, fearing an attack of delirium tremens. "I only see one thing to be done," Weber wrote, "to put him on board a Steamer for New York. . . . I should not like to cable Mrs. Taunt that he is a drunkard & that I have to send him home."

30

Sanford's news of Taunt's collapse at Banana quickly reached Mary, at the time at home in Washington. It prompted an anguished response to Sanford on April 19, 1887, written on black-banded stationery. That notepaper's use, part of the era's elaborate mourning ritual for close relatives American society borrowed from its Victorian counterpart, might have gotten Mary some transient sympathy, but it did not save Taunt's job.

"I cannot tell you how fearfully your kind letter of April 7th (just received) has made me feel," she wrote to the general:

> It is a great misfortune but I hope that it yet may be remedied.
>
> I trust that you will look with leniency upon my husband, these fearful attacks come upon him at times and he seems to have no controls over himself. What it was I am in utter ignorance of for he has not written me he feels too badly for that I know. . . . Mrs. Sanford is his friend and I ask her to plead my cause. He can do so much I feel sure. . . . Please try to think of all he has accomplished for the company and try to forgive this mistake for my sake and for the sake of our little daughter.

That plea for pity made, Mary wrote about what might have been, had things gone differently on the river. Here revealing she knew more than expected about distant events, she noted, "It was most unfortunate that Mr. Swinburne had not gone down the river as Mr. Taunt expected he would do to look after the steamer loads, then Mr. Taunt would not have had to go down to Banana where all the mischief was done." If only her husband had not been tempted, she suggested unpersuasively, this collapse might never have happened.

There is nothing in Taunt's Navy service record of the prior eleven years, since 1876 when he and Mary were wed, that hints at the other "fearful attacks" of binge drinking and uncontrolled behavior she revealed to

Sanford in that letter. No way to tell how many there were, how frequently they came, how long each lasted and how disabling it was, or why she described them as "fearful."

The arc of her husband's decline was beyond Mary Taunt's influence. One event followed another. The March binge at Banana Point's hotel ending in besotted collapse. A surprise appearance in England in April, during which Forrestt and Son reported delicately they saw him on the twenty-seventh "very far from well." A stay in Washington "under strict treatment" to recover his health in May, followed by an optimistic return to the Congo via Antwerp, "prepared to stay for two years," that never got farther than Belgium.

Taunt arrived in the middle of June in Antwerp from New York City in the Red Star liner SS *Rhynland*, an immigrant transport that had been sailing between the two ports for years. Presumably as he sailed east expecting to resume work for the S.E.E., Taunt was berthed in one of *Rhynland*'s 150 first-class cabins, not in the one-thousand-steerage-passenger space below decks that made the business case for the transatlantic shuttle. It took him only a few days on the ground in Belgium to provoke Baron Weber to fire him.

Weber's letter to Sanford at Gingelom on June 22, two days before news of Taunt's sacking was sent to Weber's correspondents, was a near–carbon copy of the one from two months ago. This time Taunt was described not as "lost" but as "impossible":

> Today I went to the hotel he did not let me go in his room but I found out that he drinks for 4 days he gave me a bill of 120 Fr. & had a private bill of 105 Fr. for drink which he said he would settle himself. . . .
>
> I took him to the office & he began in the same style as formerly when he was drunk & he was evidently so.
>
> So I told him simply Mr. Taunt you are drunk again. . . . You are disciplined & you shall not go out any more to the Congo for me.
>
> All he answered was You cannot prove it. . . . This is done and I shall under no circumstances send him back. . . . Just think the matter over and let me know your opinion whom to appoint.

The formal termination announcement went out from Weber and Company two days later. "We have the honor to inform you," a June 24 note sent to the S.E.E.'s mailing list read, "that Monsieur Lieutenant Emory H. Taunt no longer speaks for the Sanford Exploring Expedition, consequently his powers are annulled." Weber now began to pursue his former employee for the return of cash advances paid.

31

During 1888, while the Sanford Exploring Expedition continued to implode, Sanford tried to raise more money. His original investors in Belgium and France refused to contribute more, so he turned next to American businessmen he knew or knew of. The first group included several manufacturing executives, including two whose business used rubber as a raw material; all politely declined the opportunity. The second group centered on John D. Rockefeller, the nation's premier money man, whom he approached through Rockefeller's partner in the Standard Oil Company, Henry Flagler, the Florida developer and railroad magnate. Flagler explained to Sanford in May 1888 that Rockefeller had begged off, claiming lack of time to consider the proposition. A last-ditch resort later in the year to an English financier also failed to bear fruit.

Rather than marking the birth of a revitalized S.E.E., 1888 ended instead with the newly formed Société Anonyme Belge pour l'Industrie et Commerce du Haut-Congo absorbing what remained of Sanford's venture, its six riverfront stations, two steamboats, merchandise inventory, and ivory on hand. The acquisition was a step in the second phase of the commercial exploitation of the Congo River basin, the consolidation of trade in Belgian hands. (The first phase had been at least nominally international; the third and last would be under the aegis of the Belgian Parliament.) *Florida* was valued in the acquisition at $36,000, *New York* at $41,000, and ivory on hand at $1.89 per pound.

In June 1892 the three surviving liquidators of the Sanford Exploring Expedition, Messrs. Jules Levita, Baron Weber de Treuenfels, and Georges Brugmann, concluded nearly four years of investigative accounting and financial damage control. The original group of four—their number once included the late Henry Sanford; he'd died in 1891—had begun its work in October 1888. Soon thereafter its autopsy of the company revealed there wasn't much of value left in the partnership, chartered under such apparently bright prospects just a few years ago.

"Our company lasted three years," the liquidators reminded former shareholders, conceding "of which eighteen months went by before being organized, then the requisition of [*Florida*] by the [Emin Pasha] Relief Committee left us unable to function. It is only for about one year that we could work usefully." The three men somehow managed to hint at a guilt-free explanation for failure from this chronology: It had been Stanley's fault. *Florida*'s two-month diversion and her several additional months out of service under repair had, as Sanford claimed to de Winton in 1889, "nearly ruined" the enterprise. Worse yet, steps taken to obtain "a just indemnity" from the Emin Pasha Relief Committee for the disruption "caused by Mr. Stanley's requisitioning of our boat 'La Florida'" were entirely unsuccessful. No surprise: Donors to the relief committee had seen their charitable contributions vanish into what became an embarrassing fiasco. They had no desire to send good money after bad to bail out the S.E.E.

"Your work was not for naught," the liquidators bravely assured their former partners, denying the evidence. Although failing to make money, investors could still find satisfaction in having been pioneers in an honorable cause—the civilization of equatorial Africa. "The goal of creating a lucrative enterprise was not the only reason why we decided to establish a partnership," the liquidators told associates, busy picking through the wreckage. "We also had in mind to open the way to Belgian commerce, whose support is necessary so that our King's glorious enterprise succeeds, [the goal of which was] civilizing the populations of the vast territories of the center of Africa. This humanitarian idea elicited a response from all the nations of Europe, who considered it a duty to follow his example."

Unremarkably, Taunt is invisible here. He exists anonymously embedded in the eighteen months that Levita et al. said the S.E.E. took to get organized. In fact, he was the reason for much of that lost time. The only employees mentioned by name in the Expedition's obituary are Parminter (who until he departed for Europe managed the S.E.E. toward the end, after Swinburne had left) and two Belgians, Camille Delcommune and Arthur Hodister. The latter two, old Congo hands, were S.E.E. alumni from the period after Taunt.[25] Delcommune would become Joseph Conrad's nemesis and Hodister would rise to be a candidate prototype for Conrad's possessed station chief, Kurtz.

Sanford's estate's share in 1892 of what remained totaled just under 16,000 Belgian francs. That sum was delivered to his widow, Gertrude, who spent her remaining decade of unhappy widowhood trying to get more from men she imagined to have been in debt to her husband.

6

The Court-Martial

There is some prospect of a naval court-martial being ordered in a few days for the trial of an officer of the navy upon a somewhat disagreeable charge. . . . Soon after his return home from Africa, the Lieutenant was ordered to the Nipsic. It is charged that he failed to report for duty, and that a search resulted in finding him in New York living in a clandestine manner. Lieutenant Taunt is regarded as a bright officer, and it is deeply regretted that he has placed himself in such a position.

Baltimore Sun, *November 12, 1887*

32

On Monday, October 10, 1887, Lieutenant Taunt returned to active duty from extended leave and his failed second African adventure and reported as ordered to USS *Nipsic* at her berth in the New York Navy Yard on the Brooklyn waterfront. At 1:00 p.m., with her new captain, Taunt, four other wardroom officers, and four navy yard quartermasters on deck watching, *Nipsic*'s commissioning pennant was hoisted. The small flag-raising ceremony marked the moment of turnover of the ship from the yard to her crew, represented that afternoon only by the handful of assembled officers.

Work now began to prepare the gunboat for her coming Pacific deployment. *Nipsic* was scheduled to sail in mid-January for the usual three years with a squadron on station. After bringing Admiral English home, she'd been in port New York, out of commission, for the past four months. Taking the ship as she now was, an empty, inert vessel watched over by a duty officer and a single, bored shipyard sailor, and turning her into a man-of-war ready for sea took every day of the next three months.

Nipsic's commanding officer, Cdr. Dennis Mullan, USN, her surgeon, and her only officer of marines reported on board the same day as did Taunt. So did Lt. John Sherman, USN. Lt. John Hawley, USN, also joined the ship on the tenth. Hawley was two years and some fifty numbers senior to Taunt on the U.S. Navy's lineal list of lieutenants. He became *Nipsic*'s second in command. A third lieutenant, Richmond Davenport, reported on board November 1 as the navigator. Had Taunt made the cruise, he would have been the junior lieutenant on the crew.

First Lt. H. Clay Fisher, USMC, was in charge of the detachment of Marines: twenty privates, four junior noncommissioned officers, a drummer, and a fifer. Fisher's Marines came on board Saturday. They constituted *Nipsic*'s landing party, her disciplinary muscle, and part of her gun crews. The two musicians were embarked to dress up any ceremonies the ship might be required to mount and to keep marchers in step on shore.

Nipsic's enlisted sailors, her "people" (as distinguished from officers, who were referred to as "gentlemen"), started dribbling on board in small groups from the receiving ship, USS *Vermont*, during the next several days. The stores required for long months at sea—everything from foodstuffs to engine parts, from corn brooms to inkwells—began to arrive that first week, too. So did her armament, four 9-inch "great guns" firing 13-pound balls or 10-pound shells, and two pivot guns. Gunpowder, shot and shell, seventy-five Springfield rifles, sixty-five Colt and Remington revolvers, seventy cutlasses (the tradition of boarding parties died hard), and small-arms ammunition would all be delivered later.

Tied up at the yard's Cob Dock, in the very early stages of being brought back to life after four months in ordinary following her South Atlantic cruise, *Nipsic*—1,375 tons, 183 feet long, bark-rigged, with two compound steam engines driving a single screw—would have promised an austere existence for the next three years. Bleaker still when Captain Mullan told Taunt he should bed down temporarily in the unfurnished wardroom, under a blanket on a mattress atop the after berth deck. Taunt would later observe in explanation of his bizarre behavior that there were as yet "no accommodations for living in the ship" immediately after commissioning.

Taunt was the duty officer Tuesday night, October 11. Wednesday morning around 7:00 he was off the ship early, stiff and cold following an uncomfortable night, to wash up and get breakfast on shore. He failed to return by 9:00 a.m., the prescribed time, an absence duly noted in the ship's deck log by Lieutenant Sherman, who was standing the forenoon watch. Sherman seemingly paid no more attention to Taunt's failure to reappear than that required to write a single, offhand sentence, right after a log entry noting the delivery of six mattresses and six pillows. He spent the balance of his four hours on deck busily logging in stores as they moved from shore to ship and were struck below. At 9:30 the morning of October 16, with Taunt still absent, Captain Mullen mustered his crew on deck for the first time and read aloud orders assigning him to command.

As reconstructed from testimony later, during the nearly three weeks while Taunt was absent without leave from *Nipsic*, he'd crossed the East River to New York City and then shuttled between three downtown hotels.

And not always alone. At the Sturtevant House hotel on October 18 he'd checked into Room 232 as "Lieut. Emory H. Taunt and wife." The woman in room 232 with Taunt was generally believed by *Nipsic*'s officers not to have been Mary Taunt, a suspicion heightened by the fact that Taunt "positively refused" to permit her to be seen by them.

Lelands' Sturtevant House, at 1186 Broadway Avenue, seven stories high and occupying nearly the full city block between Twenty-eighth and Twenty-ninth streets, was one of New York's more popular hotels in the 1880s, despite having been the site of a sensational society parricide in June 1873, when Mansfield Walworth (novelist, son of a powerful New York state jurist, and quite possibly a lunatic) after years abusing his former wife was shot four times by their nineteen-year-old son.[1]

Built in 1871, Sturtevant House offered three hundred rooms for the upper-class traveling public and a number of elegant residential apartments for some of the city's wealthy citizens. Its American plan dining, offering guests five meals a day from six in the morning until midnight, was a great attraction. Some ate all five. Neither the Grand Hotel, at Broadway and Thirty-first Street, nor the Grand Union Hotel, on Park Avenue and Forty-second Street, across from the Grand Central Depot, boasted as fine an address.

Near the middle of his flight, on October 22, escorted by the ship's Marine detachment commander and *Nipsic*'s surgeon and heading back with them to Brooklyn from Sturtevant House, Taunt got only a few blocks. On the corner of Fifth Avenue and Twenty-eighth Street, Fisher later recalled in testimony, Taunt told the pair he could go no farther but promised them that he would report on board the ship for dinner at 5:30 that night "if well enough or alive (or some such remark)." Instead, Taunt surreptitiously changed hotels and continued to hide. All this aimless dithering either in malarial pain and confused by fever, his explanation for absence, or besotted with drink and in an alcoholic fog, the Navy's view.

Taunt didn't return until Tuesday, November 1. When he did, in a carriage from Manhattan's Grand Hotel escorted by the ship's surgeon and a civilian, that was noted in the log, too: "Lieut. Taunt returned to the ship and was placed under arrest by the commanding officer," also without editorial comment.

November 14, two weeks after Taunt finally returned to *Nipsic* and after the shipyard's commandant had asked him to, the acting secretary of the navy charged Taunt with absence from his station and duty without leave, with disobedience of the lawful orders of his superior officer, and with scandalous conduct. It fell to a general court-martial to determine which explanation for Taunt's strange behavior was correct, disease or drunkenness.

33

The charge of unauthorized absence stood on its own, but the navy secretary's two other charges against Taunt together encompassed three specifications. In order these were, "that the said Emory H. Taunt, a lieutenant in the United States Navy, attached to and serving as such on board the United States Ship *Nipsic*, at the Navy Yard, Brooklyn, New York . . . did"

> Positively refuse to obey, and did willfully and knowingly disobey [a lawful order from his commanding officer . . . to report immediately on board], this in contempt of the authority and orders [of Commander Mullan].
>
> For the purpose of concealing himself and avoiding his arrest and forcible return to his station and duty . . . refrain from communicating his whereabouts, or causing the same to be communicated to his commanding officer, or other authority, and did . . . prevent the enforcement of the aforesaid order requiring him to report; all this to the great scandal and disgrace of the service.
>
> During his absence from his station and duty without leave . . . by the prolonged and excessive use of intoxicating liquor, incapacitate himself for the proper performance of his duty as an officer of the Navy, and on his return . . . was, in consequence of such prolonged and excessive use of intoxicating liquor, so ill as to require medical treatment on board.

Members of the general court-martial convened to hear the charges against Lieutenant Taunt gathered together for the first time just after noon Thursday, November 17, 1887, at "the U.S. Navy Yard New York," in Brooklyn. Although Taunt was held on board his ship after he was arrested, *Nipsic*'s small size and ongoing preparations for sea forced relocation of the court to the navy yard's Lyceum Building, a square stone structure that housed on its three floors the offices of the yard's commandant, Rear Adm. Bancroft Gherardi, USN, of the captain of the yard, and of their staffs and clerks.

The same day the court convened the *New York City Sun* explained to its readers that Taunt's many friends, anticipating his defense, "can account for his actions only upon the ground of mental derangement. They say that the hardships suffered by him on the Greely relief expedition and later in the Congo explorations have undermined his constitution and unsettled his reason." Spinning the story of his sacking by Baron Weber, the *Sun* continued helpfully, if not completely accurately, "Members of his family and intimate friends have been worried about his condition of mind and body ever since

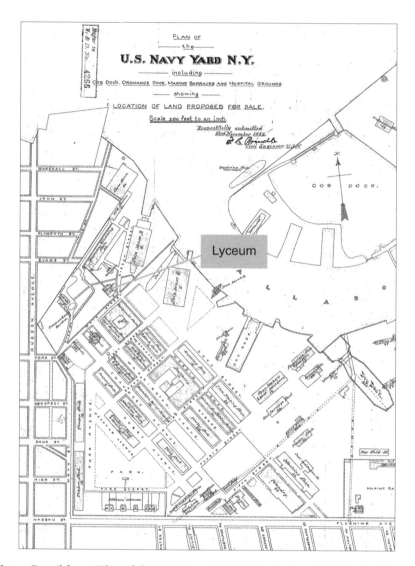

Map 4. Detail from "Plan of the U.S. Navy Yard N.Y. including Cob Dock, Ordnance Dock, Marine Barracks and Hospital Grounds. 1882." The Brooklyn Navy Yard was a major industrial site in the 1880s. Two huge ship houses, two dry and six wet docks, and dozens of shops and storehouses filled the grid of streets on the property facing the East River. During the day two thousand men filled the yard with the clamor of their work and talk. The Navy Lyceum, site of Taunt's court-martial, was a handsome building on the west side of the federal property, just a short walk up the yard's main street from the commandant's elegant quarters and garden. In a past life it had been home to a small museum of curiosities and lecture hall, hence the name. *Y&D 4266, New York State Archives; Courtesy of the Brooklyn Navy Yard*

his return from Europe, when he surrendered the remainder of his leave, which had been granted in order that he might continue his work in Africa and applied for sea duty. By the advice of his physician he was compelled to give up further travel in the tropical regions. His friends are emphatic in the belief that only impaired reason can account for actions which endanger his high standing and reputation in the navy."

Taunt's court-martial included four captains (Ramsay, commanding officer of USS *Boston*, its president, and Farquhar, Kane, and Schoonmaker) and five commanders (Shepard, Coffin, Wadleigh, Whiting, and McCalla). Together the nine members of the court represented more than two hundred years of navy service in peace and war and more than a century afloat. Captain Farquhar might have remembered Taunt. Years ago he had witnessed Rodgers' written critique of Taunt's performance in USS *Franklin*. For his part, Schoonmaker had commanded *Nipsic* in the early 1880s while she cruised with the European Squadron.

Lt. Adolph Marix, USN, in 1887 beginning three years of special service in the Navy Judge Advocate General's office, sat as the trial judge advocate, the prosecutor, and counsel to the court. Like the nine members, Marix was a line officer, not a lawyer. He'd served generally at sea since graduating from the Naval Academy in 1868, the year before Taunt. In a student body of several hundred men, the two must have known each other at Annapolis.[2]

Five members of Taunt's court-martial constituted a quorum, but all were present during the six days the court sat to hear the testimony of witnesses, nine for the prosecution and one for the defense, and to determine guilt or innocence.

Taunt's adventures in the Congo had made his name familiar outside of Navy circles. For that reason, and because the charges against him—disappearance, disobedience, drunkenness—were unusually colorful, Taunt's court-martial attracted civilian attention, especially in the big cities of the Atlantic Coast. The *New York Herald*, because of its relationship with Stanley and Africa going back fifteen years to the famous search for Livingstone, covered the proceedings with almost proprietary interest. "Taunt is a man of striking appearance," it told its readers while the navy secretariat and the White House wrestled through early 1888 with what to do after his trial and medical evaluation, "and was a great favorite with his brother officers." And then, even more inventively because Taunt had not stayed on board long enough to make himself at home in any of the ship's ten tiny wardroom cabins aft, "His stateroom on the Nipsic was hung with trophies that he had collected on his various cruises including a head of a polar bear which he shot when with the Greely Relief Expedition and a necklace made with human teeth which he captured from a cannibal chief in Central Africa."

Other city newspapers and some elsewhere were attentive, too. The story popped up in Cincinnati and other places far from salt water, thanks to the journalism conventions of the period that encouraged newspapers to fill blank spaces by appropriating each other's work and to U.S. post office practices that moved exchanged newspapers between editors free of change.

The day after Taunt's court convened, the *Herald* told its readers that, among other things, it was alleged Taunt had "by the excessive use of intoxicating liquor . . . incapacitated himself for the proper performance of his duty and was . . . in consequence of such prolonged excessive use . . . so ill as to require medical treatment" when finally in Navy custody. Anticipating lengthy trial proceedings scheduled, the paper thought, to begin in earnest on November 19, the *Herald* mused hopefully that the testimony would "doubtless present many interesting features."

If he were quoted accurately by the *Herald*'s reporter, Taunt's defense might well have been interesting to a lay readership. "I returned from the Congo broken down with fevers, liver troubles and malaria, and I have not felt myself at all," he explained to the *Herald*'s man. "I was under the care of my family in New York when Captain Mullin [*sic*] sent for me, and it was my intention to return to the 'Nipsic' at once. I did not mean to disobey orders, and I was not drinking anything stronger than some wine which my doctor ordered for me. My mind is a blank as to what transpired from the time I was found at the Sturtevant House and the time that I was brought here. I think that my case will appear quite differently after the trial, and I hope my friends will suspend judgment until then."

And what if he were convicted? "Well, I would return to Africa and join my friend Henry Morton Stanley. But I never was intoxicated, and the moderate allowance of the champagne I took was, from my experience, the best remedy for the fever from which I suffered."[3] Mary Taunt, who had lived through something very much like this before, must have read her husband's words with foreboding. She might have been surprised, too, by the description of Stanley as Taunt's "friend." There's no evidence the two ever met.

34

At his court-martial in 1873 Taunt had represented himself. This time he would not, although he did conduct much of the questioning. Taunt's request that Lt. Samuel Lemly, USN, and Passed Asst. Surgeon Cumberland Herndon, USN, be assigned to act as his co-counsels was approved.

Four years behind Taunt at the Naval Academy, Lieutenant Lemly was his former shipmate in USS *Thetis* under Schley's command in the heady days of the Greely rescue expedition, now a long three years ago. Taunt chose his legal counsel wisely. Lieutenant Lemly, in some sources "Lemley," was a comer. In July 1892 he was nominated to the Senate for promotion to the grade of captain and assignment as the Navy's judge advocate general. Beginning in September 1901, Captain Lemly sat as the judge advocate of the Navy's highest profile legal proceeding since the court-martial of the brig USS *Somers*' mutineers in 1842, the court of inquiry that condemned the conduct of his former CO, Commo. Winfield Schley, while in command of the Flying Squadron at the Battle of Santiago in the Spanish-American War.[4]

Herndon was an experienced ship's surgeon. He'd been at sea in *Canandaigua*, *Colorado*, *Franklin*, and *Albatross*. At the time of the court-martial Herndon had just finished three years special duty in Washington and would soon report to *Enterprise*. How Herndon and Taunt first connected isn't known, possibly through an introduction by Rixey, Taunt's Navy surgeon brother-in-law and a close contemporary of Herndon's. The two were separated by just two numbers on the surgeons' seniority list.

The unusual pairing reveals Taunt intended that his defense focus on persuading members of the court that he had been ill, not insubordinate. Presumably Taunt drew on advice from counsel when he entered his pleas: "guilty" to the first charge; "guilty" to the second, subject to the elimination of language in the first specification that indicated his misconduct was willful, knowing, and intentional; and "not guilty" to the third. Taunt's pleas accepted what was irrefutable and set the stage for a defense based entirely on the disabling and disorienting symptoms of tropical disease contracted during honorable service on the ground in West Africa. The *New York Times* described to its readers later that "he explained his seemingly strange behavior on several occasions by asserting he was compelled to drink liberally of champagne in order to overcome the effects of a fever contracted in Africa."

With Lemly and Herndon sitting next to him, the trial began with the prosecution's first witness, Commander Mullan, *Nipsic*'s commanding officer. Mullan was one of four naval officers Marix called to testify. It was Mullan who had ordered Lieutenant Fisher to conduct a search for the absent Taunt in New York City's "principal hotels and smaller public houses" along Sixth, Seventh, and Ninth avenues, and to bring him back to the ship. Fisher had the good sense to hire a civilian detective to help him in the hunt, and the two were soon successful in tracking down their prey.

Rear Adm. Bancroft Gherardi, USN, was the next witness. Gherardi, the senior Navy officer in Brooklyn, much more than Mullan seems to have been the chief impetus behind the search for Taunt. He ordered *Nipsic's* medical officer, Passed Asst. Surgeon Ezra Derr, to join the hotel checks with Fisher; he also asked for permission to offer a reward for Taunt's apprehension and return and authorized the use of an ambulance, if necessary, to bring Taunt back. "By force," Gherardi testified, "providing the medical officer did not object on the ground it would injure his health." Finally, his letter to the secretary of the navy prompted the charges that were being tried.

The last day of October Gherardi received a Western Union telegram from Rear Admiral English, then some twenty months into retirement and worriedly following the antics of his son-in-law from his home in distant Culpeper, Virginia. By then the two admirals had been in informal contact for several days, perhaps longer, about Taunt's travels. Its text was ruled inadmissible and never read into the trial record, but the telegram is in the National Archives and so we know that English told Gherardi his AWOL son-in-law was at the Grand Hotel, ill, and suggested that whatever Gherardi had written him on October 27 about Taunt's absence from his ship might have been based on misinformation, that what was afoot was nothing more criminal than a man too sick to travel from New York City across the river to the City of Brooklyn.

English had also been behind two surprise visits to the navy yard of a civilian, Samuel Russell Smith, thirty-five, chairman of the Culpeper National Bank, a business partner, descendant of one of Rappahannock County, Virginia's old families, and the third of the three English sons-in-law. (He'd married the youngest English daughter, Frankie, just months earlier.) Smith materialized in Brooklyn on October 18, with a promise to bring Taunt to the yard from New York City by midmorning the next day, but he couldn't pull the surrender off and after this first cameo appearance disappeared quietly from the scene to report his failure to his new father-in-law. But only for a while: On November 1 Smith reappeared at the shipyard's gate in a carriage, this time with Taunt and Dr. Derr.

Next Lieutenant Fisher took the stand to report on his several excursions into Manhattan in pursuit of Taunt, the first accompanied by Derr, to deliver written orders to the wayward officer instructing him to return. According to the *New York Times* of November 26, 1887, First Lieutenant Fisher barely finished his testimony at Taunt's court-martial before his own trial began on what the item's headline described as a "Strange Charge to Try a Marine," and the text explained was "the ignominious charge of stealing chicken feed."

Fisher was accused of stealing bread and "other provender" to feed to a flock of handsome game birds he was raising as a hobby at the sleepy League Island Ship Yard in Philadelphia, where he'd been previously assigned. Fisher had also, Maj. James Forney, U.S. Marine Corps, alleged at trial, bought a hay cutter to "masticate the tough Government loaves" and billed its purchase to the government's account "on the ground that if the bread provided by the Government was unfit for food, the Government should pay for its improvement." Two trials, one after the other, of ship's company officers led the *New York Times* to observe that *Nipsic* "seems to have been converted into a prison ship."[5] The *Herald* played the same story uncharacteristically straight.

Derr, the last Navy witness to testify, saw Taunt in New York City three times during October's oddly diffident campaign to bring him in. Each time (and also on November 1, when Taunt finally returned to his ship) Derr's diagnosis was the same: Taunt's illness was "very largely if not wholly the result of excessive indulgence in alcoholic stimulants," although he'd later concede he had not smelled alcohol on Taunt's breath. It was Derr who put Taunt on *Nipsic*'s sick list November 1, where he remained for a week, observing that Taunt was "not in condition for the proper performance of his duties as an officer of the Navy." Mullan shared that judgment by testifying that he would refuse to put Taunt on a watch bill. He told the court he thought Taunt's absence was caused because "he was spreeing or laboring from alterations of a disordered mind."

The testimony of the civilian prosecution witnesses, four hotel employees (Messrs. Toner, Pierson, Mason, and Marigan) and a cab driver (Dignan), established a rough schedule of Taunt's erratic movements during the last three weeks of October: six days at the Grand Hotel, followed by four at Sturtevant House, then two at the Grand Union Hotel, and finally a week back at the Grand. He may have also ridden the West Shore Railroad up the Hudson River to Albany and back during October 24–27, although this excursion was not proven.

At 2:00 in the afternoon on Monday, November 21, right after a recess following the cross-examination of Marigan, the head porter at Sturtevant House, the prosecution rested its case.

35

Taunt's defense included several elements. The first was testimony by Dr. Samuel Smith, a civilian physician and surgeon with a practice at 24 West

Thirtieth Street, who provided on-call medical attention to downtown hotel guests and said he saw Taunt in this role "five or six times" in October.

Smith helpfully ascribed everything, Taunt's conduct and his complaints, to fever (perhaps malaria) and to an enlarged liver. He reported that Taunt had responded well to his prescription, combining a mercurial with bromide of potash, quinine, and sponge baths. In reply to a leading question posed to him by Taunt—"Would a person who had returned a few months ago from a tropical climate be very apt to suffer from such an attack as mine when exposed to the weather such as prevailed for the last month?"— Smith was able to agree that he would. He'd earlier told the prosecution "no," that Taunt's symptoms had not suggested to him a diagnosis of excessive use of alcohol.

Long after the court-martial, in mid-April, Smith would less helpfully try to boost Taunt's case for clemency with a letter that described his sometime patient as suffering from "mental hallucinations and acts of insanity," so great as to require confinement. Taunt was, Smith wrote then, "not a responsible being and ought to be retained in some institution for that purpose."

The second part of the defense was a letter dated April 18, 1886, written and signed by Rolph Leslie, M.D., Stanley's principal medical officer during the construction of the river stations and the former chief physician of the Congo Free State. "Lieutenant Taunt, US Navy," Leslie had written to no particular addressee, "is suffering from congestion of the liver and other malarial troubles, the result of his sojourn in Africa. I consider a few months absence from duty advisable, to enable him to follow out the regime ordered by his physician which I consider necessary to the reestablishment of his health."

Leslie's letter had originally been part of the cover story for Taunt's first drinking bout at the Banana Point hotel, the collapse early in the year that was the beginning of the end of his employment with the Sanford Expedition. Now in Brooklyn eight months later, the old letter was being recycled for the same purpose, to provide a medical explanation for a relapse.

The third part was several depositions from senior Navy officers, attesting to Taunt's character, good conduct, and general worth. One, by Capt. Gilbert Wiltse, USN, the commanding officer in 1876 of USS *Shawmut*, looked back ten years to the time the two were shipmates. Wiltse recalled that Taunt's conduct as a watch and division officer was "unexceptional, he was strictly temperate and performed his duty" to satisfaction. This sounds tepid but was meant to be more supportive than that.

Another, from Lt. Cdr. Albert Snow, USN, the former executive officer of the training ship USS *Portsmouth*, was more enthusiastic. Taunt and Snow overlapped in *Portsmouth* for almost two years. "His record as an Officer was excellent, and his character was good," Snow said. He could "recall no occasion during their official relations when any infraction of regulations was committed by Lieutenant Taunt which demanded either the interference of the Executive Officer or report made to Commanding Officer." The last part was Schley's general purpose letter of recommendation after the Greely expedition. The same letter had been used in 1886 to solidify Taunt's grasp on the S.E.E. job. It now was being repurposed as an omnibus character recommendation.

The centerpiece of Taunt's defense was presented on Monday afternoon, November 22, in the form of his seventeen-page letter to the members of the court, read by his counsel and added to the trial record as Exhibit H. This procedure, counsel reading his statement, reflected Taunt's decision not to take the stand. He had that right—just as he could examine witnesses and otherwise participate actively in his defense—but this approach allowed Taunt to get his story into the record without being vulnerable to questions from the judge advocate or members of the court.

The essence of Taunt's statement was an assertion that he was not in possession of his full faculties during his weeks-long absence, not because of drinking to excess ("I drank moderately of champagne believing that it would benefit me") but because of fever. "I firmly believe and I ask the court to consider while I admit my inability to prove it that my trouble was the result of malaria brought on by exposure of some eighteen months in an extreme tropical and malarial climate," he said. "I do assert and beg you to believe that brain action was to some degree affected by my condition [and I] did not fully realize what I did."

Accounts in the press often speculated that the hardships Taunt had endured in Arctic Canada and equatorial Africa had "undermined his constitution and unsettled his reason." Here Taunt was agreeing that this was so, the point being that although he'd been absent without leave in October, he did not have the capacity or the intent to violate Navy regulations. In his *Military Law and Precedents* (W. H. Morrison, 1886) author Col. William Winthrop, U.S. Army, called this "a defense of the second class," a proof that although the act was committed, it did not constitute the offense charged. ("A defense of the first class" was proof that the offense charged was not committed by the accused.)[6]

With Taunt's statement delivered, the defense closed, leaving Lieutenant Marix to submit the case to decision by the members of the court. "After full and mature deliberation" they found unanimously that Taunt was guilty of "absence from his station and duty without leave," by plea and proof.

The members also found him guilty of the second charge, "disobedience of the lawful orders of his superior officer," by proof. The third charge, "scandalous conduct," resulted in two minor technical victories for the defense. Those judgments recorded, the court nevertheless concluded that Taunt was also guilty of the third charge. It sentenced him "to be dismissed from the Navy of the United States."

Taunt's history did elicit some sympathy. "In view of the previous good conduct of the accused," Captain Farquhar, Captain Schoonmaker, Commander Shepard, and Commander Wadleigh wrote in a petition for clemency, "as given by the depositions of two of his Commanding Officers and an Executive Officer, and of his arduous services on the Greely Relief and Congo Expeditions, we, the undersigned members of the Court, do recommend Lieutenant Emory H. Taunt to the clemency of the [?] Power." The seventy-one-page record of trial was sent to the secretary of the navy.

36

On December 1 Taunt appealed to Henry Sanford for help, at least a week too late to effect the outcome of the court-martial but in good time to influence the consideration of clemency or to support some other last-minute Washington maneuver. Taunt believed his old boss would help him by confirming his story line. "Certain reports have been circulated at Washington to the effect that I was recalled from the Congo in April last by the Sanford Ex. for the reason that I drank up all your wine &c," he wrote the general:

> Where this is coming from I don't know but it has taken such a turn that I need hold positive proofs to the contrary in order to protect my official life.
>
> I beg that you will forward me either the originals or a certified copy of the two medical certificates I sent you from Liverpool last April—one was in German the other in English. And also please send me a certificate either from yourself or from Weber & Co to the effect that I returned from the Congo [to Europe] of my own free will *against your wishes* by authority of these medical certificates and it was intended that I should return to the Congo as soon as my health was reestablished but that in July last my resignation was accepted....
>
> You will confirm a great favor by sending what I wish at once as I have learned today that I may need them....
>
> It is of vital importance to me to obtain what I have requested of you.

Technically true. Taunt had left the Congo in March entirely on his own. The surprise news that he'd abandoned his post and employees flabbergasted Weber in Antwerp when he learned it while Taunt was still at sea in SS *Lualaba* and due to arrive at Liverpool in just a few days. "The Congo Mail is in with very bad news," Weber had written to Sanford April 6, 1887. "Taunt has left for Europe without leaving a word of instructions nor leaving powers. . . . It appears he is an incorrigible Tipsomaniac [*sic*] & cannot be sent out again. . . . Take all powers from him as he can only do mischief." The rest of many letters that month between Weber and Sanford dealt largely with how to manage the Expedition in view of the fact "there is no doubt we cannot employ him any more on account of his condition."[7] Given this history, Taunt's appeal to his former boss seems surreal, an invitation to lie.

Protecting Taunt's "official life" immediately after the court-martial could not have been easy for anyone else willing to try, either. December 7 in the morning, while under arrest in *Nipsic* and awaiting action on the verdict and sentence in Washington, Taunt was discovered partly dressed on his stateroom bunk in a drunken stupor, having somehow smuggled three bottles of whiskey on board and emptied two and half of the third. The search of his stateroom by Dr. Derr that uncovered this stash was prompted by Taunt's failure to emerge on deck anytime during the past two days, not even for meals.

The next seven months were filled with furious lobbying in Washington, attempts by Taunt's family and supporters to stave off a sentence that, once executed, would indelibly blot his reputation (and English's) and likely make Taunt unemployable. The initial delay in action on the sentence was laid by the press to Secretary Whitney, who during January 1888 was described as "charitably" withholding his approval of the court's decision because of the possibility that Taunt was not sane.

The idea for a medical board to examine questions of sanity and responsibility, which Taunt had raised repeatedly as the heart of his defense during the court-martial, seems to have been not Whitney's but Taunt's mother, Marie's, then living in Syracuse, New York, with her husband, James, in the rectory of Trinity Episcopal Church. Beginning with a personal call on President Grover Cleveland in the White House (she called it "an interview," and the fact that he met with her in the White House suggests how different those times were from ours), sometime in November Marie appears to have taken on the leadership of her son's claque.

In between two follow-on letters to President Cleveland (the first in December, coincidently on the day Taunt was found stupefied in his stateroom; the second in April, both on church letterhead), his mother sent a letter to Secretary Whitney. "I most respectfully ask," she wrote on January 9, "before the case of Lieut. E. H. Taunt, U.S.N. be acted upon, that he may be ordered before a medical Board or Survey":

> I am confident that he was not in his right mind, and not responsible for the misconduct at the Brooklyn Navy Yard for which he was tried by Court-Martial.
>
> From the time he came home he acted very strangely and was observed by all the members of his family and we attributed it to the fever he contracted while on duty in Africa. If you will kindly comply with my request you will do an act of justice to Lieut. Taunt, and confer a great favor upon his mother.

Whitney quickly accepted Mrs. Taunt's suggestion, perhaps because three days earlier he'd received a letter from (the famously corrupt) Senator "Boss" Quay, Republican of Pennsylvania, "to express his earnest trust that the extreme recommendations of the Court Martial may be remitted, or at least mitigated and modified." Attached to Quay's letter was a petition he and twenty members of the state's caucus in the House of Representatives had signed urging executive clemency in view of Taunt's "admitted capacity and distinguished service upon the Arctic Relief and Congo Expeditions." Whitney, like President Cleveland, was a Democrat, but 1888 was an election year and some sensitivity to what the pols on Capitol Hill were saying and thinking probably wasn't a bad idea.

Taunt happily accepted the medical board suggestion, too. "In accordance with the wishes of my Medical Advisors in New York City," he wrote the secretary on the nineteenth, "I accept the Department's [January 13] offer for a medical examination and will proceed to Washington as soon as possible."

Acceding to such an exam after a general court-martial had considered and rejected Taunt's medical defense suggests that Secretary Whitney was not fully convinced that Taunt's crimes did not have their source in fever and mental confusion or that he was under terrific pressure to find a way around the court's sentence that did not look as if the Navy had been rolled. A Navy medical board had the power to find that Taunt was physically unable to serve because of disabling disease contracted in the line of duty. In that case, subject only to President Cleveland's approval, Taunt might have been removed from active duty in 1888 for medical reasons and collected half or more of his pay during years of retirement. On January 14 Whitney referred the case to Medical Director James Suddards, USN, president of the medical board, to establish Taunt's "mental condition at the time of commission of the offenses of which he was found guilty."

A medical director in the Navy's medical corps—there were only fifteen—corresponded in rank to a captain in the line. Only the surgeon general of the Navy was senior to a medical director, beneath whom in the pyramid stood the ranks of medical inspectors, surgeons, passed assistant surgeons, and assistant surgeons that made up most of the sea service's two hundred physicians. Dr. Suddards was an experienced Navy surgeon. He'd been on active duty since before Taunt was born and had been promoted three times (in 1861, 1871, and 1875) during a career that began in the frigate USS *John Adams* on antislavery patrol off West Africa in 1849, not long after Master's Mate Lawrence had sailed the same waters in USS *Yorktown* only to die. Suddards' career ended abruptly with his sudden death on August 31, until that day sitting as the president of the board that had in January first reviewed Taunt's mental health.

The board (Suddards and members Peck and Browne, both also medical directors) reported to the secretary on January 25 that Taunt was mentally sound and that its members were "of the opinion that the plea that 'Lieutenant Taunt's mental faculties were impaired by exposure to climactic influences during six month's journey on the river Congo, and that, as a consequence, he was not morally responsible for the offenses of which he was convicted,' is not sound." That's what the senior Navy line officers sitting on the court had concluded, too.

On March 6 Whitney told Suddards to do it again, this time to see if Taunt was physically qualified to serve at sea. Suddards, almost certainly swallowing hard, wrote on March 9 that, yes, he was qualified. (A finding that he was not could have presaged a move directly to the retired list, finessing the unpleasant questions raised by the court's sentence entirely.) That same day President Cleveland—an iteration behind his responsible department head—wrote a short note, apparently for the record, in "the matter of the Court Martial of Lieut. Emory H. Taunt":[8]

> Lieut Taunt was convicted on the *22nd day of November 1887* and sentenced to be dismissed the service.
>
> There are some things in the record of this officer and there is testimony as to his efficiency and worth, added to the recommendation of four out of nine officer members of the court which appeal somewhat to clemency.

But as a serious offset to these matters in his favor, it appears from reports before me that on the 7th day of December 1887, he was in his room on the ship in a half stupefied condition, his breath smelling of liquor and his appearance showing in other ways that he had been indulging in its use; and that two empty whiskey bottles and another partly filled were found in his room.

I hardly think I can with a clear regard to duty and in the interests of our Naval Service, exercise clemency upon the record and facts now before me.

But there is an intimation that the fever and malarial condition, induced by exposure to tropical influences to which this officer in the line of duty had been subjected were related to his offense and prejudicial [?]; and I am given to understand that an examining Board will be convened for the purpose of ascertaining Lieut Taunts present physical condition, and the causes of any impairments there may be of his health.

I think justice can be perhaps more satisfactorily meted out after the finding of this latter named Board; and I therefore withhold my action upon the Court Martial record [?] until the result of the retiring Board is made known to me.

March 9, 1888.G. C.

37

Through the spring of 1888, while the Navy and the White House grappled awkwardly with the case of Lt. Emory Taunt, he was exploring his options, too. None saw him remaining in the Navy. Even before President Cleveland penned the above note, Taunt was sampling the life of a civilian businessman. That's when he wrote Sanford to test his interest in an invention by a naval academy classmate, James Weir Graydon, that Taunt inflated into "the biggest discovery in explosives of the century." (Certainly not true. Nobel's invention of dynamite in 1866 held that distinction.) Graydon had resigned his commission in 1886 and now was doing business as the Graydon Dynamite Projectile and High Explosive Company of Washington, D.C., with Taunt as an associate. The two were hardly an all-star team. In 1869 Graydon had graduated sixty-eighth in their class of seventy-five (the three men at the bottom were not commissioned), eight below Taunt, and fifty-eighth in conduct, fifteen below Taunt.

The offer to Sanford was the franchise for sales of the newly patented Graydon Dynamite Shell to the governments of France, Belgium, and Sweden and a share in the ensuing "magnificent benefits." Allegedly his new associate's invention was a gun round with four to seven times more explosive power than commercial No. 1 Dynamite, itself about six times more powerful than the familiar black powder.

Since Nobel's invention of dynamite a handful of engineers in the United States and Europe had been working on the idea of high explosive rounds. All were frustrated by the explosive charge's sensitivity to the heat and shock of firing. Such technical hurdles didn't trouble Taunt. "Rest assured that if you do take it up there is a fortune in it," he confidently told the general, who like his correspondent had never heard artillery fired in anger. But that sensitivity bedeviled Graydon, too, who tried unsuccessfully to deal with the problem of heat by lining the inside of the shell case with asbestos.

Taunt continued his sales pitch by broaching a sensitive subject: "There will be no question of your vouching for me or for any one else. In all probability I will not be brought into personal contact with you as I have engagements in England, Turkey and China.... I simply mention this in order to do away with any hesitancy you might have arising from a reluctance to associate with me personally in this matter. Although I still claim that I did more for the advancement of the [Sanford] Ex. Ex. than all the others combined."

Unfortunately, Taunt's heady expectations for rich sales to governments of shells packed with what was being called "Graydonite" were disappointed. According to Manuel Eissler's *Handbook of Modern Explosives* (Crosby Lockwood and Son, 1890), tests of them in December 1887 by the U.S. Army at Sandy Hook, New Jersey, against targets were unimpressive. So too was a test of Graydonite's stability when fired into by a rifle round. It exploded. Those failures slowly absorbed, Taunt went back to thinking about his future.

All of Taunt's real alternatives to service in the Navy involved going back to the Congo in one role or another. The most attractive possibility was to return there as a U.S. diplomat accredited to Boma, but in May that seemed to him increasingly unlikely, whether because the new post might not be funded by Congress or because his personal failings would deny him the appointment is not clear. That's when he began pursuing a place in the "Scientific Corps" of the Smithsonian's National Museum (precursor to the Museum of Natural History), even while he continued to plan on a return to the Sanford Exploring Expedition in late June—despite Baron Weber's determined opposition.

38

On June 29, 1888, almost on the nineteenth anniversary of Lieutenant Taunt's graduation from the Naval Academy and his twelfth in grade, President Cleveland accepted his resignation, to be effective the next day. "Considerable pressure was brought to bear upon the President," the *New York Times* reported on June 30, "to prevent his dismissal, and the President finally consented to allow him to resign." Taunt's court-martial had reported out to the secretary of the Navy in the last week of November. It took Secretary Whitney and the president the seven intervening months to figure out how to pass through the political thicket that had grown up around the court's sentence, between those insisting on dishonorable dismissal and those pressing for honorable medical retirement or some other escape from disgrace.

That they did figure it out is clear from a letter Rear Admiral Walker sent to Sanford the day before. "Taunt is to retire to private life," the chief of the Bureau of Navigation wrote to Sanford, still loyally but inexplicably working the case. "He has been warned that he must resign or the sentence of the Court-Martial, which is dismissal, will be approved at once."

Although it took months to percolate, Taunt's general court-martial conviction terminated his Navy career—the second time in twelve months that he lost his job and was cast adrift—but it had a benefit of sorts. The conviction meant that he didn't sail in USS *Nipsic* when she left New York in mid-January 1888 for what was to be a routine three-year deployment with the Pacific Squadron but turned out to be something else.

39

Nipsic loaded gunpowder, shot, and shells off Ellis Island just before Christmas, spent a day in sea trials on the Long Island Sound, and, finally, on January 19, 1888, set out for the Pacific via the Cape Verde Islands, a rendezvous with the rest of her squadron in Montevideo, an impending summertime passage through the Strait of Magellan, and a port call at Callo, Peru. Her first day under way from New York was in "threatening weather," snow showers and heavy squalls. Pushed by a heavy following sea, *Nipsic* pitched uncomfortably, water leaking through all the air ports in the hull "due to carelessness or inefficiency in navy yard workmanship" and seas occasionally washing over the bow.

In the middle of March 1889, approaching the midpoint of her cruise, *Nipsic* was crowded in Apia Harbor, at Upolu in Samoa, with six other

Figure 22. An *Adams*-class steam sloop in port, probably New York, in the 1880s. Photo by E. H. Hart. Commissioned October 1879, the *Adams*-class sloop *Nipsic* was the last major combatant constructed in the historic yard on the Potomac River. She was only eight years old when she sailed for the Pacific with Captain Mullan, 14 other officers, 137 enlisted sailors, and 26 Marines on board—but without Taunt. He had been detached from the ship, Ensign Purcell recorded in the log, on December 12 and ordered to report under arrest to the yard's commandant to await the final decision on the general court-martial in his case. Naval photographer Edward Hart had offices in Manhattan on Broadway in the 1880s–1890s. He is remembered for his book *The Official Photographs of the U.S. Navy, with Group Pictures of the United States Cabinet, Army and Navy Officers, and Equipment*. NAVAL HISTORY AND HERITAGE COMMAND PHOTO *NH 44798*

men-of-war: two American (the squadron flagship *Trenton* and USS *Vandalia*), one British (HMS *Calliope*), and three belonging to His Imperial Germanic Majesty (SMS *Adler*, the nearly new SMS *Eber*, and the largest of the three, SMS *Olga*), and nine merchant ships.

Interest in the Samoan Islands, especially among Germans, was high because of their status as some of the few habitable places on earth still unclaimed by European colonial powers. That interest, and an ongoing election for the next Samoan king that Germany and the United States both hoped to influence, accounted for the cluster of combatant ships of three

Figure 23. Cdr. Dennis Mullan, USN, commanding officer, USS *Nipsic*, in Lima, Peru, in early 1889, while *Nipsic* was on the way to become the station ship in Samoa. Born in Annapolis, Maryland, Mullan (1843–1928) was the son of the Naval Academy's postmaster. He graduated with the accelerated class of 1863 and served in the Union navy during the Civil War, most notably with Admiral Farragut at the Battle of Mobil Bay in 1864. After the war Mullan went to sea with the Pacific, North Atlantic, and Asiatic Squadrons. He was promoted to commander in 1882, five years before taking command of USS *Nipsic*. NAVAL HISTORY AND HERITAGE COMMAND PHOTO NH 47631

nations in the open harbor, crews eying their foreign counterparts nervously. Tensions were so great in this congested anchorage that on March 13 the *New York Times* printed a rumor about a deadly surprise attack by the corvette *Olga* with one of her Schwartzkopff torpedoes on *Nipsic*, after which "the chances are less than one in a thousand that the little vessel did not go down like a rock with not a timber in her holding together."

Not true. It didn't happen. The actual disaster a few days later was much greater.

A monster typhoon blew through the islands on March 15–16 across open water from the northwest. At its low point on the sixteenth, the barometer stood at 29.07 inches of mercury, producing a storm surge of perhaps ten feet and winds of approximately seventy-five knots blowing straight down the throat of the unprotected, reef-lined harbor. On March 15 all the captains in port misread what the dropping barometer and roiling clouds ahead of the tempest were signaling—either that or none wished to lose face by getting under way unnecessarily. The American combatants were stripped and raised steam, but all three remained at their moorings, expecting to ride out the storm safely in the harbor instead of prudently putting to sea.

When the typhoon struck, *Nipsic* was farthest from open water, in line behind *Trenton* and *Vandalia* on the east side of the anchorage. *Calliope*, *Olga*, *Adler*, and *Eber* lay at anchor on its western side, with the British ship closest to deep water and *Eber* farthest from it. We know this because the U.S. squadron's commander, Rear Adm. Lewis Kimberly, USN, was an amateur artist, and his dozen or so drawings of the anchorage before, during, and after the storm provide a graphic record of the disaster.

After the typhoon passed through Samoa and the skies cleared, fourteen ships lay sunk or aground, badly battered in Apia. Four men-of-war were destroyed, as were all the merchantmen. *Trenton*, Kimberly noted about his flagship, had sank to her gun decks, *Vandalia* to her mast. The eighteen-month-old *Eber*, he remarked, had "entirely disappeared." Only HMS *Calliope* had managed to break successfully for the sea after the heavy weather struck and so escaped the worst.

Two of the officers who had sat on Taunt's general court-martial and recommended clemency, Capt. Norman Farquhar and Capt. Cornelius Schoonmaker, were also in Apia during the typhoon. The former was in command of USS *Trenton*, with Admiral Kimberly embarked, and the latter in command of the screw sloop USS *Vandalia*. Schoonmaker was washed overboard and drowned, one of sixty Americans, forty-two of his crew, and four officers to die in the storm. (His body was recovered and he was buried on the island.) Farquhar lost his ship but kept his life. Seven of *Nipsic*'s people, the entire crew of the ship's gig, drowned while they were bravely trying to run a line to shore.

On March 25 Mullan, still in Apia and looking back on the past ten days, wrote a letter to his brother:

> The Nipsic is again afloat, but without rudder or propeller, the only man-of-war here now. I stood at my post throughout that dark, long, stormy night and saw death at my door two or three times. Oh! What an anxious time it was. All is gloom now here and sadness. I am bruised in body, and my cabin is all torn to pieces. It was all filled with water . . . seas as high as [the] Annapolis State House, 215 feet. . . . We are all alone at anchor and have the whole harbor. God be praised for a safe deliverance from the jaws of death. Nothing like this has occurred since the loss of the Spanish Armada in the English Channel. No talk of war here, but of the late hurricane and its disasters.[9]

Two other combatants survived the typhoon together with *Calliope*, but just barely. The German navy's SMS *Olga* was patched together and sailed to Sydney, Australia, for comprehensive repairs. USS *Nipsic*, intentionally beached during the storm, also made voyage repairs at Apia. She sailed for Auckland on May 9 but ran into heavy weather and soon returned to Samoa. On the fifteenth *Nipsic* again cleared Apia, this time for Honolulu via Pago Pago and Fanning Island. She finally arrived in Oahu on August 2, but without Commander Mullan. A few days out of Apia for New Zealand, Mullan had brought *Nipsic* about and returned to Samoa, claiming the ship was in no condition for a South Pacific crossing. Admiral Kimberly immediately relieved him from command and sent *Nipsic* steaming under her first lieutenant in the other direction.

Commander Mullan's sudden relief from command marked the beginning of a decline in his career that, like Taunt's, eventually ended in disgrace. After idle months at home in Annapolis awaiting orders, during which the spat between Admiral Kimberly and Mullan cooled only slightly, Mullan was finally ordered to active duty as New Orleans district's lighthouse inspector, the officer in charge of the sixty-four lighthouses, beacons, and lightships on the Gulf Coast between Florida and Texas. Two brief ship commands in the Pacific were next, followed by what became his last tour of active duty, command of the sleepy and, since the Civil War, neglected navy yard near Pensacola, Florida.

Figure 24. Apia Harbor, Samoa, soon after the storm. *Nipsic* is beached in the fore-ground, and *Vandalia* is sunk off *Nipsic*'s stern. *Trenton*'s masts are just visible to the right. On March 19 Rear Admiral Kimberly wrote to the Navy Department "to report the disastrous injury and loss sustained" by his squadron at Apia. His dreadful news first got to the secretary in Washington via a telegraphic cable that ricocheted westward from him to Washington, through New Zealand, and then via Australia, Singapore, ports in India and on the Arabian Sea, Egypt, several Mediterranean islands, Gibraltar, Lisbon, and London, a kind of thirteen cushion-bank shot. Secretary of the Navy Benjamin Tracey's sympathetic answer to the admiral on April 27 declined to order a court of inquiry, as requested by Kimberly and Farquhar, viewing the calamity as an example of a "visitation of Providence in the presence of which human efforts are of little avail" and confirming the wisdom of Kimberly's decision to keep the squadron in port. Tracey's decision made Kimberly into a two-time survivor, once from the typhoon and once from the investigation that his squadron's ship handling surely merited. In Washington rumors picked up by the press were that "King" Walker was behind the secretary's decision not to convene an inquiry. NAVAL HISTORY AND HERITAGE COMMAND PHOTO 2151

Mullan was commandant of the Pensacola Navy Yard for only eight months in 1896–97. While in command, and days away from promotion to captain, he was charged with being drunk while on duty and also while at leisure, charges that the *San Francisco Call* and other friendly West Coast newspapers attributed to spiteful gossip by officers' wives living at the iso-lated yard. The *Call*'s cascade of headlines on its first page of April 15, 1897, summarized the whole story from the perspective of Mullan's defense: "Mullan a Victim of Intrigue; to Scandal-mongers the Naval Officer Owes his Troubles; Plots Hatched by his Subordinates Connected his Name with that of a Young Woman Living at Pensacola; Idle Rumors Brought about an Inquiry; He was not Popular with Navy-yard Officers and they Plotted Against him."

A one-officer court of inquiry—Capt. Norman Farquhar, again—sitting in Pensacola heard forty-nine witnesses on the two charges and each of their six specifications and then found against Mullan, findings that made him liable to discharge. He then successfully petitioned Secretary of the Navy Long to have the charges reheard by general court-martial.

Sitting in Washington, that court, five senior officers chaired by a com-modore, found Mullan guilty and sentenced him to dismissal, a sentence mitigated by President McKinley in July 1897 to a reduction in rank and suspension for five years on half-pay. Later, when the last year of his sus-pension was remitted, Mullan sued in the Court of Claims for four years' half pay and again lost. In early 1909 (eight years after his retirement) the Supreme Court heard his appeal of that negative decision and also found against him.[10]

None of Mullan's unhappy legal history appeared in his biography in *Men of Mark in Maryland* (Johnson-Wynne, 1907), a collection of short, admiring bio sketches of the "Leading Men of the State." Mullan's entry ended mildly with, "In 1896 and 1897 he was in command of the navy yard and station at Pensacola, Florida, and was retired in July, 1901, under the act of congress allowing an officer of the navy to retire after forty years of service."

7

Emory Taunt, U.S. Commercial Agent

I am very grateful for your kind wishes for success and for your words of encouragement. Such encouragement will go a great ways towards making a man firm and strong in his determination to go straight and make a success in life and thereby gratify his friends and chagrin his enemies.

I fully realize how true it is that there will be jealous, watchful eyes observing my every move on the Congo, but I will disappoint them all, I assure you. I go down filling a position of dignity and trust, and I shall so conduct myself and so carry out my instructions that my country will be proud of me in the future. But, of course, I know that words go for little, but I hope that my deeds will now speak for me and if my health is spared my record shall be a brilliant one.

Taunt, from Washington, D.C., to Henry Sanford, December 27, 1888

40

On July 1, 1888, the day after his resignation from the Navy became effective, Emory Taunt was again unemployed. The next day he sent a letter "To His Excellency The President" to petition for a job. "Sir:" he wrote, "I would respectfully request that I may receive the appointment of U.S. Commercial agent at Boma, Congo River, Congo Free State, which Agency has been provided for by Congress in the recent Consular and Diplomatic Bill." A second, longer letter to President Cleveland on July 30 (both written in Washington but from two different street addresses in the city) pressed his case politely but urgently.

Taunt was betting on the come when he wrote the president the first time. The bill, "An act making appropriations for the diplomatic and consular service of the United States for fiscal year eighteen hundred and eighty-nine [the budget year that began on the first of July]," was not passed by Congress until the middle of the following week. The act's language establishing a post at the Congo capital seemed to presume that the United States might have a long-term economic interest in the country.

The key paragraph, under the heading of "Miscellaneous Expenses Foreign Intercourse," was, "For salary and expenses of a commercial agent at Boma, in the Lower Congo Basin, with authority to visit and report upon

the commercial resources of the Upper and Lower Congo Basin, their products, their minerals, their vegetable wealth, the openings for American trade,
and to collect such information on the subject as shall be thought to be of
interest to the United States, four thousand dollars."[1] That ambitious charter, Taunt later explained to the State Department, represented eighteen to
twenty-four months' work, because travel to and up the Congo's tributaries could only be done hitchhiking on Leopold's steamers running on their
own schedule.

Unmentioned in his July 2 letter to the president but explicit in the
one at the end of the month was Taunt's sense of entitlement to the new
agency: "I hope that you will agree with me, that, to a certain extent, I have
a claim upon this place on account of the work I have already done on the
Congo. Work carried on during the most unhealthy season the Congo has
known for years." A stronger claim was tactfully also left unmentioned: By
determined lobbying in the Senate, focused on several key members of the
Committee on Foreign Affairs, Taunt and Sanford had manufactured the
new position he hoped now to fill.

The legislative initiative to establish and fund the Boma commercial agency in fiscal year 1889 had come originally from Senator George
Edmunds (Republican, Vermont), fronting for Henry Sanford, the bill's
ghost writer. The two exchanged more than a dozen letters during 1886–
89. In the 1880s Senator Edmunds (1828–1919; he left the Senate in 1891
after twenty-five years in office) was chairman of his party's caucus in the
Senate and of the Committee on the Judiciary. He also sat on the Committee
on Foreign Relations. Edmunds is better known for his sponsorship of the
Edmunds-Tucker Act of 1887, a law prohibiting polygamy, de-incorporating
the Church of Jesus Christ of the Latter-day Saints, and seizing church property. Six years earlier Edmunds had shepherded an act through Congress
that made polygamy a felony and took away civil rights from its practitioners. His pressure on the LDS church, and especially on its polygamists, had
the intended effect, pushing some of them to seek foreign sanctuary, Mitt
Romney's grandfather among them.

Sanford had generously proposed a $25,000 budget for the new agency
in Africa in his draft and persuaded Senator Edmunds to introduce the
bill with that rich provision. It might have passed into law as part of the
State Department's appropriation had not Representative Perry Belmont
(Democrat, New York) blocked it in the House. The compromise amount
that emerged from the legislative mill was a paltry four thousand dollars.
That sum, Taunt knew and the others soon heard, was barely enough to
keep a single white man alive at Boma, never mind sufficient to pay for his

travel through the river's huge upper basin collecting commercial information while supporting a family of two at home.

In 1884 Willard Tisdel had sailed off to Africa bolstered by a $15,000 appropriation. In 1885, Navy pay aside, Taunt's expenses during the half-year he'd spent in the Congo, he alleged, had come to two thousand dollars. In 1888 everyone involved in Washington agreed that four thousand was too little for twelve months' expenses and salary for a commercial agent, but that was the most that could be extruded from the thrifty members of Congress who had moved the appropriation through the legislative process. The small sum was described to Taunt, when he testified before a conference committee on the subject, as an "experiment" to see what could be done for the money with a promise, perhaps only a suggestion, maybe just a hint, that it would be increased the next year.

Taunt appealed for an additional $1,200–1,500 to Assistant Secretary of State George Rives before he left for Africa and by mail from there to Senator John Sherman (Republican, Ohio) and Representative Belmont, the chairmen of Congress' committees on foreign relations. If he had succeeded, this amount would have constituted his salary, roughly equal, he knew, to what the Europeans who would be his opposite numbers in Boma were getting paid.

In April 1889 Rives was replaced as assistant secretary of state by William Wharton, forty-two, an 1873 Harvard Law School graduate from Boston, who served until March 1893, and then returned to Massachusetts and the private practice of law. Once in Boma, all of Taunt's correspondence with the State Department was addressed to Wharton, who, during Secretary Blaine's several illnesses in 1892–93 was acting secretary twice.[2]

These overt efforts failed, but Taunt was working behind the scenes, too. In December 1888 he laid out a plan to his former boss. Sanford was to get Senator Sherman or Senator Edmunds to propose a five-thousand-dollar add-on to the Boma agency budget that Senator Quay and Senator Cameron had already committed to support. Both were, Taunt wrote, in on the scheme. That done, Taunt boasted to Sanford, "I will see that the bill is passed." As a quid for Sanford's part in the process, every three months Taunt would forward *"private reports"* to Sanford from the Congo, which would place the general "in a position to *discuss absolute facts*" and to advance his own business interests on the basis of expert, inside information. Nothing came of this either.

Taunt tried again the next year, going so far in November 1889, while on the way in SS *Cameroon* back to the Congo after a summer spent recuperating in the United States and Europe from malaria and other fevers, as to include sample language for a "Bill something of this nature" that Sanford could float in Washington: "I enclose a suggestion as regards the bill you say you will put in. I hope you will put it in the first of the session then it can be rushed and I can get to work with a will. I will do good work for you rest assured of that. I have my whole life now at stake and this is my hope for the future. Two years or perhaps eighteen months will place me on my feet with a good hope for the future." But four thousand dollars annually was all there was; it would have to be enough. Not until two years later—too late for Taunt—did Congress agree to an increase, and then only to five thousand dollars.

What could *not* be had for four thousand dollars was much of an annual salary for the agent-to-be. Trying to demonstrate the scope of his experience, and the austerity of the appropriation, Taunt's second letter to President Cleveland appended a one-page budget for "Necessary Expenditures/Year on Congo River." Its fourteen line items totaled $3,935, leaving only $65 unbudgeted for the agent's annual salary above room (a "double roofed, water proof tent made for tropical work") and board (imported canned food), a balance $10 less than that alone required for his "medical outfit," or for ammunition for a double-barrel, breech-loading Express rifle, one of three firearms in the agent's personal armory.[3]

It was a microscopically small salary, but for Taunt the appointment offered something more important: a commercial agent ranked with a Navy captain, an Army colonel, or a State Department consul on the U.S. government's precedence list.[4] The job promised not only honorable employment but also a promotion . . . and impoverishment for anyone without private wealth. The miserly appropriation was a time bomb, almost certain to blow up in bank overdrafts by the end of the second fiscal year, if not at the end of the first. Taunt's desperate need for a job, and confidence that his political friends could hustle a supplement through Congress, blinded him to the risk.

"Living expenses in Congo including European food, servants &c, &c." for three hundred days were the major item on Taunt's sample budget, $1,500. One hundred native porters for twenty days, to carry loads from Boma to Stanley Pool, took $700. Round-trip transportation via Europe and expenses in transit consumed another $700. And so it went. The least item was $20 for ammunition for a "self-acting revolver." Taunt was planning to go well armed. His third firearm was to be a "double barrel breech loading fowling gun." In fact, he ended up with four, two shotguns and two handguns.

Congress had considered naming more senior diplomatic representation, but despite the fact that Belgium, Holland, Italy, Portugal, and Great

Britain were represented in Boma by consuls, in the end Washington opted for an agency rather than a consulate as the more appropriate instrument to advance what were, after all, limited American interests in equatorial Africa and limited enthusiasm to pay for plumbing them. (The British consul resident in Portuguese Angola was accredited to the Congo Free State and to Gaboon. The other four European diplomats lived in Boma.) For a while, in fact, the idea of sending a three-man expedition into the countryside instead of opening an agency in the Free State's capital had enjoyed some support in Congress, but a resident agent won out over that alternative, too.

The product expected from this investment in representation was modest: yet another report to Congress, the third in four years, on commercial opportunities for Americans in the Congo. The first two appear to have been published, ignored, and filed. The same fate would have likely faced this report, notwithstanding that one focal point was to be the neglected great basin draining the highlands between the cataracts above Stanleyville and those below Leopoldville.

Taunt's first letter to President Cleveland sketched his qualifications for the job: sixteen months exploring the Congo's upper and lower basins, the first seven months under Navy orders and the last nine "in Command of an Exploring Expedition." Familiarity with the state's government and its officials, with resident diplomats, with the laws and customs of Congo natives, with French and native trade languages, and (thanks to the Naval Academy curriculum) with international law and with surveying practices were further arguments for his selection. Any other candidate chosen would have to start from square one, but not Taunt; he'd literally been there before and done that already.

A postscript to his letter, signed by Senator George Vest (Democrat, Missouri, and a former legislator for the Confederacy) and Senator Matthew Quay (the "Boss" would be a big reason why Cleveland lost to Harrison that autumn), endorsed Taunt's application with the request that he be appointed to the new position. Several unnamed others were also interested in becoming the new commercial agent in Boma, and the competition inevitably became political. Endorsements such as Vest's and Quay's constituted decisive votes in what had become a contested election.

Sometime after the first of August Taunt relocated from Washington to the English family home in Culpeper, a grand, columned mansion on North Main Street built in the early 1830s by William "Extra Billy" Smith, a future state governor, for his new bride. On September 16, with no progress visible and Taunt still awkwardly camped with his wife and daughter at her father's downtown property, he wrote again to Assistant Secretary Rives.

In this letter Taunt didn't claim the endorsement of Alabama's Senator Morgan (a more powerful player in the formulation of American foreign policy than either Vest or Quay), but he did claim the senator's support, a slender distinction. Reporting on a September 12 meeting he said he had with the senator, Taunt wrote Rives that Morgan told him "he had no candidate for the place. He then stated *that he hoped I would receive the appointment*, as my former experience there had eminently fitted me for the place, and he thought that I deserved it, for service already rendered in the Country."

The letter was also meant to hurry the process along, pointing out to Rives, a New York lawyer who knew nothing of tropical climates, that Boma's sickly season would begin the next month and that starting in November heavy rains would flood streams and render travel near-impossible into May of next year—or raise the cost of hiring porters to unaffordable levels. He feared that if the president left on a scheduled vacation without a decision, the delay would make a successful trip impossible in 1888.

Senator John Tyler Morgan, Democrat of Alabama, former Confederate general, and emeritus Grand Dragon of the Alabama Realm of the Ku Klux Klan, stood in the front rank of those few American politicians engaged in Congo policy making near the end of the century. Beginning in 1877, Morgan served thirty years in the Senate, during which he and some political allies championed cotton exports, white supremacy, and something the *Encyclopedia of Alabama* later called "'southern nationalist' philosophy." That philosophy included a tenet to repatriate American blacks to Africa.

Morgan quickly denied making any recommendation. Writing to Secretary of State Bayard four days later, he described Taunt "as 'a man with a mission,' bright, intelligent and unreliable as to his powers of self control." The senator went on:

> If this little expedition [?] is to have any success, reasons I stated to you in my first letter on this subject demand that a man of sobriety, will and enterprise should be selected.
>
> Mr. Taunt has recently been forced to resign from the Navy on account of his habits. I have no desire to inflict on him any penalty for a matter of this kind, but I could not advise his selection in view of these facts.
>
> I am aware that social considerations that are considered important strongly influence his selection but I cannot accept them as an excuse for my giving a recommendation in his favor, when there are so many good men to select from.

"I did not tell [Taunt] that I thought he ought to be appointed," Morgan continued to Bayard, "I said I thought him well qualified by experience and abilities for the place and advised him to see you, but I said nothing about recommending him. . . . He has been very eager and persistent in seeking the place and, while he has worried me with importunities, I have thought that a good augury of his success in this mission. Now I beg you to proceed in this matter without any reference to my wishes, for I have none."

41

Experience was one argument for his selection, motivation was the other. Here, like a wrestler, Taunt attempted to convert his weakness, a professional reputation sullied by forced resignation from the Navy (not as bad as dismissal, but a close second to it), to a strength, powerful motivation to recover his public standing through an admirable performance in Boma.

Taunt was candid with President Cleveland, a reflection of the fact that he could conceal nothing from the man who, after a personal review of all the court-martial and medical board records, had agreed to compel his resignation:

> I am willing and most anxious to undertake this work. Not for the money, there will be nothing left from this small appropriation if the work is properly done, but I believe that with my experience . . . I will be able to make a successful trip and return to this Government a complete and exhaustive report upon the resources of the Upper and Lower Basin of the Congo River. If I accomplish this, the reputation that it will give me will go far to re-establish my good name, so recently hurt by my trouble in the Navy. And this reward, Mr. President, will be the recompense I look forward to, and will be the incentive I would carry with me to make a success.

He made the same general point to the assistant secretary of state, minus any specific reference to the Navy and embarrassing details possibly unknown to Rives. "Of course you know," he wrote Rives, "that my great anxiety arises from the fact that by hard, faithful work in Africa I can make a reputation that will greatly influence my future. I aim to be successful there, and with such success will come a reputation that will be invaluable to me in the future. . . . Should I be appointed you will have no harder worker serving under you and certainly no one with such an incentive to gain the approbation of your Department."

On November 14, 1888, Taunt got the job. His strongest competitor, a man named Benton, had withdrawn from consideration, "his [Benton's] mother being strongly averse to his taking the risk of a climate that was fatal to his father," explained a supporter, and the rest of the field also failed to finish for one reason or another. Taunt's government appointment came only several months after his being one day away from disgraceful dismissal from the Navy. This despite the fact that after Dr. Suddards' second examination, no one in the State Department or Navy Department, anywhere in Congress, or at the White House had any reason to believe that Taunt's flagrant misconduct in *Nipsic* could have been anything but the product of alcohol abuse.

Whatever the favorable "social considerations" that Senator Morgan had alluded to were, they had worked powerfully. Taunt credited his selection to the support of Secretary of the Navy Whitney and to that of Senators Quay, Cameron, Vest, and Morgan, support the *Boston Daily Journal* had knowingly described on June 19 as "potent influence." Taunt's elder brother-in-law, Presley Rixey, might have been a voice heard during the commercial agent selection process, too. Rixey was a personal friend of President Cleveland; the two were close enough that later Cleveland personally recommended him to President Theodore Roosevelt for the post of surgeon general.[5] On November 15, the necessary documents for signature, the oath of office and allegiance, and the bonding papers, were mailed to Culpeper from Washington.

Ten days later, November 25, Taunt wrote from Culpeper to announce to Henry Sanford in Brussels the good news about this "turning point" in his life and to make a generous and inappropriate offer:

> I shall be very glad to carry out any wishes you may have in regard to the Congo, and more especially do anything *in your interest* to help the Sanford Ex. while I am down there. And from what I know of the feeling of the members of the Expedition and of Baron Weber's many schemes, perhaps it will be just as well for you to have a man devoted to your interest on the spot to keep you posted.
>
> Before going I should be glad to have a long talk on the subject and get your ideas, for I am told that upon my reports will depend the ultimate establishment of the Congo Steam Ship Line from this country, and the interchange of commerce generally. . . .
>
> What I wish you to understand is that I shall do anything in my power there in your interest, I don't exactly know now what shape it may take, but anything you may suggest I will certainly carry out.

Figure 25. Lieutenant Emory Taunt, United States Consul to the Congo State. In December and January the news Taunt had already shared by letter with Sanford appeared in many American newspapers. The most impressive coverage was the 1888 year-end edition of *Leslie's Illustrated Newspaper*. The short piece in *Leslie's* included a few paragraphs under this drawing of Taunt's head and shoulders. Taunt asked Sanford to help him get the news of his appointment published in *Le Mouvement Geographique*, thinking the publicity would boost his status in Congo on arrival. *FROM A PHOTOGRAPH BY JOHN THOMSON OF LONDON;* FRANK LESLIE'S ILLUSTRATED NEWSPAPER, *DECEMBER 29, 1888*

Later the deal he proposed to Sanford was even more explicit and corrupt. It was a trade: Sanford was to lobby Congress in ways helpful to Taunt, and in exchange Taunt would work for Sanford while he was on the State Department's payroll.

Taunt's appointment to Boma provoked some sharp press criticism. "Cleveland's Bad Break" was the headline in the *Wisconsin State Journal* in mid-December, the paper picking up a distant story from East Coast newspapers. "The appointment of Henry [*sic*] H. Taunt as commissioner to the Congo country is very severely criticized," the *State Journal* wrote, getting almost all the details correct. "Mr. Taunt was formerly an officer of the navy, and only a few months ago was dismissed from the service by order of a general court martial for drunkenness and general dissolute habits . . . but his conduct has been such that his wife was compelled to leave him and has instituted proceedings for divorce":

> On his trial before the court martial his friends pleaded insanity as a defense, and appealed to the president to set aside the verdict of the court as an act of mercy to a young man who was not responsible for his acts. The evidence, however, showed that the lieutenant behaved himself well enough when sober, and only disgraced himself when he was drunk, so the president refused to intercede in his behalf. He has, however, to the surprise of everybody, appointed him to an important position and there is general indignation, particularly among the officers of the navy.

That Mary Taunt filed for divorce in 1888 seems to have been the reporter's invention. In 1902, identifying herself as Taunt's widow, Mary filed in the Court of Claims to recover the $105 difference between sea and shore pay for a distant period during her late husband's Navy service. (The claim was validated, but payment was denied on a technicality, as having accrued before the effective date of the relevant legislation.) She would hardly have risked perjury for such a sum. The rest of the short page-one piece probably struck the *State Journal*'s readers at home in Madison, Wisconsin, as small news from very far away.

42

Mid-November, he thought, was too late to start off for the Congo. Instead, Taunt immersed himself in scholarly preparations at the Smithsonian

Institution for his new opportunity. Taunt's training there during early winter was most likely a private course of instruction arranged informally, perhaps with Thomas Wilson, curator of prehistoric anthropology. (The two exchanged letters several times during the next two years.) Whatever they were, these studies were completed sometime near the start of the new year. On January 17, 1889, and now equipped to start work "in an intelligent manner," Taunt left the United States for Africa via Belgium with some of the Smithsonian's photographic equipment and a field guide to collecting mineral specimens in his baggage. His plan was to make diplomatic office calls in Brussels en route and then to catch a steamer arriving in the Congo in late March. (If Taunt had kept to this schedule, he would have been at sea somewhere abeam the great bulge of West Africa heading south about the time that USS *Nipsic* was in port Samoa, losing her fight against the great typhoon.)

Taunt actually got to his destination more than a month later. "I had expected to sail from Liverpool on Feb'y 27th," he explained to the assistant secretary of state in a letter written on board the Dutch transport SS *Afrikaans* on April 20, "but was obliged to delay my departure in order to obtain the necessary letters from Gov. Janssens. . . . Later I was taken quite ill with Bronchitis (See medical certificate) and confined to my room some two weeks. I have availed myself of the first steamer possible, that belonging to the Dutch African Trading Co., and will reach the Congo the first week in May."

"Think of me amongst the cannibals," he wrote the same day to Dr. F. O. St. Clair, chief of the department's consular bureau and a personal friend, whom Taunt had enlisted in the unsuccessful campaign to increase the agency's congressional appropriation.

After a stop on the way, Taunt arrived at Boma May 1 and quickly opened the newest diplomatic post in the Congo Free State's capital town. In view of his official status, Janssens, in a sick bed in Brussels, had granted Taunt certain privileges, including the right to be attended by Zanzibari guards, to travel on the river in the state's steamers, to stay at government stations, and to employ as many as twenty-five porters. All these benefits to be paid for at established rates.

Taunt's first tour of duty at his new post in 1889 was abruptly cut short. On June 6, after barely five weeks back on the ground in Africa, he was once again afloat off Banana Point in *Afrikaans*, this time heading to Rotterdam, having suffered attacks of "bilious hematuric fever" and "catarrh of the stomach and intestines" so serious at Boma, he wrote Sanford from Holland on June 29, that doctors there insisted he sail north to save his life. In the month or so between arrival and medical evacuation, he'd only had time for two short "caravans" around the lower Congo and completed just enough research to be able to write part of an update to his 1886 report.

Had it not been for the ministrations of an American Baptist missionary from Boston, the Reverend John Camp, who during the first few days of June discovered Taunt in bed at Banana's hotel (feverish, vomiting, and "totally dependent on a little stupid negro boy to whom he could not speak nor understand"), managed to lodge him in an officer's cabin on the departing ship, and cared for him at sea, it is possible that Taunt would have died in 1889. To set his suffering in context for a man whose business interests in Africa had only once and then very briefly taken him to the continent, Taunt's June 29 letter to Sanford reported that early 1889 in the Congo had been the "most fatal season in the memory of the oldest trader." Sixteen white men had died since January, three in one month from among the Dutch traders. When SS *Afrikaans* sailed, five other whites were left behind dangerously ill at Boma and four more at Banana. Almost certainly most would die.

Anticipating Sanford's immediate suspicions of what would have sounded like an echo from the unhappy past, Taunt quickly explained, "This was not brought on through any of my old weakness. I have been abstemious, not touching anything except table wine and only Madeira when I was ill in Boma at the request of [the state medical officer] as likely to allay my stomach troubles. All this I have taken care to have certified to by Mr. Camp, the missionary who nursed me through it."

Writing from Rotterdam on July 2, 1889, Taunt told Assistant Secretary Wharton the news about his health, diagnosed as "a bad malarial attack, which finally terminated in bilious hematuric [blackwater] fever." That letter included two enclosures: one from a German "practical physician" at Banana confirming "a speedy return home urgently requisite" and the other in Reverend Camp's spidery hand, written afloat in the Bay of Biscay June 27, describing Taunt's near-death experience and his successful efforts to keep his fellow American alive.

Taunt planned to write his report on the lower Congo during a stop in Brussels to catch Sanford up on what his former expedition employees were doing and to share news from the Congo and Washington with him. After that, sometime in midsummer, he intended to leave the Belgian capital and return to Africa. "I am gaining strength daily," he told Sanford, "and will certainly return to my post in August." Instead, he asked for and received permission from the State Department for a month's home leave to recuperate and sailed to the United States. His first, and as it would turn out only, report to the State Department (on the lower Congo, No. 12 in the sequence of his despatches to the department) was written in Virginia and sent to Washington from Culpeper on August 1.

43

In the report Taunt wrote that on his return to the Congo in 1889 he had found "a well-equipped Government, with a full corps of officials, court of law, post offices, customs stations, a standing army of from twelve to fifteen hundred men, currency in gold, silver, copper—in fact, every thing in proper shape to successfully conduct a well-organized government." This first report was limited largely to news from Banana Point and Boma, because an outbreak of smallpox that began first in the lower Congo in September 1888 soon spread its terrible lethality upriver into the highland drainage basin. "An unfortunate obstacle," he described the outbreak, to moving freely about the country. The epidemic made it "not only difficult to travel but to gain information."

Estimates, Taunt reported, placed the death rate from smallpox for natives of the lower Congo Valley during this outbreak—not the first—at about 50 percent.[6] Victims died swollen and in great pain, their heads and bodies covered with encrusted pustules. Whites, vaccinated against the disease, "didn't suffer at all." Smallpox epidemics typically produced fatality rates in unprotected populations ranging between 25 and 60 percent of those infected, so Taunt's figure is horrifying but reasonable.

Under ten headings, Taunt's brief report (nine typeset pages) summarized how the Congo had changed since his report to the navy secretary nearly four years earlier. The principal change was the appearance of a new trading company in the country, "organized on a large scale, backed by immense capital," the Belgian Joint Stock Company of the Congo. Five subsidiaries clustered under its umbrella, the most important of which, at least in the beginning, was the Compagnie du Congo pour le Commerce et l'Industrie. This was the entity holding the concession to build the railroad between Matadi and Stanley Pool. The other four included a company to build and manage hotels and retail emporiums, a second to produce palm oil and raise cattle on Matabe Island in the river, a third to operate plantations to raise tropical products for export, and the last—the successor to Sanford's failed "Exploring Expedition"—to promote commerce on the upper Congo.

Taunt neglected to draw the obvious conclusion from the omnibus enterprise he'd just sketched out to Washington: The Congo Free State was no longer to be open to all comers on an equal basis. Instead, Leopold had determined to smother Dutch, English, French, and Portuguese competition in the Congo, and this hydra-headed, Belgian-owned company was his instrument for that. Taunt wrote,

> While the Belgian Joint Stock Company of the Congo is not officially connected with the Government of the Congo Free State, it is unquestionably greatly favored by them, and will prove a formidable rival to any commercial company operating in the valley of the Congo. . . . The present inspector-general and acting governor at Boma is a director of the joint stock company. A large number of their agents are on temporary leave from the state. The constitution of the joint stock company provides that the bulk of merchandise, supplies, etc., for subcompanies must be purchased in Belgium.

"I am not ready," he concluded after sharing this intelligence, "to pass upon the prospect for American trade throughout the Congo Valley." Obviously any Belgian competitor big enough to threaten the powerful Dutch-African Trading Company and its three European counterparts would wipe out any American start-up as collateral damage.

Another obvious conclusion also escaped Taunt, or he kept it to himself. The wages for porters hauling loads of freight on their heads through the cataract region between Matadi and the Pool had nearly tripled since his first expedition upriver. A cause for this inflation was a shortage of food for porters, because there were no markets along the caravan route, "the villages having been moved to the interior. Along here in 1885 we would come to a native village every few hours, now in 1889, there are two villages between Matadi and Stanley Pool." Taunt didn't explain why villagers had fled to the remote interior, but he must have known. They did it to escape extortion and capture by agents of "the well-equipped government."

On August 28, 1889, Taunt left home to return to the Congo via Brussels. His plan was to ride SS *Afrikaans* in mid-October from Rotterdam to the Congo (a favorite because of her twenty-two-day, one-stop schedule), arriving during the second week of November. On November 10 he wrote Assistant Secretary Wharton from somewhere "en route" to report without explanation that *Afrikaans* did not sail from Europe as planned. He'd left from Liverpool instead, in SS *Cameroon*, and would get into Boma weeks after *Afrikaans'* scheduled arrival. Taunt told Wharton he intended to depart for the upper Congo soon after that, "before the wet season has well advanced." He planned to take a camp kit and six months' supplies with him because the influx of white men working on the new railroad and for other new Belgian companies was sopping up the state's food reserves and spare lodging.

In the late spring of 1890, following a first trip upriver, Taunt again fell seriously ill. His collapse prompted a second, long medical evacuation to Europe. On August 20, finally back in Boma after more months away from his post, he wrote Wharton to report he'd been sick with a "strong malarial fever" complicated by "ulcerative gastric trouble." The letter included statements from two doctors, one in Liverpool dated June 18 diagnosing malaria and recommending he leave England for a more congenial climate and another from Milan dated July 4 saying he'd arrived in Italy "to obtain the benefit or cure of the change in climate" and was anticipating a month-long stay for recuperation.

"For some time after my arrival in Europe the doctors despaired of my recovery," he told Wharton, "but I am now in good health and will at once continue my work on the Upper Congo River." Caravans leaving Matadi for the interior had stripped the area of porters, he said. His plan was to sail to Loango and proceed from there to the upper Congo by this new route, one "never visited by me," to collect his gear—eighteen months of supplies—already shipped to Stanley Pool and begin his market research.

There's no evidence that he had much time to do any of this. Taunt's obituary in the April 24, 1891, edition of the *New York Times* only hinted at the life that came to an end on January 18, 1891: "Lieut. Taunt was one of the officers who went on the Greely Relief Expedition in 1884, and in the following year went to the Congo and made a successful and creditable trip to Stanley Falls. He injured his health at that time and never fully recovered. He was one of the brightest young officers of the Navy. In 1888 he resigned and was appointed United States Commercial Agent to the Congo Free State, which position he held at the time of his death." The newspaper got most of its short story right, all but the last phrase.

His death was miserable, as most white men's deaths along the river must have been in that time, nothing like the "good death"—painless, in bed at home surrounded by decorously grieving family and friends, and at peace with God—that was the end-of-life model for late-nineteenth-century Americans in the comfortable classes of society.

"I called to see Mr. Taunt at Boma on Jan. 14 and found him in bed, partly paralyzed, and utterly helpless," the Reverend James Teter, the veteran Methodist Episcopal missionary at Vivi, wrote to Mary Taunt in a letter that arrived in April and was quoted in the *Times'* obituary. "On the 16th I brought him to Banana, with the intention of sending him to the United States, hoping that change of climate would help him. He stood the trip quite well, but the next day grew worse and died on Sunday, the 18th. He was buried at Banana with the Methodist Episcopal form."

An international group of pallbearers, Taunt's peers in government service at the capital and the cream of Congo Free State society among whom the Portuguese consul in full diplomatic regalia must have stood out conspicuously, carried his body to its grave. A uniformed company of the Congo Free State's Force Publique grandly escorted the party to Banana's graveyard. None in the small, brave parade could have known that the coffin carried not the remains of an American diplomat but of a disgraced civilian.

On November 21, 1890, the U.S. consul in Marseilles, Charles Trail, had mailed the text of a brusque cable (like civilian users of undersea cables, the department paid for telegrams by the word) from Secretary Blaine to Taunt, instructing him, "Your commission as Commercial Agent at Boma is hereby revoked and you are removed from office. Your accounts are largely overdrawn." Just a week after passing his second anniversary in the post, Taunt had been fired. During those twenty-four months nominally in office, he'd been in place in Africa for fewer than five of them.

44

Taunt's successor as U.S. commercial agent in Boma, and the last American diplomat of this rank to serve in the Congo capital, was Richard Dorsey Mohun of Washington, D.C. R. Dorsey Mohun, then twenty-eight, was appointed to Boma on January 22, 1892, one year after Taunt's death. Congress had learned something about subsistence in Africa in the four years since the late Emory Taunt filled the same post, and Dorsey Mohun's agency had an annual budget of five thousand dollars.

Mohun's family credited his selection for the assignment in Boma to the influence of two-term Secretary of State James Blaine of Maine, a Republican and fellow Catholic whose familial ties to Notre Dame University paralleled their own. The Reverend John Camp, longtime master of the Baptists' steamboat *Henry Reed* and the same "exploring and mechanical missionary" who in June 1889 had escorted an ailing Taunt to Europe in SS *Afrikaans*, had been interested in the job, too.[7] On December 29, 1891, he asked the secretary of the Smithsonian Institution to support his candidacy. "The Congo Government wishes me to accept a position as general scientist & wishes me to go exploring as soon as my time can be engaged," he wrote to the new secretary, Samuel Langley. "I may accept their position in about 1 years time if my own country does not want my services. But as you are at the Capital

& know that my interests in scientific matters are not personal, but for the general welfare of my people, as I have been contributing to the Smithsonian Institute for the last 7 years as often as my searches justified I trust that you will feel justified if you will kindly take a step for me by proposing my name as a proper person for commercial agent to Boma Congo S.W. Africa."[8]

Camp, entering the campaign from afar and too late, wasn't a contender. Besides, the honorable secretary of the National Museum didn't have the thrust in Washington that Senator Blaine had, whose extraordinary career in government included years in the House, the Senate, in three presidential cabinets, and in 1884 a failed campaign for president, losing to Cleveland. In 1894, after seven years with the mission, Camp returned home to Ohio for the second and last time, a victim of some unspecified Congo fever. He continued to correspond with the museum for another thirty years.

Mohun left New York in the North German Lloyd steamer SS *Werra* on February 27 with his sister and younger brother, Louis, who was going to join him at Boma as his deputy and the post's vice commercial agent. He and Louis arrived in the Congo April 28 after a leisurely ocean passage that included the traditional stopover in Brussels, where on March 23 he called on resident U.S. diplomats and on the Congo's secretaries of state and of the interior. While he was in the Belgian capital, Mohun saw King Leopold II twice, first during an hour-long audience at the palace on March 26 and then at a royal family dinner in his honor on April 3.

In his practiced fashion, the king had used both opportunities to charm the young American, who very near the end of the month steamed in B&ASN's SS *Congo* up the river to Boma as Leopold's enthusiastic partisan, persuaded that the king "was perfectly familiar with every detail of the workings of the Government of the Congo State. It is stated here in Brussels," he'd written to Assistant Secretary of State William Wharton before sailing from Antwerp, "that no move is ever taken without his knowledge and support." Mohun would forever be a Leopold enthusiast and Congo Free State apologist. His offhand comment about Leopold's omniscience should have undercut the king's know-nothing defense when reports of atrocities later began to emerge from his colony, but for several more years nothing seemed to stick to Leopold.

Boma on arrival, Mohun wrote in a consular report, "presents a pretty appearance, all the trading houses on the beach being whitewashed and looking very clean":

> The large hotel, of two stories, is in the center of town, the trading house
> of Hatton & Cookson, of Liverpool, on the right, and the machine

shops of the government on the left. The grounds on the beach are well laid out and look very attractive with their many palms and banana trees. At the back of the town, on the plateau, is the governor's house, a large sheet-iron structure, situated in well-kept grounds; around it are the different offices and back of it the houses belonging to the chief officials and also the sanitarium. These are made either of brick or iron, and are very cool and comfortable. A great deal of taste has been displayed in their construction, and the whole effect is very pleasing.

This is the Boma that Taunt would have known near the end of his life.

The Mohun brothers' first official duty was to deal with what was left of Emory Taunt, his body and his papers and effects, whatever Congo's heat, humidity, and insect life had not already consumed. Taunt's personal effects and papers had been shipped from Boma after his death by an unknown party to the Brussels office of the Congo's secretary of state for foreign affairs, Edouard Count de Grellé-Rogier, where they were delivered to Mohun days before he sailed for Africa. On June 30 he forwarded the assembled papers to Washington. They amounted to fourteen letters from the department, seven from his bankers, five salary statements, and a dozen or so miscellaneous documents, including a letter from a collector interested in postage stamps of the Congo now that mail service had been established. Those in the first two categories catalogued a growing wave of financial problems that washed over Taunt and eventually overwhelmed him. Separately, two *process verbals* in French detailed a $557 debt to the Congo Free State. Curiously, sadly, the cache included no letters from Mary Taunt.

Under instructions from Assistant Secretary Wharton to repatriate the remains, Mohun had bought a coffin while he was in Brussels calling on officials and the king, with the idea of exhuming Taunt and shipping him to the United States. Conducted in sandy ground below the saltwater table twenty-six months after interment, the search was unsuccessful. Taunt's body was never found. In November 1894 Mohun filed a claim with the State Department for his expenses associated with this macabre quest. Apparently there was nothing to the "peculiar rumors" about Taunt's death that Dorsey Mohun told Wharton in May 1892 he would investigate because nothing more was ever written about them.

Throughout his time in the Congo and later, Mohun took the king of the Belgian's side in the debate. "It has been the fashion during the past," Mohun was quoted as saying in 1903, and between jobs in Africa, "for travelers who have been in the Congo State to run it down in every way, but it gives me the greatest pleasure to be able to affirm that only the most captious critic would be able to find fault with its administration today."⁹ In an essay a year later in *Messenger Magazine*, "The British Government versus the Congo Free State," he urged the United States not to "meddle in the affairs of the Congo Free State." For ten pages he refuted accusations that natives were not afforded useful training (counting 15,000 in station craft shops, manning river steamers, or working on plantations), described the Force Publique's 16,500 troops and reserves as "a splendid body of disciplined men," and denied that the state's labor tax—forty hours per month, he claimed, collecting rubber—was onerous or excessive.

Mohun (1865–1915) was an extraordinary man, but one miscast as an American diplomat in a foreign colony. His career as a diplomat included only two posts, Boma (January 1892 to May 1895) and Stone Town, Zanzibar (May 1895 to November 1897, a span that included the famously short Anglo-Zanzibar War, fought for thirty-eight minutes on the morning of August 27, 1896). Beginning in the Congo in the spring of 1892, Mohun spent the next twenty years or so in and around Africa. In 1898, after a stint prospecting, he led a telegraph wire–laying expedition north from Lake Tanganyika to the Nile through Stanley Falls before returning to prospecting and then becoming a rubber company executive.

His obituary in the *New York Times* on July 15, 1915, aptly described Mohun first as a "soldier of fortune." Not until its fourth paragraph did it mention his official role in the Congo capital. In another place he was described, awkwardly but accurately, as "an opportunistic . . . masculinist hunter/prospector."¹⁰ In his spare time in the Congo, Mohun had acted as the chief of artillery for the Congo Free State in its war against the Arabs and participated in a Belgian expedition to establish if there were a water route between Lake Tanganyika and the Lualaba River. In gratitude for this service, Leopold made his American volunteer (Mohun had rejected pay from the king for his services) a knight of the Royal Order of the Lion, the junior of the Congo service order's five grades and distinguished by a handsome silver medal worn on the left breast.

45

Her husband's death on the Congo left Mary Taunt, not yet forty, a widow in Washington, D.C., with two small children, Earlena and Frances. A few years after Taunt died Mary married her widowed brother-in-law, Samuel Russell-Smith, with whom she had a third daughter, Elizabeth. Russell-Smith had been married to Frances English, Mary's youngest sister, until Frankie died in childbirth June 15, 1888, less than a year after the two were wed.[11] He was the same man who in late 1887 had unexpectedly appeared at the navy yard in Brooklyn twice and offered to find Lieutenant Taunt across the river in New York and to escort him back to Navy custody.

The new Russell-Smiths lived in Culpeper, where Mary's husband was the county treasurer for more than fifty years. She was widowed for a second time in early September 1933 following her second husband's years-long illness. Mary English Taunt Russell-Smith died in New Jersey at her daughter Earlena's home July 19, 1946, six days after her ninety-fourth birthday. She'd outlived Taunt by almost sixty years. When she died, King Leopold's Congo had been the Belgian Congo for nearly forty years and the Belgian Parliament's writ had fourteen more years to run in equatorial Africa before independence was granted and chaos followed.

Following the English style, nineteenth-century American obituaries were usually written about prominent men and often included very little information about wives, family, or other survivors. Reading them, it would be possible to conclude that the movers and shakers of the English-speaking world took vows of chastity and were unacquainted with women. That journalism practice began to change as the nineteenth century yielded to the twentieth. By the time Mary Russell-Smith died, a little over a year into the sudden first presidency of Harry Truman, her obituary in the Culpeper, Virginia, *Exponent* contained a remarkable amount of information about the Englishes, the Taunts, and the Russell-Smiths, and the way the three families with their roots in three states had merged together.[12]

The obituary's last paragraph was three sentences about her first husband: "Lieut. Emory Taunt, U.S.N., was a member of the Horace Greeley Expeditionary Relief [*sic*] in the 1880's, and it was Lieut. Taunt who discovered the cache with maps and papers by which the survivors were saved from perishing after 3 years in the Arctic regions. Several years later Lieut. Taunt was assigned to a naval force for scientific research in the African Congo. While on this expedition he contracted a jungle fever and died."

The truth was something like that. Adolphus Washington Greely was the Arctic expedition survivor. Horace Greeley (1811–1872) was the founder in 1841 and the longtime editor of the influential *New York Tribune*. Greeley ran for president as a Democrat in 1872 against U. S. Grant but died before the electoral vote revealed his crushing posthumous defeat. Greeley lived long enough, however, to survive his wife, to be victimized by a hoax, to see control of his paper wrested from him, and to lose his mind. Had Horace Greeley known of the Culpeper *Exponent*'s confusion, he would not have been amused.

8

Heart of Darkness

Sometimes we came upon a station close by the bank clinging to the skirts of the unknown, and the white men rushing out of a tumble-down hovel with great gestures of joy and surprise and welcome seemed very strange, had the appearance of being held there captive by a spell. The word "ivory" would ring in the air for a while—and on we went again into the silence, along empty reaches, round the still bends, between the high walls of our winding way, reverberating in hollow claps the ponderous beat of the stern-wheel. Trees, trees, millions of trees, massive, immense, running up high, and at their foot, hugging the bank against the stream, crept the little begrimed steamboat like a sluggish beetle crawling on the floor of a lofty portico.

Joseph Conrad, Heart of Darkness

46

In October 1889, three months after the State Department's new man in equatorial West Africa, former lieutenant Emory Taunt, mailed his report on "The Lower Congo" to the State Department from Culpeper, George Washington Williams of Pennsylvania had a royal audience with King Leopold II. The call, at the palace in Brussels, was an astonishing first for both men. Williams, soldier, pastor, journalist, lawyer, legislator, and historian, had never met a European king before, and Leopold had never before hosted what amounted to a one-on-one press interview with an American black man.[1]

Williams was no rube, but he was impressionable at such high altitude: He was dazzled by the king, "a pleasant and entertaining conversationalist," who clearly went out of the way to charm his extraordinary guest, much as he had done in his first meeting with another American in transit to Africa, Willard Tisdel, five years ago. The tall king's "eyes flashed with intelligent interest," Williams wrote after his audience with Leopold, "his mouth showed both strength and generosity, and his chin was indicative of decision and courage." How Williams saw either concealed within Leopold's great, shovel-shaped beard is a mystery. He politely wrote nothing about one royal feature he actually could see, Leopold's impressive nose, a promontory the king's new acquaintances invariably commented on, to each other in private.

Figures 26 and 27. Leopold II, king of the Belgians and sovereign of the Congo Free State. This slightly battered equestrian statue by Thomas Vinçotte was first erected in 1928 on a site planned to be in front of the colonial governor's new residence when the capital was moved from Boma to Leopoldville. The statue was taken down in 1971 on Mobutu's orders as part of the dictator's "authentication campaign." It stands now largely unseen on the grounds of the national museum on the slope of Mont Ngaliema above the capital. The statue is a duplicate of an original erected in 1926 in Brussels' Place du Trône. Both were cast at La Compagnie des Bronzes, a foundry in Brussels well known after 1870 for its sculptures. Baron Vinçotte (1850–1925) was a Belgian sculptor and medalist with close ties to Leopold's court. His heroic sculptures adorn parks and other public sites in Belgium. Unlike Arthur Dupagne, Vinçotte never spent time in Africa. *AUTHOR'S PHOTOGRAPHS*

Forty when he first called on the king of the Belgians, Williams had already held serious conversations in the United States with a president, cabinet officers, congressional committee chairmen, and a wealthy industrialist during a remarkable career for a young black American in the decades after the Civil War. He'd recently fallen into a crack between two presidential administrations and so just missed being appointed the American minister to Haiti; the post went to Frederick Douglass instead.

In late 1889 Williams was drawn to Europe for a second time that year, this time by an international antislavery conference at the Belgian foreign ministry. While some good would come of it, the event was chiefly an opportunity for Leopold to maneuver an end to the Berlin act's twenty-year prohibition against duties on imports to the Congo. This initiative to cramp and then throttle commercial competition—private trading companies would pay duties, state traders would not—was disguised by the king as the funding source for a new, aggressive campaign against slavery.

There's something of Henry Morton Stanley in George Washington Williams: the same sense of coming on hard from behind, the same deliberate fogging of the biographical details of his life, the same careful polishing of image. Both were ambitious opportunists. Denied a diplomatic post, Williams had hoped to be named as one of the U.S. delegates to the Brussels conference, but he was not. He thought not because of politicking by Henry Sanford, who was a delegate. Instead, carrying newly minted press credentials from Samuel McClure's Associated Literary Press, Williams used his status as a syndicated reporter to observe the start of the seven-month meeting and to navigate around the Belgian capital near year's end.

His first royal audience, plump with the king's descriptions of the motives behind his good works, had impressed him greatly. The next, in January 1890, much less. (In between he had returned to the United States, called on the president, and tried unsuccessfully to recruit young American blacks at the Hampton Institute to work for Belgian companies in Africa.) The second time the king met with Williams it was to hear his visitor confirm that he intended what amounted to an informal inspection tour of the Congo Free State. Leopold's minions had tried energetically but unsuccessfully to dissuade Williams from making the trip anytime soon. So did the king. Facing prickly opposition to his upcoming trip, Williams began to fantasize about being the target of obstruction or even assassination.

Palace rumors hinted that Sanford had set Leopold against Williams, but that was not necessary. Ever since Tisdel's final report, Leopold had feared and fought losing control of the message emerging from Africa. That's why, for example, his employment contract with Stanley gave the king complete editorial control over anything the explorer might write. With Williams sitting in front of him, Leopold feared that again now.

By the end of the 1880s the Congo was served by regular passenger and cargo service to Boma by several steamship lines sailing from Liverpool, Hamburg, Lisbon, and (newly) Le Havre. A fifth line ran on a less frequent schedule to Congo's port from Rotterdam. On January 30, 1890, Williams sailed from Liverpool in the Glasgow-built screw steamer SS *Gaboon* of the British and African Steam Navigation Company, then a few years into what would become a decade operating on the company's West African service. *Gaboon* could make turns for only ten and a half knots—she was slow even by the standard of the day—and thanks also to stops at many West African ports on the way, the ship took nearly eight weeks to reach the Congo, a voyage that usually required fewer than four. When Williams arrived, Taunt was somewhere upriver, back from his first rest cure and summer at home and not yet gone to England on what passed as a second medical evacuation. There's no indication that the two men ever met.

Nearly four months after disembarking from *Gaboon*, having finally arrived at Stanley Falls, Williams wrote an "Open Letter to Leopold II," dated July 18, 1890. It was a stunning, lengthy indictment of Leopold's Congo property and of everyone—Stanley by name—who had conspired in its design and participated in its operation; nothing like Taunt's year-old, admiring quick sketch of the organization of the Congo Free State.[2] Comparing their conclusions, he and Taunt could have been describing different places on the globe, or two different planets. Their only overlap was the common observation that the Congo government was trading for its own account, competing unfairly by taxing the others but exempting itself.

47

Addressed cheekily to his "Good and Great Friend," the king, Williams started strong. "How thoroughly I have been disenchanted, disappointed and disheartened, it is now my painful duty to make known to your Majesty in plain but respectful language," he wrote, and then he went on to wire brush the "Sovereign of the Independent State of Congo" in earnest. Williams began by announcing that Leopold had "no legal or just claim" to the land. The treaties Stanley had negotiated with African chieftains were fraudulent, the product of tricks, lies, and "boxes of gin."[3] Later, in a claim that Tisdel would likely have endorsed, Williams argued that the land thus stolen was misrepresented in Europe as fertile where it was sterile and unproductive.

Paragraphs illustrating Leopold's failure to honor the expansive promises Henry Sanford had made to Congress during the recognition debate in Washington introduced Williams' specific charges. Most began with "Your Majesty's Government," assigning to Leopold personal responsibility for the crimes described.

Williams' "Open Letter" powerfully and for the first time exposed the crimes being committed in the Congo and ascribed them to the king:

> All the crimes perpetrated in the Congo have been done in *your* name. . . . Deceit, fraud, robberies, arson, murder, slave-raiding, and [a] general policy of cruelty. . . . *You* must answer at the bar of Public Sentiment for the misgovernment of a people whose lives and fortunes were entrusted to you by the august Conference of Berlin, 1884–1885. I now appeal to the Powers, which committed this infant state to your Majesty's charge, and to the great States which gave it international being; and whose majestic law you have scorned and trampled upon, to call and create an International Commission to investigate the charges herein preferred in the name of Humanity, Commerce, Constitutional Government and Christian Civilization.

It's an indication of how far ahead of contemporary opinion Williams' appraisal was to observe that more than ten years later reformers took up the case against Leopold's Congo using very similar language.

48

Williams' July 16 "Report on the Proposed Congo Railway," written at the same time as his letter to the king, was a curious digression from his principal business in Africa. He had no civil engineering or railroad experience, in fact, no specialized knowledge of any kind relevant to evaluating a railroad's business case, its right-of-way survey, construction schedule, or associated cost estimates. Moreover, the railroad's surveyed route between Matadi and N'dolo (its planned eastern terminus some seven miles down slope from Leopoldville and almost on the Stanley Pool shoreline) ran on average some thirty miles off the porter's trail that connected Matadi to Leopoldville along which Williams was hiking. Still, out of Matadi until some distance past M'Poso, the two were not far apart, and for these first miles and for the last few Williams could not have escaped moving overland upriver generally along the proposed right-of-way. That coincidence presented Williams with an opportunity to comment on the status of the Congo Free State's major, practically only, infrastructure project.

Henry Morton Stanley had been the first to realize that the lower Congo's cataracts had to be skirted by rail, that no reluctant army of porters walking in line like pack animals to and fro alongside the river could carry the fortunes the king and traders planned to wrest from the continent's interior. That army had grown to horrific and tragic proportions by the time railroad construction was under way. Belgian senator Edouard Picard was quoted by Conan Doyle in *The Crime of the Congo* (Hutchinson, 1909) as describing it this way:

> We are constantly meeting these carriers, either isolated or in Indian file; blacks, blacks, miserable blacks, with horribly filthy loin-cloths for their only garments; their bare and frizzled heads supporting their loads—chest, bale, ivory-tusk, hamper of rubber, or barrel; for the most part broken-down, sinking under the burdens made heavier by their weariness and insufficiency of food, consisting of a handful of rice and tainted dried fish; pitiful walking caryatids; beasts of burden with the lank limbs of monkeys. Pinched-up features, eyes fixed and round with the strain of keeping their balance and the dullness of exhaustion . . . jogging on, with knees bent and stomach protruding, one arm raised up and the other resting on a long stick, dusty and malodorous; covered with insects as their huge procession passes over mountains and through valleys; dying on the tramp or, when the tramp is over, going to their villages to die of exhaustion.

It wasn't just the constraints on moving exports to the Atlantic that made a railroad look like a good idea, it was also the exorbitant cost of delivering to Stanley Pool the prefabricated, European-built stuff and other goods necessary to make the colony a going concern. In 1885, Francis de Winton told Tisdel, shipping freight from Europe to the Pool cost four hundred dollars per metric ton: twenty-five dollars to haul twenty-two hundred pounds across the Atlantic to Banana, seventy-five dollars from Banana to Vivi, and three hundred dollars—more than a dollar per mile—to transport the same ton of goods and gear the last two hundred-plus miles from Vivi past the cataracts to Leopoldville on loaded heads.

Even so, some weren't so sure that there was enough moving on the Congo in both directions to make economical use of a costly railroad regardless of its design. Tisdel, whose merchant shipping background translated in 1886 to no special railroad expertise (that came later), had made his view known. "It is possible to build a railway around the rapids or even across to Zanzibar," he once wrote. "But I venture to say that to take out one dollar's worth of produce by means of this road the cost will be $3." At one point Roger Casement suggested, to no one in particular, the construction of a road suitable for wagon and cart traffic instead of a railroad. Separately, Sanford and Taunt exchanged a few letters on the subject of mule or donkey trains on an improved track paralleling the river, with Taunt proposing a trial of the idea. Neither animal alternative faced up realistically to feed requirements (for even a small mule more than ten pounds of forage and more than ten gallons of water per day, and some salt), the possibility of sleeping sickness devastating the beasts, or to the problems posed by pressing wary pack animals to cross flooded, rushing streams in the wet season.

The late professor John Hope Franklin, his biographer, speculated that Williams wrote his critique on plans and estimates for the railroad as a service to Collis Huntington, the Connecticut-born California dry goods merchant whose ambition and sharp practices morphed a wagon road survey through the Nevada Territory into the Central Pacific Railroad, fabulously enriching him and several associates. The two men had first met some six months earlier and fairly quickly developed a curious relationship that saw the wealthy industrialist occasionally acting like Williams' sponsor, introducing him to Hampton Institute's leadership (the school where Booker T. Washington taught was a favorite Huntington charity) and providing cash on several later occasions for travel expenses.

Huntington probably wasn't interested in Williams' amateur analysis of what amounted to the railroad's business plan or its construction schedule and cost estimates anyway. He hadn't been interested much in that kind of information on his own railroads in the American West, which he saw more as steam-powered machines to deliver money from Washington than as national infrastructure. If the fact that the extension of America's railroads to the Pacific Coast was ten or twenty years premature didn't concern him, then surely the doubtful viability of the Congo railroad's economic model wouldn't either.[4]

Stanley had done some back-of-the-envelope revenue and construction cost estimates for a Congo railway, but like his population estimates, his arithmetic was not much more than hopeful, bad guesses enrobed in his prestige. He didn't know any more about railroading than Williams did. This did not stop him from telling the *New York Times* in April 1891, when only a few miles of rail had been laid, "The engineers report that all the estimates I made are coming out exactly correct." Instead, the cynics at the *Engineering News and American Contract Journal*, who in 1886 had described Stanley's as "one of the estimates it is well to add ten percent to and then double," were vindicated. Stanley had guessed the railroad would cost $6 million; in the end it cost $12 million.

The only serious effort to see how a narrow-gauge, single-track railroad could be constructed between Matadi and Stanley Pool was made by the Belgian Compagnie du Congo pour le Commerce et l'Industrie. Its costly survey, done between August 1887 and November 1888, concluded that a 435-kilometer (270-mile) railroad could be built in four years for 25 million Belgian francs ($5 million).

The final plan contemplated a seventy-five-centimeter, single-track main line with terminals in "first-class stations" at Matadi and N'dolo, the latter near the riverside flats below Leopoldville at the far western end of Stanley Pool. A second-class station near midway (for overnight stops; trains were to run only in daylight), two third-class stations, and fifteen water tanks, spaced as required, completed the railroad's furniture. Rolling stock required by the end of the fourth year was projected to be 15 engines and 150 cars.

Belgian engineers' estimates, as Williams would soon charge, like Stanley's, turned out to be wildly optimistic. By April 1897 it was possible to ride the rails only as far as Tumba, 110 miles from Matadi, a twelve-hour trip and only 40 percent of the way. The first locomotive didn't steam into N'dolo Station at the head of a train until nearly a year later, on March 16, 1898.

Williams and his porters came trudging through the right-of-way work site in May and June 1890, four months after work began on the line in Matadi by the Compagnie du Chemin de Fer du Congo (the surveyors' firm renamed and recapitalized to do the construction). Looking back on what he'd seen, Williams didn't like the railroad any more than he liked the colony. "The difficulties were," Williams said, "almost insuperable." They included, he thought, the treacherous waters between Boma and Matadi, mountainous rocks at Matadi, and everywhere on the way to N'dolo tight curves, steep climbs, and cross-cutting watercourses to bridge.

Labor availability for what was going to be a hand-built railroad posed another huge problem. The Compagnie du Chemin de Fer du Congo expected that its European engineers would supervise native laborers, recruited or impressed from local tribes. But because building the railroad proved to be brutal work, tribal levees were loath to remain in place, and foreign workers had to be brought in to augment them. The most distant, 529 Chinese "coolies," came from Macau to Matadi from around the Cape of Good Hope. During their first four months in equatorial Africa more than 200 of these Chinese withered and died, many from beriberi or dysentery.

Others dropped their tools and fled east, hoping to reach their distant homes in Asia on foot. Some absconders, the *Railway Gazette* reported improbably in December 1907, were later found as far as six hundred miles in the continental interior.

"The projectors of the Congo Railway scheme have been too boastful and too profuse in their promises to shareholders, and under these circumstances disappointment and confusion are sure to cover them, as heat follows light, and the rising sun," Williams wrote. By the time engineer Nicholas Cito eased his tiny engine into N'dolo in early 1898 some 60 million francs and an estimated 1,900 lives had been consumed in the railroad's construction.

Even so, the start of operations on the line was met with celebration, or at least admiration, in distant places. October 22, 1898, the Denver, Colorado, *Evening Post* exulted that Africa had finally been opened to civilization, presenting as proof the fact that 8,815 miles of rail were now either operating or under construction on the continent. (At the same time, 200,000 miles of train track crossed the United States.) The most important segment, said the *Evening Post*, exceeding in significance even the line from Alexandria, Egypt, to Khartoum in the Sudan, was "being built to follow the course of the Congo" through topography as challenging as "the Swiss or Tyrolean Alps" and across terrain infested with "much-dreaded wood ants" that devoured wooden ties and trestle timbers from the inside out.

There was more to the idea of a narrow-gauge railroad, however, than just lowering costs by updating Bronze Age African logistics to nineteenth-century transportation technology. The railroad would also serve, in *New York Times* columnist David Ker's words, to "bridge over the most unhealthy tract of the Congo Valley and to enable immigrants to get past it as quickly as possible into the more wholesome districts that the new railway has projected." If, Ker thought, great communities could exist in St. Petersburg, New Orleans, and Calcutta, despite their wretched climates and endemic dangers, then surely one could flourish in the Congo. Speeding would-be European settlers past the contagion was the idea. This, of course, was written in the naive time when significant white immigration and settlement were still imagined to be possible.

Ker's long piece in the June 20, 1886, edition of the *Times* was subtitled "Why Capitalists Hesitate to Invest Their Money in the Proposed African Road." His answer was that reluctance came from more than "that chronic distrust of everything new and startling which is so prominent a characteristic of the sober British mind" or from the idea that attempting to establish a colony of Europeans in the country constituted the "wanton sacrifice of human life." It arose, instead, from doubt about the anticipated wonderful commercial results. "Many of the tribes on the Upper Congo are mere brutal savages, and cannibals to boot," Ker wrote. "The only articles which such creatures would care to import are muskets—with which no one but a fool would trust them—and rum, with the possession of which no one but a scoundrel would think of cursing them. . . . The chief exports of the Congo have hitherto been slaves (which are not in our line) and ivory, which must necessarily be exhausted sooner or later."

49

Williams' "Open Letter to Leopold II" drew a flash of attention in Europe and the United States. The stories broke in the United States months after the same news began circulating in Europe and while Williams was in Egypt preparing to sail for England in the British India Steam Navigation Company's nearly new SS *Golconda*. In the middle of April 1891, the *New York Times* and the *New York Herald* ran long, front-page stories about the Williams letter, as did papers in smaller American cities soon thereafter.

The piece in the *Times* included all of Williams' charges practically verbatim and contained several long paragraphs about Stanley that quoted Williams as saying, among other things, that mention of Stanley's name in the Congo "produces a shudder among this simple folk," who remember his "broken promises, copious profanity, hot temper, and heavy blows" and "his severe and rigorous measures by which they were mulcted of their lands."

But the *New York Times* wasn't entirely supportive. Under headlines that read "Williams in Middletown [New York]. He Prospered for a Time, but his True Character was Learned," the same April 15 issue of the paper described Williams in the early 1880s in that city as a social climber who had lied about his means, motives, and marital status ("said he was a widower and intimated that he was desirous of marrying a white woman with money"), leaving some parties to "have substantial pecuniary reasons for regretting that Williams ever came here."

Stanley, who happened to be in New York at the Plaza Hotel in mid-April when the story broke and had known about the letter for months, was quoted in the *Times'* April 14 edition as replying that he and King Leopold were the targets of "blackmailing on a big scale" by Williams, whom he described as an unsuccessful job seeker in the past. Stanley told the *Herald* the same thing. The suspicion was that the goal of Williams' alleged blackmail was to get the Congo railroad contract thrown over to Huntington's American interests.

Leopold quickly launched his formidable public relations machinery in reprisal. The king's and his allies' response to the "Open Letter" took two forms: an assault in the media and in the Belgian parliament against "Colonel" Williams personally, and on the substance of his charges. *Le Mouvement Géographique*, still in 1891 Leopold's reliable defender, published a long article in its June 14 edition attacking "le Colonel noir" and rejecting his accusations. The *Journal de Bruxelles* did too, in several issues in midmonth, as did *La Nation*, *Le Patriot*, and other conservative papers on the continent.

Publication of Williams' letter stirred up a short-lived flurry on both sides of the Atlantic. Although some politicians, journalists, and other activists took his charges seriously, the letter changed nothing. Nothing perhaps because Williams was unable to stump for his cause (he died at forty-one on August 2, only two months after he arrived in London from Ismailia, Egypt, where his tour of Africa had ended) or perhaps because public sentiment and government policy were not yet ready to rally behind what a black man thought and wrote about Africa. Not until Edmund Dene Morel's discoveries pierside in Antwerp became public, and after Roger Casement's official report was published, did King Leopold's definition of what was happening in the Congo face an effective challenge.

50

In 1890 *Le Mouvement Géographique* counted 175 Belgians, 58 Portuguese, and in descending rank order smaller numbers of Dutch, British, Danish, Swedish, French, and American citizens in the Congo Free State at the end of 1889. Most of these 430 whites—traders, state agents, missionaries, and a few foreign diplomats like Taunt—were living and working on the lower river below Stanley Pool. None of the resident foreigners were settlers. The number of transient foreigners increased the next year, driven sharply upward by the Compagnie du Chemin de Fer du Congo's requirement for engineers and supervisors to build its railroad.

It's possible, but confirmed nowhere, that late that year Joseph Conrad met Emory Taunt in the Congo, while Taunt was in his last few months as the U.S. commercial agent in the Congo Free State (and his last alive) and Conrad was back on the lower river from Stanley Falls. The former U.S. Navy officer and the British mariner, two among several hundred white men

living and working along the river, overlapped in the colony for a while during the second half of that year.

George Washington Williams and Conrad were also in the Congo at
about the same time, and for roughly as long. The chief product of Williams'
travels through Leopold's fiefdom was two acerbic letters condemning
everything he saw. Conrad mined his six months of wretched experience in
equatorial Africa to write his best-known work, the haunting novella *Heart
of Darkness*, and a single public letter.

Before he became a published author, Conrad was a merchant seaman.
In 1866, after a dozen years at sea under French and British flags and with
experience in eleven different ships, Conrad received his master's license in
the British merchant marine. That same year he became a naturalized British
citizen. Most of Conrad's time afloat and his only time in command, fifteen months as master of the small Australian bark *Otago* and her crew of
twelve, was under sail in Far Eastern waters.

Taunt and Conrad had more in common than time at sea and white skin:
Both were unemployed when each mounted his successful campaign to find
work in the Congo, Taunt in Washington in 1888 for his third and last time
and Conrad in London in 1889 for his first and only. In mid-January 1890,
thanks largely to an aunt's machinations in Brussels, Conrad was able to
write a relative that he was "more or less under contract . . . to be master" of
one of the river steamers belonging to the year-old Société Anonyme Belge
pour le Commerce du Haut-Congo. How Conrad imagined his future command isn't clear, but in *Heart of Darkness* he has his avatar, Marlow, describing his own vessel dismissively as "a two-penny-half-penny river-steamboat
with a penny whistle attached."

Conrad's first steamer command was to have been the defunct Sanford
Exploring Expedition's *Florida*, in 1890 flying the flag of the Congo Free
State and then operated out of Kinshasa by the Société Anonyme Belge
(SAB), successor to the assets of the S.E.E. Her captain, a young Dane named
Johannes Freiesleben, had been killed January 29, shot or speared during an
argument with a chief over a gift to a woman or perhaps over two black
hens (accounts differ, the latter would be an especially insufficient reason
to die). When the news of Freiesleben's death finally reached Antwerp, the
position opened that Conrad was slated to fill.[5]

His contract with the SAB was for three years. Had things gone well on
the upper Congo River, Conrad would have remained in Leopold's isolated
colony at least through the spring of 1893, with an unknowable effect upon
his future life as an author. When he left Europe for Africa his first novel,
Almayer's Folly, existed only as seven handwritten chapters in his baggage,

and Conrad might have put the manuscript aside and vanished from history had he found job satisfaction as a riverboat captain for the SAB.

Newly employed, Conrad sailed from Bordeaux for the Congo on May 10 in the French steamer SS *Ville de Maceio*, already ten days out of Antwerp on her regular service between Belgium and Leopold's colony (and according to *Le Mouvement Geographique*'s issue of May 4, on this passage carrying in her cargo hold the first rails and ties to be laid for the new railroad). *Ville de Maceio* called at seven ports during her month at sea with Conrad on board. After bouncing down the West African coast and pausing for a day at Banana, Conrad finally arrived at Boma on June 12, 1890, about the time that Taunt was passing through Liverpool and Williams was approaching Stanley Falls, the halfway point of his tour of the Congo Free State.

Boma's two-foot gauge trolley was then only three months old. Shuttle service between the jetty on the riverfront (Boma Rive) and a stop two kilometers away in the upper town (Boma Plateau) had begun on March 4th. The new hotel, assembled from double-walled, galvanized iron plates rolled by the Oiseau Iron Works of Belgium, stood on a half-acre of ground at Boma Rive. Its parts had arrived in the Congo from Antwerp in June 1889. Their assembly took the next ten months.

Conrad was in the colonial capital his first time only long enough to pass through overnight, ample time not to like what he saw. Not the kit-built Government House; not the prefabricated hotel where sallow-faced public officials were fed twice a day; not the nearly new, steam-powered trolley; not even an enormous baobab, a tree species he might not have seen before, holding its bare boughs above "soldiers' huts, wooden shanties, corrugated iron hovels." The next day Conrad caught a steamer to Matadi, where after two weeks he left at the head of a party of porters for the long hike to Leopoldville.

Distressing news soon reached him on the trail: None of the steamers on the upper Congo was seaworthy and one, his *Florida*, was the victim of a recent wreck. In *Heart of Darkness* he blames the accident on some "volunteer skipper," who in a sudden hurry to get up the river on June 27 ran *Florida* on the rocks not ten miles from her home pier and tore the bottom out. In this account it took months to effect repairs and to refloat her. That accident explains why, when Conrad finally left Kinshasa for Stanley Falls Station, it was in *Roi des Belges* and not *Florida*.

During their weeks on the river pressed together, Camille Delcommune, thirty-one, and Conrad, then thirty-three, came to despise one another. In those same weeks Conrad's prospects as a Congo riverboat captain evaporated, in part because of Delcommune's hostility and in part because of

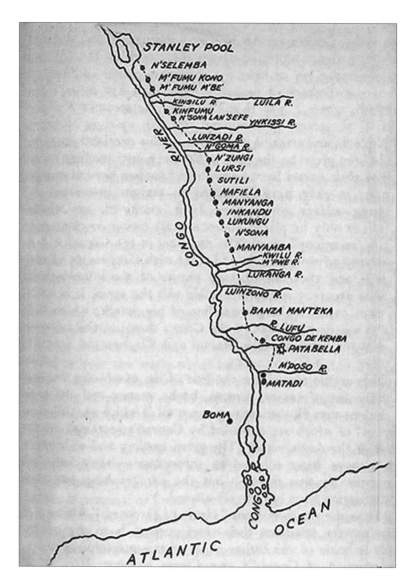

Map 5. Sketch of Conrad's route along the Congo. Conrad's caravan moved only nineteen of the thirty-five days it spent bypassing the river's rapids, averaging more than ten miles made good every day actually on the march. The spelling of place names is Conrad's. (North is to the left.) August 1, with the caravan's destination almost in sight, Conrad granted he was "glad to see the end of this stupid tramp." The next day the party reached Kinshasa, on the flats below Leopoldville Station. It arrived ten days or two weeks behind two Southern Presbyterian missionaries, Reverend Sheppard and Reverend Lapsley, who later built their church's first mission near Luebo Station. CURLE, *"CONRAD'S DIARY,"* 255

Figure 28. The steamboat *Roi des Belges.* On August 3, 1890, *Roi des Belges,* under Captain Ludvig Koch (another Danish captain in the Congo) with Conrad, the company's local station manager, Camille Delcommune, and several other SAB employees on board, got under way on Stanley Pool for distant Stanley Falls Station, where Georges-Anton Klein, the company's French resident agent, had fallen ill with dysentery. The small steamer took the rest of the month to get there. Klein, twenty-seven, died on the downriver leg. In time his death turned into a plot device in Conrad's dark novella about the Congo. Captain Koch fell sick not long after departure from Stanley Falls, and on September 6 Delcommune temporarily promoted Conrad from supercargo to acting master. *Roi des Belges* did not return to Kinshasa until September 24. Belgian-built *Roi des Belges* was constructed in 1887 and went into the water at Stanley Pool in March 1888, after assembly following the usual trek in pieces past the cataracts. DELCOMMUNE, VINGT ANNÉES DE VIE AFRICAINE

his own fragile health. Conrad confessed in a letter to his aunt to suffering four attacks of fever and five days of dysentery during his two months in *Roi des Belges*. Command of *Florida* was granted when she was repaired to a certain Carlier, and Conrad was put to doing chores ashore, where Delcommune told him that contracts written in Belgium were not necessarily valid in the Congo and not to expect promotion or a pay raise. (Conrad got his revenge on Carlier for this usurpation in "An Outpost of Progress," a short story written in 1896, by recycling his last name. The fictitious Carlier in the story, assistant trader at a miserable, isolated station, was accidently murdered by his boss, who then killed himself, after both had gone insane having first acceded to the enslavement of their employees in exchange for six tusks of ivory.)[6]

Instead of assuming command, Conrad spent the next two months on shore back at Boma, sick and waiting to escape Africa. "I arrived at that delectable capital," he wrote wryly in *A Personal Record* (Harper & Brothers, 1912), "where before the departure of the steamer that was to take me home, I had the time to wish myself dead over and over again with perfect sincerity." Not so much a comment on Boma's meager attractions as a reflection of his health. Conrad sailed for Europe December 4, barely alive, just weeks before Taunt died at Banana Point. His experience on the river had been a shattering one, and nearly fatal. He would return to the Congo only in his imagination.

The next year *Almayer's Folly* was published by T. Fisher Unwin of London, followed several years later by *The Outcast of the Islands* from the same publisher. As other authors, among them Melville and Stevenson, had discovered, readers in England and America were eager to peer through the pages of a book at life lived badly in exotic places they could never expect to see in person. *Heart of Darkness* was all that and more in just 40,000 words.

Heart of Darkness was first published in serial form in *Blackwood's Edinburgh Magazine* in February, March, and April of 1899 and reappeared in serialized form several times elsewhere before, in 1902, it came out as a bound book. It remained in print through the last century and into this one, a staple of high school and college reading lists during much of the recent past. Only in small part because it's so short it can be read in an hour and a half. In the book's relatively few pages Conrad went on to create evil incarnate upriver in a hellish jungle and quickly let him die, leaving generations of readers who knew of the author's African experience to wonder how much was fact and how much was fiction, and what any of it meant.

"There was an air of plotting about that station," he has Marlow say of the Middle Station, Kinshasa, after only a few days there, "but nothing came

of it, of course. It was as unreal as everything else—as the philanthropic pretence of the whole concern, as their talk, as their government, as their show of work." Conrad understood that everything visible was a pious fraud. Taunt, seeing the same evidence, told Washington that a fully formed government was functioning effectively in the Congo. So did most other observers.

Most reviewers of *Heart of Darkness*, John Masefield in the January 1903 issue of the *Speaker* was a conspicuous exception, were impressed with the story. None, curiously, seems to have used the obvious opportunity to segue from writing a book review about the essence of evil discovered at the Inner Station to expressing any interest in what was really going on in the Congo Free State, even less in commenting on those events. Odd omissions, given that all of these men would have known of the autobiographical dimension of Conrad's novella.

Soon after British consul Roger Casement finished his bombshell report of evidence of horrifying abuses in the Congo, but before it was published in early 1904, Casement attempted to recruit Conrad into a group of reform activists. They had roomed together briefly in Matadi before Conrad left to steam upriver in *Roi des Belges*, and a visit and exchange of letters in 1903–4 renewed the passing friendship. The product of Casement's appeal was a scathing letter Conrad wrote to him on December 21 for publication. In it Conrad described the Congo Free State as "the monopoly of one small country established to the disadvantage of the rest of the civilized world in defiance of international treaties and in brazen disregard of humanitarian declarations. . . . A Congo State created by the act of European powers where ruthless, systemic cruelty towards the blacks is the basis of administration, and bad faith toward other states is the basis of commercial policy." But that's as far as Conrad went. He did nothing further for the reform movement, leaving it to Casement, Morel, and others to expose the crimes being committed in the Congo.

9

Exposing the Crime of the Congo

The fact is that the running of a tropical colony is, of all tests, the most searching as to the development of the nation which attempts it; to see helpless people and not to oppress them, to see great wealth and not to confiscate it, to have absolute power and not to abuse it, to raise the native instead of sinking yourself, these are the supreme trials of a nation's spirit. We have all failed at times. But never has there been failure so hopeless, so shocking, bearing such consequences to the world, such degradation to the good name of Christianity and civilization as the failure of the Belgians in the Congo.

Arthur Conan Doyle, The Crime of the Congo

51

Emory Taunt died too soon to see the beginning of the end of Leopold's plantation, but given the evidence of the anodyne report he filed with the State Department in 1889, had he lived longer in Boma, Taunt still would have missed what was unfolding around him.

In 1890, the same year George Washington Williams launched his first assault in prose against Leopold's colony, Edmund Morel, a French teenager, and his widowed mother moved from Paris to Liverpool. There, for sixty pounds sterling a year, Morel became a junior clerk in the offices of Elder, Dempster and Company, a commercial juggernaut with financial, mining, and agricultural interests on three continents.

The firm he had just joined, Morel said later, lay at "the centre of West African interests . . . in England." Supporting those interests, eleven ships of the company's huge merchant fleet steamed on schedule every month between Europe and West Africa.[1] At the company's center stood the round-faced, handsomely mustachioed Alfred Jones (after 1901, Sir Alfred), simultaneously the company's senior partner, chief of the Africa Section of the Liverpool Chamber of Commerce, and the Congo Free State's consul in England's second port city. Triple-hatted Sir Alfred and his company's great reach gave Elder, Dempster an influential voice in the British capital.

Morel's discovery, made while examining the company's books and observing its operations pierside, that the value of exports from the colony

far exceeded the value of its imports, confirmed that the Congo was being sucked dry by the king of the Belgians.

In 1900 Morel left the company to become a full-time journalist, and three years later he started the *West African Mail,* a weekly that became his pulpit for preaching reform for the Congo. From him also flowed a stream of letters, pamphlets, and books, all documenting Leopold's injustices and the tragic lot of natives in the Congo, victims of a system that he believed was inherently criminally abusive. His revelations, substantiating the dreadful stories slowly leaking out of the Congo, triggered the campaign against Leopold that Williams' brave letter years ago had failed to ignite.[2]

Morel's agitation finally stirred Parliament to have the government dispatch Roger Casement, Taunt's former employee and now HMG's consul in Boma, to investigate. The publication of Consul Casement's damning confirmation of upcountry atrocities in February 1904 led in March to the creation of the Congo Reform Association (CRA), followed by what grew into a torrent of shocking revelations and accusations that energized history's third great civil rights movement.

Just before the end of September 1904, Morel, now the new association's secretary, arrived in New York City from Liverpool on board White Star's new steamship, RMS *Baltic.* The first purpose of his month-long visit was to deliver a memorandum to President Theodore Roosevelt from the Congo Reform Association, urging the United States to take on a leading role in the movement. "The historical basis for our appeal to this Government," the *New York Times* on September 30 quoted Morel as explaining to its reporter, "lies in the fact that this country was the first to recognize the flag of the International Association for the Exploration and Civilization of Africa under the auspices of which the Congo Free State was founded. . . . In order to gain the recognition of this country, King Leopold made specific pledges to protect the right [sic] of the natives and not to do anything to suppress commerce. All these pledges he has since violated."

While Morel's message was percolating through official Washington he went to Boston. During the first week of October the city (once the heart of abolitionist sentiment in the United States) was home to the thirteenth Universal Peace Conference, a convention of activists that offered a sympathetic audience and a place to find recruits for an American counterpart to the Congo Reform Association. As Morel expected, the conferees unanimously adopted resolutions supporting an international inquiry into the status of the Congo, this despite a letter from the absent James Cardinal Gibbons, the influential archbishop of Baltimore, who urged peace activists to stay out of the Congo debate.

Like most Roman Catholic prelates, Cardinal Gibbons was a vocal Leopold enthusiast, who volunteered to admiring Leopold's "noble ideals" and the splendid results of his humane policy.[3] That month Gibbons wrote Morel, "It is only some score of discontented men, depending largely on the untrustworthy hearsay evidence of natives, who have raised an outcry against the Congo administration, out of a great band of 500 or 600 missionaries, both Catholic and Protestant, who are working on the Congo, and who give thanks to the Congo administration for its support of the missions, and for its successful efforts to introduce Christianity and civilization into Central Africa."[4]

Not everyone else responded with natural sympathy to what Morel was urging either. Representing these skeptics, the *New York Times* editorialized on October 8, "We imagine a general feeling of relief will follow the announcement from Washington that the President does not see his way to intervene with respect to the administration of the Congo Free State. . . . In this matter . . . our interest is infinitesimal, whereas the interests of more than one European country are substantial. If there are abuses in the administration of the Congo Free State, and we think the general American opinion to be that decidedly there are, let some Government concerned undertake the belling of the Belgian cat."

Roosevelt's initial response to Morel's importuning was negative, but that wasn't his last thought on the subject.[5] Roosevelt was no activist on the subject of race relations, but as his astonishing private dinner with Booker T. Washington in the White House soon after he took office showed, he was ahead of his times. Two years after the Morel call, Roosevelt revisited Congo policy, pushed to reconsider it by growing public revulsion at the flood of stories reporting on the horrors of life in the Congo, and by his own instincts for justice.

Leopold reacted to the CRA's charges with characteristic determination and guile. Among other actions he quickly stood up "the Federation of the Defense of Belgian Interests Abroad" (a name that glossed over the fact that the interests to be defended were not national but exclusively his). The lobby's chief in the United States was the Belgian minister in Washington, Baron Ludovic Moncheur, who'd come to Washington in 1902 from diplomatic service in Mexico. Recently married to the daughter of his American counterpart in Mexico City, Moncheur's connections in the American capital were especially congenial.

Unfortunately for the king of the Belgians, his hired American point man, a San Francisco lawyer named "Colonel" Henry Kowalsky, turned out to be a cunning low-life with a colorful history, if contemporary press reports are believed. Less flashy members of Leopold's lobby in the United States included lawyer and author Henry Wellington Wack and James Whiteley, the Congo's resident consul in Baltimore.[6]

In a report published on October 18, 1904, the *Times* wrote that Kowalsky had called on President Roosevelt to deliver the party line the day before, that negative reports from the Congo came only from self-interested missionaries and agitation in Great Britain had as its goal not helping natives but reopening settled territorial questions to the United Kingdom's advantage. "I called the President's attention to the fact," Kowalsky was quoted as saying,

> that all this uproar over the fearful atrocities in the Congo Free State is fathered by missionaries whose applications for big concessions were turned down by Congo authorities. Not a single charge of cruelty and atrocity has been made except by those who have been seeking material advantage in that region and have not been permitted to exploit it at the expense of others.
>
> This fact, and the fact that Great Britain has failed in her effort to open up the Congo question, accounts for the attempt now being made to work upon the sympathies of the American people by trumped up stories of cruelty to the Congo natives.

Much later the *Times* revealed from unidentified sources that the meeting in the White House had been a "60-second chat" during which nothing of substance had been discussed. From this distance, it's hard to tell who was spinning the story, Roosevelt or Kowalsky.

The following March, and now describing himself as the Belgian government's legal representative in matters related to his client's rights and possessions abroad, Kowalsky wrote a thirty-five-page brief "in reply to [the] memorial presented to the President of the United States of America concerning affairs in the Congo State by the Congo Reform Association, Supported by the British and Foreign Anti-slavery Society and the Aborigines' Protection Society." Complete with a several-item appendix, it was an articulate if fundamentally dishonest defense of the Congo Free State's government against allegations that it had treated natives cruelly and inhumanly, absorbed all unoccupied land into the public domain, and "imposed upon natives the obligation to work," Kowalsky's euphemism for "slavery." Kowalsky would soon prove himself to be a scoundrel, but he was not incompetent. The brief was the product of a glib publicist making the best case possible for a tainted client.[7]

52

Edmund Morel's prize American convert to the cause of reform was Mark Twain, a contender for the title of best known man in the English-speaking world. Morel's recruitment of Twain into the leadership ranks of the Congo Reform movement was a brilliant coup. Until he got discouraged and withdrew, Twain, then back in the United States after almost a decade abroad, practically submerged himself in the work of the new American branch of the Congo Reform Association.

For nearly eighteen months, until February 1906, when the demands of the CRA overwhelmed him and he grew frustrated with the prospect of change, Twain devoted himself to writing and lobbying for reform in the Congo. His exertions included sitting for newspaper interviews and, around the end of 1905, meeting several times with President Roosevelt, Secretary of State Elihu Root (Hay's successor), and the new first assistant secretary of state, Robert Bacon.

Twain's sharpest attack came in *King Leopold's Soliloquy: A Defense of His Congo Rule* (P. R. Warren, 1905), a book-length pretend admission by a sullen, uncomprehending king of his sins in Africa. Its text was hot emotion forged into words, pure Twain but not Twain at his best, not even at his pretty good. (Sample, playing Leopold's ventriloquist: "They can no more keep quiet when my name is mentioned than can a glass of water control its feelings with a seidlitz powder in its bowels.")[8]

The Free State's press bureau in Belgium was concerned enough by Twain's attacks to prompt publication of an anonymous forty-six-page pamphlet rebuttal, *An Answer to Mark Twain* (A. & G. Bulens Brothers, 1907), rightly accusing Twain of being the Congo Reform Association's mouthpiece but wrongly accusing him of lying.

King Leopold's Soliloquy didn't get much traction, but Twain didn't wait to get a reaction from the royal court before he went after Leopold again. At the end of a seventieth birthday interview at home on Thanksgiving Day 1905 with the *New York World*'s Sunday magazine, Twain granted that "we have much to be thankful for." Then he specified, "Most of all (politically), that America's first-born son, sole & only son, lovechild of her trusting innocence & her virgin bed, King Leopold of the Undertakers, has been spared to us another year, & that his (& our) Cemetery Trust in the Congo is now doing a larger business in a single week than it used to in a month fifteen years ago."

A little later Twain wrote a short, never published essay in the same vein, the obscure "On Leopold, About 1906," but by then the old man was tired out by his take-no-prisoners campaign against Leopold.

Figure 29. "An Answer to Mark Twain." This illustration of the pamphlet's cover shows Twain and Morel as two serpents spewing lies and slander down on "the present Belgian Congo," a bucolic scene of order, development, and prosperity, while across the river in the Congo of the past a war party attacks fleeing natives. "No Belgian would take the trouble of discussing such filthy work," the pamphlet's unknown author wrote. "Truth shines forth in the following pages, which summarily show what the Congo State is—not the hell depicted by a morbid mind—but a country which twenty years ago was steeped in the most abject barbarity and which to-day is born to civilization and progress." *Courtesy Special Collections, Alderman Library, University of Virginia*

53

Twain's was not the only household name attached to Morel's cause. From mid-October 1881 into January 1882 (while Lieutenant Taunt was on board the training ship USS *Portsmouth* and when Henry Morton Stanley was back in the Congo, busy building Leopoldville Station), Arthur Conan Doyle, twenty-two, the new ship's surgeon in the African Steam Navigation Company's SS *Mayumba,* sailed from Liverpool to Old Calabar, Nigeria, and back, drawing all the while twelve pounds sterling per month for his professional services to crew and passengers and by his own account drinking too much. This was his second time at sea as a ship's surgeon. The first, on board the Atlantic whaler *Hope* while he was a third-year medical student, was recorded in a recently published journal, *Dangerous Work* (University of Chicago Press, 2012).

Conan Doyle described the miserable experience in SS *Mayumba*, punctuated with several malarial collapses and a fire at sea on the return leg that could have destroyed the old, 1,500-ton vessel, as steaming from "one dirty little port to another dirty little port," under an "apoplectic sun glaring down . . . in a disgusting manner." Sounding something like Conrad would ten years later, Conan Doyle summed up his experience: "The deathlike impression of Africa grew upon me. One felt that the white man with his present diet and habits was an intruder who was never meant to be there, and that the great sullen brown continent killed him as one crushes nits."[9] Again like Conrad, once Conan Doyle left equatorial Africa, he never returned. Nor, despite his mother's encouragement, did he ever go to sea again as a ship's surgeon.

In 1891 he gave up his medical practice entirely, to concentrate on his writing career that by then had seen *A Study in Scarlet* and *The Sign of the Four* published, launching his brilliant sleuth, Sherlock Holmes, into the world. Much later, in late 1909, in between writing his enormously popular mystery stories and the several weird explorations of fairies and spiritualism with which he closed out his life as an author, Conan Doyle wrote *The Crime of the Congo*. The short book, some five thousand words longer than Conrad's *Heart of Darkness*, was one of a number of his nonfiction "pamphlets" on assorted subjects that prompted his support.

Like *King Leopold's Soliloquy*, *The Crime of the Congo* was written in a fury. Conan Doyle was "driven" to do it, he said in Chapter XIII, "by a sense of burning injustice and intolerable wrong." Powered by this heat, he dashed off the book during eight frenetic days sequestered in a London hotel room, sleeping four hours a night and sustaining himself on coffee, or so he claimed to Edmund Morel, who'd asked for his help in the campaign against Leopold. The product of Conan Doyle's labors reads better than such a caffeinated state might lead one to expect.

Conan Doyle came at his subject with a purity that must have seemed otherworldly to most of his countrymen, an idea that would have set eyes to rolling in Manchester and Liverpool: that making money from a colony was persuasive evidence of wrongdoing. "It is proof of the honesty of German colonial policy," he wrote, "and the fitness of Germany to be a great land-owning power, that nearly all her tropical colonies, like our own, show, or have shown a deficit."

He believed that Leopold's announced "civilizing and elevating mission" may have been authentic at the outset, "vaguely philanthropic" and not consciously hypocritical. It was only over time and by degrees, as the king came to understand the potential for wealth in what he held, Conan Doyle thought, that the Congo Free State morphed into a privately owned slave labor camp camouflaged beneath the trappings of a state.

While the truth about the horrific abuses in the Congo slowly leaked out, Leopold remained largely unsullied, even as observers tried to make the connection. Finally, in 1905, Arthur Conan Doyle did. "Trace back the chain," he wrote in *The Crime of the Congo*, "from the red-handed savage, through the worried, bilious agent, the pompous Commissary, the dignified Governor-General, the smooth diplomatist, and you come finally, without a break, and without a possibility of mitigation or excuse, upon the cold, scheming brain which framed and drives the whole machine. It is upon the King, always the King, that the guilt must lie."

"*Any* change must be for the better," Conan Doyle argued in his final, "Solutions," chapter, anything but "Belgian occupation." A fix on the ground, he believed (his preferred solution was partition of the "outlaw state" among England, France, and Germany, around a central core encompassing a "great native reservation"), had to include compensation for the victims. "Surely," he concluded, "there should be some punishment for those who by their injustice and violence have dragged Christianity and civilization into the dirt."

54

American, British, and eventually Italian prying behind the scrim that obscured from outsiders what was going on in the Congo Free State produced a stream of accusations charging atrocious cruelties.[10] As these accumulated, Leopold determined to co-opt the process by building a backfire. On July 23, 1904, the king launched his own, tame Commission of Inquiry. The commissioners' report was published November 5 in the Congo's *Official Gazette*. Astonishingly, the report substantiated much of what had been charged during the past fifteen years.

Leopold's response was to assemble a reform commission and on June 3, 1906, to announce implementation of its recommendations, a bogus process capped off by a prickly signing letter to his government that revealed the old king, seventy now, wasn't willingly giving up anything while he still lived. "The Congo is essentially a personal undertaking," Leopold wrote, putting down his marker. "The law of nations regulates the relations between sovereign Powers; there is no special international law for the Congo state. . . . My rights in the Congo are indivisible: they are the product of personal labor and expense. You must miss no opportunity in proclaiming these rights; they alone can render possible and legitimate my bequest of the Congo to Belgium, which has no title but what reverts to her through my person." The king was quoted in the *Boston Evening Transcript* as going on to say that "attempts at interference with a sovereign's right to manage his own finances have assumed the proportions of usurpation," or worse. The old bully was bridling at being bullied himself.

At first, while the Congo Reform Association pressed for outside intervention in the Congo catastrophe, the fact that the United States was not technically a signatory to the Berlin Conference's General Act, and so not bound by it, provided cover for American inaction as a response to the abuses being documented more and more persuasively by outsiders. The American administration's excuse for being a spectator was weakened by the special interest in Congo Washington had claimed by reason of Stanley's presumed U.S. citizenship and powerfully undercut by the American role in providing Leopold's Congo diplomatic recognition and political legitimacy in 1884.

That role, Conan Doyle argued in the preface appended to the American edition of *The Crime of the Congo* (Doubleday, Page, 1909), posed an obligation to act. "There is in the instance a very special reason why America and England should not stand by and see these people done to death," he wrote. "[The Congolese] are, in a sense, their wards. America was first to give official recognition to King Leopold's enterprise in 1884, and so has the responsibility of having actually put him into that post which he has so dreadfully abused. She has been the direct and innocent cause of the whole tragedy, surely some reparation is due."

55

In mid-1906 Clarence Slocum, the youngest son of the late Union major general (and for three terms a Democratic member of congress from New York) Henry Slocum, was appointed to be the first U.S. consul general at Boma. After eleven years during which no American government officer had been assigned to the African capital, and fifteen after a feverish Emory Taunt had been fired and escorted to Banana and his death, Clarence Slocum (1871–1912) replaced the long-gone Commercial Agent Dorsey Mohun, now an executive of the Anglo-Belgian India-rubber and Exploration Company.

The new consul general arrived on October 10. "A wharf forty yards long led from the steamer to the bank," wrote Richard Harding Davis in his book *The Congo and Coasts of Africa* (Charles Scribner's Sons, 1907), describing his arrival at Boma at about the same time that Slocum landed there, before continuing, "Boma is built on a hill of red soil. It is a town of scattered buildings made of wood and sheet-iron plates, sent out in crates and held together with screws. . . . In the Report of the 'Commission of Inquiry' . . . Boma is described as possessing 'the daintiness and chic of a European watering place.'" Davis saw something very different. "Boma really is like a seaport of one of the Central American Republics," he corrected. "It has a temporary sufficient-to-the-day-for-tomorrow-we-die air. It looks like a military post that at any moment might be abandoned. . . . In spite of the fact that Boma is a 'European watering-place,' all the servants of the state with whom I talked wanted to get away from it."

On December 1, not eight weeks after his arrival, Slocum sent a confidential report to the secretary of state, his seventh dispatch to Washington, "concerning the Kongo Free State as a commercial undertaking," based on "personal observation, personal reading, and conversations with officials, traders, and other trustworthy men of affairs." The report was focused on commercial issues, but it made clear that in general the Congo was nothing like the Berlin conferees had foreseen twenty-one years ago.[11]

Leopold regularly denied he was profiting from the Congo, telling a visiting Publishers' Press news service reporter in early December 1906, for example, "On the contrary, I have spent large sums of my own in developing the country, sums amounting in the aggregate to millions. . . . The betterment of the country and the improvement of the conditions of the natives are the only objects of my efforts. . . . The prosperity of the country no more affects me financially than the prosperity of America increases the means of President Roosevelt."

After a few months on scene, Slocum was unpersuaded. "I find the Kongo Free State, under the present regime, to be nothing but a vast commercial enterprise for the exploitation of the commercial products of the country, particularly that of ivory and rubber," his report began, and then went on to confirm Morel's observations of a decade ago about the imbalance of trade, noting that "with all the vast exportation of rubber and ivory, and its compensating value in European markets, not even a closed shed as a receptacle of imported goods exists in Boma."

Held in place by offsetting political pressures and a plausible, legalistic excuse for inaction, Roosevelt might have continued to do nothing about the Congo, but as sentiment in the United States grew for reform, the president found a place to stand: The United States was a party to the "Convention Relative to the Slave Trade and Importation into Africa of Firearms, Ammunition, and Spirituous Liquors." That convention, signed in Brussels on July 2, 1890, was the product of the same international conference that George Washington Williams had hoped to attend as a U.S. delegate and during which Leopold had argued successfully that he needed authority to collect duties on imports in order to fund antislavery initiatives. Its seventeen subscribers included Belgium and the Congo Free State as well as the United States. Several articles of that convention, especially Nos. 2 and 5, addressed directly the state's responsibility for the elimination of slavery.

The U.S. Senate had finally ratified the convention on January 10, 1892, after nineteen months of foot dragging by Senator William Chandler (Republican, New Hampshire; the same Chandler who as secretary of the navy in December 1884 had ordered *Lancaster* and *Kearsarge* to the Congo) and some colleagues, who shared his reservation about endorsing an agreement that could somehow be read as acknowledging the partitioning of Africa.

These senators' concerns were soothed by a disclaimer, written by Chandler, in the act of ratification that the United States had "any intention in ratifying this treaty . . . to indicate any interest whatsoever in the possessions or protectorates established or claimed on that continent by the other powers or any approval of the wisdom, expediency, or lawfulness thereof, and does not join in any expressions on the said general act which might be construed as such a declaration or acknowledgment." Ratification done, if the governments in Brussels and Boma were not performing as agreed, then the Brussels convention offered a basis for U.S. action that the unratified 1885 Berlin agreement had not.

Slocum's report, the first from an American official in Africa to describe Leopold's property accurately, wasn't essential to move Washington forward.

The essential impetus probably came instead from the senior senator from Massachusetts, the patrician Republican Henry Cabot Lodge, President Roosevelt's best friend and the closest thing to hereditary nobility in New England. On December 10 Senator Lodge introduced to the Senate's Committee on Foreign Relations a resolution that informed Roosevelt he would have the Senate's support "in any steps . . . he may deem it wise to take in cooperation with or in aid of any of the powers signatory of the Treaty of Berlin for the amelioration of the condition of [the inhabitants of the basin of the Congo]." Carte blanche. The resolution wasn't reported out of the committee until January 25, or passed by the Senate (unanimously) until February 15, but its presentation to the committee that Lodge dominated was sufficient evidence to the White House that political cover was available for any initiative.

That same December day Secretary of State Elihu Root sent a cable to the American chargé in London, John Carter, instructing him to say to the British foreign minister, Sir Edward Grey, that the United States shared his government's interest "in the amelioration of conditions in the Kongo State" and wished to participate in the realization of humanitarian reforms. Beginning with that cable, Washington and London fashioned a common approach pressing Brussels on the shape of the Congo after Leopold.

56

Reluctantly responding to this foreign pressure and to that coming from Parliament's left wing, the king and his government began to consider how to proceed. Promoting the fiction that Belgium and the Congo Free State were entirely separate entities, the eight nominees recruited in the summer of 1907 to draft a treaty of cessation and annexation included four from Brussels and four other Belgians ostensibly representing the Congo Free State, all defined as plenipotentiaries, men with authority to sign a text for later consideration by Parliament. Over a few months the negotiators dutifully produced a draft that placed "all legislative power over Belgian colonial possessions" in the hands of the king and empowered him to appoint "the functionaries of judicial law" in the colony and, if he chose, to suspend at will civil courts and tribunals, replacing them with courts-martial. "The Domain of the crown," a 120,000-square-mile property specially reserved for the king's disposition and "bounded somewhat vaguely on the west, north, and east by the basin of the main Congo, the Equator, and the basin of the Lomami, and on the south" by a line parting the drainage basin of the Kasai-Sankuru from that of the Mfini and Lukenye, was exempted from annexation. A nine-man colonial supervisory council, all nine to be selected by the king, completed what would have been the instruments of Leopold's continued domination of government, business, and life in the colony-to-be.

The text instantly drew sharp American criticism, shared with the British foreign office on November 4. "It seems to me," Secretary Root wrote to the American ambassador in London for the information of the British foreign minister, Sir Edward Grey, "that the enactment of this law would be a most unsatisfactory conclusion of the effort to redress and prevent for the future the outrages which have been committed on natives of the Kongo region under the control of the King of Belgium." Hearing of American views on November 19 Grey readily agreed, but he was chary about interfering in the political process under way across the Channel. Through 1907 and into 1908 this became the pattern: a shared negative assessment, American unwillingness to take the diplomatic lead, and—in the persons of Sir Edward Grey and HMG's minister in Brussels, Sir Arthur Hardinge—British reluctance to press the prickly Belgians, who made clear they wanted no instruction in their international obligations.

While the Belgian Parliament deliberated the bill for a new colonial law, Slocum's successor, the new U.S. consul general at Boma, James Smith, and Vice Consul Lucien Memminger were deep into yet another examination of conditions on the ground in "Kongo." The two had left Boma August 1 and sailed to Matadi, where they caught the overnight train to Leopoldville, riding there in cars that were "uncomfortably small and far from clean." The fare for these 250 miles in first class, Consul General Smith reported to Washington, worked out to about sixteen cents per mile, "exorbitantly high" he thought for the right to occupy one of twelve swivel seats in a tiny enclosed car accompanied by only sixty pounds of baggage. (Second-class transportation was on narrow benches in an open car and permitted just twenty pounds of baggage. Only Congolese traveled in second class.)

"The importance of Leopoldville," Smith explained to Secretary Root, "arises from its being the terminal of the railroad from Matadi and the port of departure for the steamers leaving for the upper Kongo, and it is also, with the exception of the region around Stanley Falls, the end of the free-trade zone. Beyond this point practically the entire territory of the Kongo is exploited by the State itself, or by concessionary companies in which the State holds a large, and in many cases, controlling interest."

Near the end of November, after traveling by boat and on foot for three months, the two submitted individual reports to the secretary of state, explaining exactly what "exploited by the State itself" meant to the Congo's fifteen—or maybe as many as thirty, no one knew—millions: a condition equivalent to slavery in which men were "taxed" their labor to collect rubber for twenty or more days per month, and women and children also worked near-continuously in the baking and cross-country distribution of the manioc root flour loaves (kwanga), which tasted like boiled chestnuts and were the chief native foodstuff. Kwanga was free to the king's concession holders because its production and distribution was inflicted as a tax on their chattel.[12]

"That the obligations of the Kongo government toward the natives, as provided for in the Berlin act," Smith concluded from what he saw, "are being openly violated there is not the shadow of a doubt. . . . The tendency of this system is to brutalize rather than civilize—to force the native into such a condition of poverty and degradation that his future is a hopeless one, and to keep him there."

For would-be foreign traders, "exploited by the State" meant something different: no access to the Congo's natural products (rubber, ivory, or gum copal, a resin used in the manufacture of varnish), despite the guarantees of free trade in the basin elaborated in the Berlin act. "The Government is but one tremendous commercial organization," Smith wrote. "Its administrative machinery is worked to bar out all outside trade and to absolutely control for its own benefit and the concessionary companies the natural resources of the country. . . . The policy of the administration . . . is to extract the riches of the country at the lowest possible cost, and with the result that the profits accruing therefrom go to swell the dividends of the Europeans interested, and neither the country nor its inhabitants receive any corresponding benefit."

On February 4, 1908, the Belgian government withdrew the draft annexation treaty from parliamentary consideration, with the new prime minister, Frans Schollaert, reportedly explaining to the king that passage was impossible unless Belgium had "unrestricted sovereignty throughout every part of the Kongo," meaning that crown lands could not be exempted from the transfer.

The challenge the Belgian Parliament faced, amid the static hum of increasingly impatient commentary from foreign governments, the popular press, and reform movements, was intimidating. It required the extraction of the king from the Congo without humiliating his supporters and other conservative Belgians, and the assumption of the Congo's assets and liabilities on a basis the small country could afford that somehow acknowledged the legal status of and economic importance of proprietary corporations and concessionary companies. These dozen-plus companies held sway over more than 60 percent of the Congo's land and dominated rubber collection, the stuff of 85 percent of all exports and the financial bedrock beneath the future colony.[13]

The cessation and annexation deal, as it was finally struck in negotiations through the spring and into summer, bought off the king through the provision of two special funds, one equivalent to $9 million to carry forward "philanthropic, scientific, or other projects" that Leopold claimed were under way and the other—a buyout described as "a token of national gratitude"—of $10 million, payable to the king in annual installments over fifteen years.

57

On August 20, 1908, the Belgian Chamber of Deputies, the country's parliamentary lower house, voted to annex the Congo Free State. Three weeks later, on September 9, the Senate did the same, and with that and after some weeks of administrative shuffling the Congo Free State officially became the Belgian Congo on November 15 with the transfer of sovereignty. Parliament agreed that the concessions granted in 1906 to the American Congo Company and others would be honored going forward.

Watching the shuffle, John Daniels, corresponding secretary of the Congo Reform Association, wrote that as king-sovereign of the Congo, Leopold had given it away with one hand, and as king of the Belgians, had taken it up with the other.[14] Many thought Leopold had done little more than moving change from one pocket to another.

Conan Doyle contemplated the change in Congo's status to Belgian colony with horror, but none of Conan Doyle's idealistic ideas for other outcomes (or anyone else's) ever got beyond appearing as paragraphs on a page. "The Belgians have been given their chance," he'd written in the final chapter of *The Crime of the Congo*. "They have had nearly twenty-five years of undisturbed possession, and they have made it a hell on earth. They cannot disassociate themselves from this work and pretend that it was done by a separate State. It was done by a Belgian king, Belgian soldiers, Belgian financiers, Belgian lawyers, Belgian capital, and was endorsed and defended by Belgian Governments. It is out of the question that Belgium should remain on the Congo." But Belgium did, for more than fifty years.

Modest ceremonies in Boma had marked the adoption by Belgium of the Congo in November 1908. On June 30, 1960, in the great circular hall of the National Palace (the same building was to have been the Belgian governor general's residence), King Baudouin I presented the Congolese with their independence—hastily, before they wrenched it from him. Some Belgians had seen colonial status extending another generation or more into the future, but the turnover had been accelerated by riots during the past year.

During the ceremony Baudouin (1930–1993), Leopold II's great grand-nephew and the fifth in Belgium's royal succession, was embarrassed by bitter remarks ad-libbed by Prime Minister–designate Patrice Lumumba. That was the second act of lèse-majesté the young king had suffered in as many days. The day before, while his motorcade was proceeding slowly through the capital with Baudouin standing stiffly in an open limousine, his handsome all-white uniform dramatizing the chasm between the Belgian royal house and its black subjects, a bystander had rushed up and snatched the king's dress sword. The bold act, caught in a photograph that found its way around the world—an exultant Ambroise Boimbo on foot, brandishing the sword behind an oblivious and disarmed Baudouin driving off—was a very small revenge for the major crimes and minor indignities inflicted on all Congolese in the past eighty-five years.

Epilogue

In the darkness of river and forest you could be sure only of what you could see—and even on a moonlit night you couldn't see much. When you made a noise—dipped a paddle in the water—you heard yourself as though you were another person. The river and the forest were like presences, and more powerful than you. You felt unprotected, an intruder. . . . You felt the land taking you back to something that was familiar. Something you had known at some time but forgotten or ignored, but which was always there. You felt the land taking you back to what was there a hundred years ago, to what had been there always.

V. S. Naipaul, A Bend in the River

Nothing in *Through the Brazilian Wilderness* (Charles Scribner's Sons, 1914), Theodore Roosevelt's book about his catastrophic expedition on a tributary of the Amazon River, or in papers about it he went on to present to American learned societies, hints that the expedition nearly disintegrated while it plumbed the Rio da Dúvida, or that he almost died on its banks. The true story can be found in Candace Millard's *River of Doubt: Theodore Roosevelt's Darkest Journey* (Doubleday, 2005) or in a broader context but more briefly in the last volume of Edmund Morris' magisterial biography of the late president, *Colonel Roosevelt* (Random House, 2010).

Roosevelt's trials on the Amazon a century ago were on my mind during the spring and summer of 2011, while my son, Jason, and I prepared for our own river expedition, a near month-long trip down the Congo from Kisangani to Banana Point on the Atlantic in first one and then another small outboard motorboat, the second of near-dingy size.

I looked forward to our trip—timed to match Emory Taunt's return to the Atlantic Coast in 1885 after his few days' stop at Stanley Falls Station, at about his speed—with trepidation. This despite the fact that river trips had been done successfully not very long ago, first by Jeffrey Tayler, seven years later by Thomas Butcher, and most recently by Arne Doornebal. All three men my juniors by a generation.

In *Facing the Congo* (Three Rivers Press, 2000), Tayler explained frankly that his determination to ride the river came from dissatisfactions with his life as an expatriate in Moscow and a desire to revitalize himself, less an exploration of any particular place than a voyage of self-discovery, the usual subtext of most road trip books. Butcher's broader motives behind his horrific *Blood River* (Grove Press, 2007) were tied to his status as the *London Evening Standard*'s Africa correspondent, making him the professional descendant of the first *Standard* correspondent to have traveled down the river, Henry Morton Stanley. Duplicating a part of Stanley's trek gave Butcher a way to reconsider his reportorial beat and to confront its history. In 2011 Doornebal, a young Dutch freelancer living in Uganda with his wife, hitchhiked down the river from Kisangani to Kinshasa on a month-long barge trip, looking for copy and for professional visibility in Europe.

One goal of my expedition with Jason was to emerge after some 1,400 miles of downriver and cross-country travel intact and in reasonable health, not necessarily trivial achievements for foreigners wandering the Democratic Republic of the Congo. Notably, during the past several years the American Embassy in Kinshasa has announced safety, health, or other warnings to American residents and tourists in the DRC at an average rate of roughly one per month. An "emergency message for U.S. citizens" issued by the embassy several days before we landed in Kinshasa, for example, warned recipients about a cholera epidemic just appearing in the capital after erupting in Kisangani in March. The last cholera epidemic in the United States was a century ago. By the end of 2011 some 20,000 Congolese from both sides of the river had caught the water-borne disease as it spread west from its origin near the great African lakes. Perhaps a thousand of them, 5 percent, died from it, a low rate of fatalities judged by the standards of the global cholera pandemics of the nineteenth century.

Moreover, registering our itinerary on the State Department's Smart Traveler Enrollment Program site, as the department recommended, brought with no promise of any help that mattered in the event of real trouble. Nothing like the saber-rattling U.S. response that in the summer of 1904 had seen Ion Perdicaris, sixty-four, and his stepson freed from the grasp of Berber kidnappers after six weeks captivity in the mountains of Morocco.[1] No one was going to dispatch two squadrons of Navy ships or even a lone SEAL to the mouth of the Congo if we were snatched and held in the equatorial bush for ransom. We'd be lucky if some official in Washington were to go as far as sending an e-mail.

My other goal was to understand through our experience how the Congo River might have appeared to and affected Lt. Emory Taunt in the 1880s, and how to describe it and that to you, the reader. Butcher, especially, helped me believe that this second purpose could be achieved. In *Blood River* he'd described a country spinning backward through time. While the rest of the world moved into the future, the Congo Butcher passed through five years ago was everywhere swirling back into its own miserable past. It was this past—the original creation of King Leopold II of the Belgians, later perfected by the home-grown despot Mobutu Sese Seku—and the tropical terrain it played out on that I hoped the trip would help me better to understand and describe. In Naipaul's words, I hoped riding the Congo River would take me "back to what was there a hundred years ago, to what had been there always."

Jason and I joined up, both of us stupid with travel fatigue, a little after two o'clock in the morning August 26, 2011, in the darkened passenger terminal of Nairobi's Jomo Kenyatta International Airport. I got to East Africa from Washington through Istanbul an hour ahead of Jason. He flew there from his home in Iowa via Chicago, both New York City airports, and Cairo, a more difficult trip. The two round-trip tickets to Kenya zeroed out the family's frequent flyer miles. Each of us was carrying a backpack with several changes of mosquito repellent–impregnated clothes, camping accessories, and the medicines that obsessive readings of the Centers for Disease Control and Prevention's website suggested no savvy central African traveler would step on the ground without. Together he and I also packed enough extra repellent to threaten extinction to entire species of "suctorial" (Reverend Bentley's descriptive word) flying insects. From inside the cloud of DEET we inhabited, we saw very few mosquitoes during the several weeks that followed, and surprisingly nothing of the Congo's wildlife, either, outside of a reserve. The explanation we got in passing from a disappointed European tourist we ran into at Lisala was "they've eaten it all." (Not all. In December 2010 a South African kayaker was killed by a crocodile on the Lukuga River, a tributary of the Lualaba known for its dangerous concentrations of hippos and crocs.)

Other than a daily dose of Malarone, an antimalarial, the only medicines we used were Gatifloxacin drops for curing eye infections and a few Loperamide capsules to combat diarrhea. The thirty-pound, waterproofed shock/trauma kit Jason hauled with us covered, I joked, every medical specialty but obstetrics, but we never used any of it. Approaching the end of our trip the intact kit was donated to the Centre de Santé Mère et Enfant in Boma, where as near as we could tell its contents represented the only sterile health-care stuff in the building.

Once together in Nairobi we spent six restless hours waiting for Kenya Airways Flight 554 to Kinshasa, on a Boeing 767, to start check-in. When it did our great adventure almost died at the departure gate, where a young, English-speaking agent misread our French-language DRC visas, wrongly decided they had expired, and denied us boarding. She explained that with invalid visas we would be refused entry into Congo and our expulsion on arrival would cost Kenya Airways a big fine and our return airfare. An hour or so of increasingly desperate cross-cultural pleading, and the failure of her supervisor to show up, got us on the aircraft among the last few to board. Had she not relented, our expedition would have been over the day after it began.

Our outbound passage through Jomo Kenyatta International, overnight September 15–16, was much less stressful. It featured a hot shower, dinner overlooking antelopes grazing stylishly behind the fence line of the neighboring game park, and a nap at the Hotel Ole-Sereni before departures just after midnight toward home through Cairo and Istanbul.

During these few hours on its paved and illuminated roads and in a modern hotel, after Kinshasa, the Kenyan capital represented the good life to us, a return to the present century in the form of twentieth-century sanitation, infrastructure, and comforts. That same night more than one hundred Nairobi slum dwellers died horribly not far away, in a flash fire at a leaking gasoline pipeline from the port of Mombasa that ran between the airport and the city center directly beneath their huts. An explosion at the site of the leak incinerated many who had gathered around the break to steal fuel. The catastrophe (a replay of several similar disasters) erased the illusion that we'd passed from the land of poor government and no regulation to the land of the good.

Our original plan had been to fly from Nairobi direct to Kisangani and to start our downriver trip the morning after arrival, but Kenya Airways' summer schedule changes put us first in Kinshasa and then two forced overnights in the capital before we could connect that Sunday with CAA's (Compagnie Africaine d'Aviation) Kinshasa-Kisangani service.

Africa is the elephant's graveyard for old commercial transport aircraft, with the result that the hardstand at Kinshasa's N'djili International Airport could double for an underfunded outdoor aviation museum. Too bad photography of this "strategic site" is prohibited. The airport terminal itself looks like the anteroom to Purgatory and operates under similar rules. We were fortunate to slide through arrival formalities, our passage greased by a helpful "protocol," a paid facilitator who ran interference for us. Absent him, Jason and I could have expected to face together the infamous gauntlet of grasping customs and immigration officials, grabby baggage handlers, and larcenous taxi drivers that challenges every arriving foreigner, before collapsing in the Hotel Invest, one of the capital's more modest hotels for foreigners.

We'd been booked out to Kisangani the same day on a Hewa Bora flight, but the airline (its name means "Fresh Air" in Swahili) had lost its operating certificate three weeks before we arrived after suffering a 727 crash at Kisangani that killed most of the people on board, Hewa Bora's third fatal accident in as many years. The rumors were that the airline's CEO had insisted that Flight 952 land in a storm instead of diverting to Goma and better weather. On July 8, when Hewa Bora's 727 hit the ground a thousand yards short of Runway 31 at Kisangani, the veteran Boeing aircraft was forty-six years old and had logged more than 52,600 flight hours. Since delivery to United in late 1965, the jet had flown in the livery of at least thirteen airlines and worn the registration marks of as many countries. A flying hand-me-down.

CAA's safety record is imperfect, but through the summer of 2011 they hadn't killed anyone, and their Flight 320 to Kisangani with us on board was uneventful. In general, domestic air travel in the Congo does not lift one above the fray. Hewa Bora's sudden grounding aside (the carrier now operates under another name), government regulation of air carriers registered in the DRC is so problematic that they are forbidden from flying in European and American airspace. Similarly, official travel by American embassy and government contract employees is prohibited on "most airlines flying domestic routes in the DRC." The guidance forces civilians, people like us who do not have the option to fly on UN or government aircraft, to take their chances. The DRC is large, the size of the United States east of the Mississippi, but it boasts operating rail and paved road systems measured in only hundreds of miles (consider that just four of Congo's provincial capitals are connected to Kinshasa by road) and has no scheduled, long-haul passenger service on its rivers. Flying is often literally the only way to go.

Our next and last internal flight, Muanda-Matadi-Kinshasa, with Kin Avia near the end of our trip on September 14, was also on time and uneventful. The airline operates Czech-built Let-410s, unpressurized nineteen-seat twin turboprops, an aircraft not fundamentally dissimilar from the smallest regional transports in the U.S. system, to eight destinations in the country. Ours was likely built sometime after 1986, but the type has been flying since 1970. Eleven hundred were built in what was obviously a successful program, and some five hundred are still believed to be in service, most in smaller, Third World markets.

Had I known of it, the Let 410's recent safety record—four fatal accidents since August 2010, the first of them in a Filair aircraft credited to an escaped crocodile causing panic in the passenger compartment on a flight from Kinshasa to Bandundu—might have caused us to rethink our return to the capital, but we had no alternative to flying. Turboprops are not inherently less safe than are pure jets, despite the complications of a reduction gear box and propeller, and I happily spent years piloting Navy four-engine turboprops, but aviation safety requires a highly proficient government oversight infrastructure and expertise in and around the aircraft. There isn't much of either in the Congo.

The story about the crocodile in the aircraft is almost certainly apocryphal, however, the equivalent of a central African urban legend. African flying crocodile stories pop up in accident reports about as often as do the stories of lamb barbeques on dung-fire braziers in the aisles of aircraft flying hajj pilgrims to or from Mecca. After investigation, the usual explanation for an accident anywhere on the globe is often much more prosaic: pilot error.

Our schedule required us to pass through the Congolese capital three times: on arrival, in between our two legs on the river, and overnight at expedition's end, just before leaving for Nairobi and home. Eight to 10 million people are thought to live in Kinshasa's twenty-four "communes," the government municipalities into which the city is divided. Together, these twenty-four span a metropolitan area (some of it very thinly settled) that encompasses some 3,800 square miles around a central, 60-square-mile core—much more than ten times the size of New York City or twice the area of Delaware—all lying on ten or so miles of riverfront and minutes away by ferry from the capital of the former French colony on the opposite bank, the Republic of the Congo.

One must be cautious coming to quick judgments about a distant metropolis, whose citizens are a different color and speak a different language and whose own government cannot fix its population within 20 percent. Our several days in and around Kinshasa and repeat passes through N'djili and the domestic airport at N'dolo (not far from the site of the original train terminal) were quick glimpses of a huge city, one whose daily life as we observed it appeared to be a demonstration of Brownian movement, the random motion of small things impelled by a mysterious force.

The Congo has beautiful places. The "mob of wooded islands" in the upper river that Conrad noted, many of which look today as they must have before Stanley first saw them. The southern shore of Pool Malebo, with palm-clad hills eroded into almost organic forms. The lush mangrove swamps between Boma and Banana on the lower river, whose open leads are larded with small fishing villages nearly obscured behind mounds of chalk-colored shells. Beautiful images, too: fishermen standing on unseen dugouts as if supported magically by the mirrored water alone, casting purse nets into the river and recovering them with almost balletic grace. Such delights are rare.

Countless thousands of dugout canoes (granted, none with paddles of silver) and many other boats have moved over the Congo River since Vachel Lindsay wrote his poem almost a century ago, but sadly his lone vulture still has it right: No angels sail on the river, equatorial Africa is not yet the "land transfigured," and Mumbo-Jumbo's spell still blights the jungle. Indeed, in November 2012, while violent warfare roils its eastern provinces, the Democratic Republic of the Congo's tragic plight seems irreversible for its nearly 74 million citizens.[2]

The United Nation's 2011 assessment of human development indicators, a rank ordering of its member nations on the basis of citizens' average health, education, and income, put the Congo dead last on the list, in the nasty neighborhood behind Burundi and Niger. In no other index then or since comparing states, rating such matters as government corruption or the ease of starting and running a business, does the DRC manage to climb out of the lowest quintile. Other statistics are unrelievedly grim. Fewer than one in four Congolese has access to pure drinking water, fewer than one in ten to even sporadic electric power. Another example: Today a male Congolese's life expectancy at birth is just forty-eight years, barely one year longer than was an American's born in 1900.

For the most part the Congo is a demonstration of entropy on a subcontinental scale. This seems especially true of Kinshasa. Known as "Kin la Belle" when its population was a fraction of today's, only a weak-eyed romantic would call the city "Kinshasa the beautiful" now. Sharp-tongued cynics substitute "la poubelle," the trash can, for "la belle." The best its boosters can claim is that Kinshasa's streets, home to long-suffering Kinois, are slowly recovering from the deliberate destruction of rampaging troops that scarred the city in 1991–93 and the impoverished neglect that followed.

The only evidence of the twenty-first century most urban Congolese see—those living outside of the better downtown neighborhoods that house walled hotels, fortified embassy compounds, and hardened UN posts—is bright billboards hawking in French the virtues of one or another brand of beer, cell phone network, hair straightener, skin lightener, or powdered milk product to a population the greatest part of which owns little more than a pair of flip-flops and a scant outfit of clothes from Goodwill.

Much more apparent than signs of the present in the four cities we passed through are the harbingers of a future world in which Reverend Thomas Malthus' terrible arithmetic about population and the food supply, and the worst nightmares of environmentalists, might yet be proved correct:

vast, claustrophobic slums suffocating in a thick, toxic cloud of dust, smoke from garbage fires, and vehicle exhaust, seasoned by rotting smells, that must be visible from Earth orbit. A few hours after arrival your throat is sore from breathing the abrasive air. Huge, fluid crowds of unemployed and underemployed people move about on foot on missions of survival. Herds of battered trucks, buses, and cars that could be licensed to operate nowhere else, migrate on traffic-strangled boulevards, hauling unrecognizable freight or packed with passengers stacked on board like cordwood. Rickety market stalls sell life's bare essentials. Often—like the bagged leaf dust from Sri Lanka that passes for tea—the detritus of other countries.

The Congo is cited as the base case of what economic geographers have described as "the tyranny of geography," a combination of isolation from world markets (think again about the cataracts between Kinshasa and Matadi), poor soils and low agricultural productivity, and endemic disease. Like North Korea, however, the Congo is a victim of history more than of geography. A century and a half of venal misgovernment has drained the wealth pried from the earth into the hands of despots, exploiters, and foreign warriors. No wonder that the arterial streets of the cities host nightly parades of lean men and women and small children apparently living on little more substance than do air plants.

We sampled several of Kinshasa's tourist attractions while waiting impatiently for CAA to fly us to Kisangani. The best known is probably Lola ya Bonobo, the ape sanctuary in the woodlands near Lukuya Falls, southwest of the city. Bonobos, somewhat smaller than their near-relatives, chimpanzees (we humans are their other nearest relatives), and no better looking, are the fourth of the great ape species. They're native only to the Congo, and the operation of this refuge represents a real commitment in a hungry country where monkeys and apes are edible protein. Their charred bodies lie, like small victims of arson, in market food stalls right next to tables displaying the catch of the day. Some of the bonobos in this sanctuary have been rescued from just such a fate, or orphaned by it.

Another of the capital's attractions is the tomb of assassinated President Laurent Kabila, the father of the current president, Joseph Kabila. His sarcophagus is in a glass case inside of a circular, flag-bedecked memorial near the Palais du Peuple, the Chinese-built home for the national legislature. A bronze statue of the late Kabila, in the massive proportions of Fernando Botero, looms in front of the mausoleum. It was cast in North Korea, and some claim that its sculptor affixed a likeness of Kabila's head to a surplus Kim Il Sung body. The monument's proximity to the government hall puts the tomb inside a security zone, and because civilians in Kin la Belle don't look for extra face time with young, armed soldiers collecting bribes, attendance at the site is sparse.

In 1997 the first Kabila (1939–2001) ousted Mobutu, Congo's native dictator and the model for the Great Man in Naipaul's 1979 novel about life in postcolonial Africa. Kabila then began his own era of corruption and misrule, a period punctuated by two wars during which the armies of half a dozen neighbors crossed Congo's borders to join the fight against one another and for its wealth, and perhaps 4 million people died. (Some say as few as 3 million. Every number in the Congo is very soft.)

Kabila's murder by one of his bodyguards in January 2001 triggered a two-year trial of more than one hundred defendants. Eventually, roughly half of them were sentenced to prison and another fifth were condemned to death. Days after the assassination Joseph Kabila, twenty-nine, was inaugurated to replace his father. He was elected to his own term in November and inaugurated in December 2011. That election was somewhat less corrupt and violent than outside observers had feared it would be, considering how weak his support in the capital was.

As one nineteenth-century travel critic gracelessly said about another place, the city's tourist sites "are secured, in a measure, from abuse by the mediocrity of their splendor and attractions." In fairness to Kinshasa, however, we didn't come to the DRC to tour its capital. We came to see the river.

Just after 9:30 in the morning, August 29, we six—Jason and I, and our Congolese crew of four—cast off from Kisangani and headed downriver. In my log I dutifully entered the GPS departure coordinates as 0° 30.49' N, 25° 10.5' E and our elevation as 1,244 feet above sea level. The night before at Kisangani's imaginatively named Palm Beach Hotel we'd met the crew over bottles of Primus beer, on a patio crowded with off-duty white troops from the local detachment of UN peacekeepers in the Congo, MONUSCO. (The acronym comes from the mission's name in French.) MONUSCO's approximately 24,000 soldiers and civilians constitute the largest deployed United Nations uniformed force in the world. Its all-white vehicles and aircraft are common on and above the ground in Congo.

My first sight of our boat for the next 1,100 miles came a few minutes before departure, while she was out in the stream with Alain, our coxswain, and Jean, his assistant, on board. The two were maneuvering to ensure her load, our fuel, food, bottled water, everyone's gear, a charcoal brazier, three plastic chairs, and a small table, was well balanced. It was, well enough, and Wivene (our cook, recruited overnight after her predecessor quit), Frederick (our interpreter), Jason, and I clambered on board.

Days later I realized that what had looked like a near-wreck at first inspection was a riverboat in sound condition by local standards. Only then did I understand how naive had been my assumption that our small vessel would be equipped with two outboard engines, the second for reliability in case the first failed in midstream on the long trip. Powerboats are uncommon enough on the Congo that the approaching sound of our motor brought excited, hand-waving children and adults down to the riverbank to watch us pass everywhere. A second engine would have represented an unaffordable and perhaps unobtainable luxury. On arrival at Kinkole days later, the same tireless two-stroke, 55-hp engine was trucked to Matadi, where we used it on our second—even smaller and much less seaworthy—boat to power us the rest of the way to the Atlantic.

Propelled by the outboard and thrust ahead by the Congo's current, we traveled downstream (and often cross-stream, Alain navigated by asking other boaters where we were) at about ten knots. Riverboats in Taunt's era could go as fast, although most cruised economically at around eight.

Two days out of Kisangani, at Bumba near the top of the great bend in the Congo, we ran low on bottled water. Alain's solution was to scour out several of our now-empty gasoline jugs with bottom sand and river water and fill them from the Congo for use in cooking. His economy move could easily have brewed up something intestinal that even 1,000 milligrams of ciprofloxacin a day times three couldn't handle. There are no sewage treatment plants anywhere in the DRC. Raw human waste is dumped directly into rivers and streams in those places where it doesn't leach there naturally. From then on Alain and I were agreed that we would do nothing with the water of the Congo beyond floating on it.

Time on the river quickly settled into a routine. Up with the roosters well before sunrise; under way on bread, jam, and instant coffee soon after; a cold lunch afloat, and a search for a campsite beginning around 5:00 p.m., so that our tent could be erected and the cooking fire started by twilight. As day's end approached, Alain would bounce us along the shore, looking for a small village or a fish camp where we could roost overnight.

Only once did village elders deny our request to camp among them. Elsewhere we were met with curiosity and grave courtesy. In several villages the campsite offered was carefully swept clean before we settled into place, a generous and welcoming gesture, as was an occasional gift of chicken eggs. I'd expected tent camping overnight. I had not expected that our tent would be erected in the middle of these small, hospitable villages, never more than a few yards away from the huts of our hosts or a few minutes' walk past the tree line to the hole in the ground that was the community pit toilet.

Figure 30. Our riverboat on the left bank at Kisangani, with Alain and Jean pre-paring to get her under way after checking trim. Most of the interior space was preempted by about three dozen twenty-five-liter jugs being thriftily recycled as unvented gasoline containers. Emptied of their original contents, "golden pure" palm oil, these bright yellow plastic jugs are the all-purpose jerry cans of the Congo and conspicuous everywhere. Everybody and everything else was wedged into the boat around our fuel supply. We had life preservers, but not until much later did I notice we carried no poles or paddles in case of engine failure. *AUTHOR'S PHOTOGRAPH*

The pattern changed only at Mbandaka, the capital of Équateur Province and our interpreter's home town. Frederick, dignified, personable, and articulate in three languages, was a Mongo, a member of one of the several largest of Congo's more than two hundred tribes. Educated as a minister, he alone among our crew had seen the outside world during six months in the English midlands. Those perspectives and easy communica-tion with us made his relations with Alain, his nominal boss, awkward as both maneuvered for status and leadership. A motorboat is a very small arena for this kind of competition.

We camped for two nights just downriver of Mbandaka and its run-down port. Here our tent went up on grass, the riverfront lawn of the vacant and for-sale brick house of a retired American minister and his family now living in the United States. While Alain scrounged for gas, often sold in the Congo in recycled liter bottles but here sometimes available at stations, we visited Stanley's stone marker on the equator (at 0° 1.5′ north, 18° 13.7′ east misplaced more than a mile north), the sadly neglected botanical garden at Eala (home of a caged, aged, and perhaps dead crocodile; we never saw it breathe), and the Bibliothèque Aequatoria, a two-room archive of molding Belgian colonial documents on the grounds of the eighty-year-old Church of the Missionaries of the Sacred Heart.

At Mbandaka we had two rival local immigration officials vying for our attention. Both insisted on a careful examination of our passports and, to no apparent purpose, on laboriously copying down our identity details and visa information into spiral bound notebooks full of other such penciled entries, every one presumably representing some amount of Congolese francs in fees. Here and elsewhere such bureaucratic procedures easily ate up an hour or more and opened opportunities for problems. We made it a practice to avoid coming ashore anywhere near a shed flying a DRC flag, the sign of an outpost of central authority. For the same reason, to avoid extra hassles, at the end of this travel leg on September 8 we disembarked at Kinkole, a fishing port miles upriver of Kinshasa's waterfront.

A powerful thunderstorm on the morning of our departure from Mbandaka kept us off the river for several hours, one of the several rain- and windstorms during our passage that marked the coming start of the rainy season. Our boat's side curtains acted as sails. Dropped into place, they made the narrow, shallow-draft hull dangerously unstable in any gust of wind. We necessarily left them up in the rain, guaranteeing in minutes a soaking equivalent to swimming.

Mbandaka was the last place our new SPOT satellite position reporting and communications system worked. From arrival in the Congo until September 5 our GPS position was regularly uplinked to an Earth observation satellite overhead, and down from it to Suzy, my wife, at our son's house in central Iowa. The AAA battery–powered system, contained in two pocket-sized devices, also incorporated a rudimentary, one-way communication channel for short text messages and "Help" and "SOS" functions. While it worked, it was marvelous: Suzy could follow our track down the Congo practically in real time. After Mbandaka we still had position, elevation, and speed information, but we were mute and she was anxious.

The only potentially serious incident came during our seventh night out of Kisangani, below the Congo's confluence with the Ubangi and some 740 miles downriver. We made camp among young fishermen, who some time before we came ashore began drinking palm wine under a tree very near to where we were invited to put up our tent. By 10:30 their discussion was nearing a bar-fight level of enthusiasm. Approaching midnight the overheard conversation turned to talk about *mundele*, "white men," the only word of Lingala either of us, unable to see anything outside the tent and now feeling very vulnerable, understood.

In Washington before departure I'd called on the State Department's DRC desk officer for a conversation about where we were going and what we planned to do there. Our useful discussion included his advice that wherever we were, we should always have an exit in mind. That counsel remembered, Jason and I now bundled up our gear, unzipped the tent flap, and walked quickly downhill to our boat, pulled up on shore with the crew bedded down on deck. Our sudden bail-out astonished them no less than it did the fun-lovers crowded around the tree, where Alain and Frederick now went to sound things out.

After a quick conversation with our hosts—some embarrassed and some belligerent—the two returned to confirm without explanation that we ought to leave. An hour or so later we made a cold camp on boggy ground on an island downriver, at the first flat place we came upon in the dark. There some kind of nocturnal marsh wildlife filled the quiet of the night with its call, "rat," pronouncing the word clearly and emphatically in competition with its fellows in a cascade of louder and louder repetitions. These could have been the chants of happy human rodent hunters, but a better guess is that we were hearing the song of the African common toad.

At 2:45 p.m., September 8, we disembarked in Kinkole, a chaotic boat landing rather than anything as orderly as a port, wet and tired after spending the day fighting headwinds in the narrows below Kwamouth. Departure from the last (ninth) camp, a small farming village called Fermesan by the few families who lived there, that morning had been a little after six—a careful walk in the dark to our boat around a large, open pit that separated the village and river from which someone was digging out thousands of clay bricks by hand.

At day's end in Kinkole, an uphill hike through a fleet of beached dugouts and other boats brought us into Kinshasa's great fish market and its stunning smells (no refrigeration and no ice), beyond it to a car and a twenty-mile ride at dusk down Boulevard Lumumba, past N'djili International Airport, into the center city and our hotel. The drive took us through traffic and pedestrian throngs so dense and determined it appeared that the city and port were exchanging evacuated populations.

Along more than a thousand miles of the river between Kisangani and Maluku, the port and sawmill at the entrance to Pool Malebo, and outside of cities and the big market towns, life is lived much as it was in the nineteenth century. Both sexes today naturally assume roles and adopt postures that have been traditional along the Congo for centuries. Men stand in dugouts on flat water to fish with nets. Women sit on low stools over cooking fires in front of huts roofed with leaves. The small, open spaces of every village are alive with young, half-naked children playing; their slightly older siblings are already working alongside their parents. Travel, by dugout, is rarely farther than to the nearest market town. Everyone is trying to cope. Life for most people has to do largely with getting, preparing, and eating food.

Rusting wrecks occasionally dot the river's banks. Here and there long-abandoned industrial buildings above the high-water line also hint at the country's past, but like the wrecks these factory ruins have little to do with the fishermen and farmers of today. Only in a few places is any use improvised from these relics. Otherwise, the Congo River is what it has always been, a source of food and water for every purpose, but—surprisingly—little else.

Stanley once, very improbably, compared the Congo to the Mississippi, but the river has not become the great transportation artery that Europeans and later Americans imagined it would be. The few commercial vessels that move along the Congo today between Kinshasa and Kisangani—tugboats under clouds of oily, black smoke pushing barge trains packed with a jumble of deck cargo and teeming with encamped squatters—look like escape capsules from the apocalypse and nothing like links in a modern logistics chain. Even more unsteady are the rafts of debarked trees chained together and pushed downriver, occupied by small communities of people and their animals riding confidently on an undulating deck a few inches above the water. We never saw any of the passenger ferries that the Democratic Republic of the Congo's National Transportation Office (ONTARA) claims it is putting into service as part of President Joseph Kabila's widely touted and largely invisible "Five Pillars of Development" program.

Since the early nineteenth century, Matadi, now the capital of the DRC's Bas-Congo Province, has been the white man's gate to the heart of the continent west of the great East African rift. Early the morning of September 11, Jason and I left Kinshasa to go there, the port of departure for the rest of our trip to the mouth of the river. Our plan was to overnight in the city and to leave the following afternoon by small boat for Banana via Boma. For the next four days, until we left for home, we'd be staying in hotels.

We chose not to fly, thinking to reduce our exposure to sudden attacks of gravity. A train would have been my choice of transportation to Matadi. Approaching the end of the run we could have watched the Erector-set girders of the M'poso River bridge flicker past our windows, signaling entrance into the S turn that feeds out to the rocky shelf excavated from the Congo's bank. A little while later we would have eased to a stop at the terminal, arriving in the old colonial town exactly as travelers might have decades ago.

Joseph Conrad wrote about the construction of this part of the railroad in *Heart of Darkness,* a few sentences about "a boiler wallowing in the grass . . . an undersized railway truck lying on its back with its wheels in the air . . . decaying machinery, a stack of rusty rails . . . a heavy and dull detonation . . . objectless blasting." He hiked past the site in mid-1890, on the way, he thought, to join his boat on the upper river and to take command. Pushing the right-of-way these first sixteen miles through and over the rocks of Matadi was the most difficult and costly part of the whole project, and it was probably as dangerous and chaotic as Conrad makes it sound. More than 1,800 Africans and Asians died constructing the railroad, together with a few dozen Europeans.

Until a decade ago it was possible to ride the rails to Matadi, twelve hours from Kinshasa, in the first-class L'Express, Train 50 or 52 depending on the day of the week. While it lasted, the Express, pulling a consist that included a buffet car with hostess service, was the successor to the Congo's name trains of the last century, the Train Blanc and the Train Bleu. Back then one could also go to Matadi more economically, but much less comfortably, in the commuter-class Train 51 or 53. These carried people, small livestock, and their associated odors from terminal to terminal in a scheduled sixteen hours, likely longer.

Twice a week passenger train service between the two cities, twenty-five dollars each way, ended in 2006, killed off by strandings on the line caused by breakdowns and by improved security on the road. That's how Jason and I went, seven hours on the N-1, a narrow, two-lane toll road (one in each direction, no guardrails, open drainage ditches) that is Kinshasa's chief connection by land to the country's principal ocean port and everything to its west all the way to Muanda on the Atlantic. Stripped and rusted remains of past wrecks and breakdowns line its shoulders, the way I imagine bleached ox skeletons marked the 2,000 miles of the Oregon Trail in the mid-nineteenth century. This shattered scrap on both sides of the road didn't intimidate our driver, François Lenta Mofiki, who cheerfully kept the accelerator on the floor and pressed on, offering us a chance to die on the road to Matadi.

The hilly, winding route took us over the Crystal Mountains, through Mbanza-Ngungu, past the derelict maintenance shops and rail yards at the old Thysville train station (the overnight stop on the original narrow-gauge line), everything rusting back into elemental iron, and finally into Matadi. In the nineteenth century Thysville was one of the Congo's colonial focal points. Serendipity put the midpoint of the railroad and the associated maintenance shops at a high enough elevation (around 2,200 feet) to ensure relatively pleasant weather much of the year. The result was a cluster of housing for European executives and employees of the railroad and of a nearby palm oil mill. The buildings are still there, their residents long since gone.

All there was of Matadi in those years hung onto a wide, stony ledge on the left bank of the river below the Congo's junction with the M'poso. The old European port town and railroad terminal (the white *ville*, still there like a time capsule with its Belgian- and Portuguese-style buildings) has metastasized up and over the surrounding hills (the black *cité*) toward Angola, more than doubling in population in the last twenty-five years. A view from atop Belvedere, at 837 feet above sea level the city's highest point, reveals a smoky vista encompassing cranes on the piers at riverside, the "strategic" Pont Maréchal suspension bridge (no tourist photos allowed here, either) across the Congo carrying the truck road west, and everywhere else a tufted carpet of small, metal-roofed block houses, homes to many of the city's third of a million residents.

Jason and I spent the next morning with Frederick and Terence Mwanza Ngombo hunting down the pieces of the porters' monument and the early afternoon impatiently awaiting a license to proceed down the river. A seventy-dollar fee to travel on the river paid and permission from the appropriate official finally in hand, we set off on the water again.

We'd dropped Wivene and Jean in Kinshasa and picked up a local boatman in Matadi as a pilot because Alain had never been on the lower river. Wivene was probably happy to leave. We'd been great disappointments to her. Jason is a vegetarian, and I became one, too, for the duration of the trip, being squeamish about what might be serving as animal protein on my plate. The result was we ate a lot of beans, rice, and plantain, with some fruit. A *lot* of fried plantain, but not enough to persuade Wivene that we liked her cooking and appreciated her contribution. She kept passing the same bottle of mayonnaise forward, and we kept passing it up, thinking about summertime midwestern picnics in the United States gone terribly wrong thanks to unrefrigerated mayonnaise.

Only very shallow draft vessels can move on the upper river, and even some of them run aground on the shifting sands. Between Kisangani and Maluku aids to navigation are limited to occasional white-painted, wooden pointers nailed to trees on the riverbanks, confirming the direction downstream but nothing more. The lower river, however, where deeper draft vessels operate—Matadi can take ships drawing twenty-seven feet—is buoyed to show the safe channel. But because dredging and other channel

Figure 31. Loading up at Matadi for the trip down the lower river. Our boat on this leg was a small, open, slab-sided fisherman, not the dugout we'd expected. Here Terence waits while Jason loads our gear. The six of us wedged on board, one behind the other, filled her. I sat forward, trying not to watch water seeping in everywhere between uncaulked boards and splashing into the air when we slapped a wave. A loose boulder bigger than a basketball rolled about in the bow in front of me. It balanced the weight of our trusty Yamaha outboard. Clad in high-topped boots and a vest full of tourist electronics, I would have beaten our ballast to the bottom if the boat had gone down. *AUTHOR'S PHOTOGRAPH*

maintenance is a sometime thing, here, too, vessels get stranded and have to wait to get towed free.

To nineteenth-century European eyes the lower Congo, flowing from the rapids through gently rolling banks on both sides, must have looked safe and familiar. Not until beyond Kwamouth on the upper river, where riverside greenery turns lush, or perhaps Bolobo, where islands first appear in the stream to confound navigation, does the Congo seem truly exotic. We powered our way downstream to Boma, "Embomma" centuries ago, through several hours of light rain and past a shipping anchorage off shore. There are several of these in the lower river, where vessels lie waiting to enter port or to head upriver to the cranes at Matadi. It all looked very twentieth century because the container carriers are small, dozens of cargo containers rather than hundreds (or thousands, which is the modern standard), their number limited by depth of water in the channel and alongside the wharf at Matadi and by the port's antiquated cargo-handling equipment.

These limitations, together with those imposed by the railroad and the N-1 highway from Muanda to the capital (a road that in the United States might connect county seats in the Ozarks), throttle the surface transportation connections the DRC has with the world economy. The Congo is not one of Africa's ten land-locked countries, but its connections to the ocean are very frail; capillaries, not arteries. The bottlenecks could be eased by infrastructure construction if Congo's economy could generate and pay for a higher level of demand for imports or produce a significant level of exports for the world market, but it's difficult to imagine that scenario.

At Boma we were greeted on arrival at the riverbank with a documents check and baggage inspection. Once freed, we passed up visits to two of Boma's tourist attractions, Stanley's baobab tree (he's supposed to have slept inside a great hole in its trunk in August 1877, exhausted at the end of his epic African crossing) and the rusty chassis of the Congo's first car, imported in 1905 and long since stripped to the frame. Our goal was to see what was left of Boma's distant decades as the Congo capital, Government House and the first cathedral.

For many reasons—one was the rate at which they died prematurely—early missionaries made very slow progress in their work of education and conversion. By the time Taunt died on the river in 1891, the work of proselytizing had been going on fitfully for centuries by Roman Catholics and not yet for decades by Protestants. In both cases, in numerical terms at the end of the nineteenth century, their accumulated successes were tiny but not vanishingly small. Despite its identification with colonialism, Christianity and especially Roman Catholicism has made the sale.

Notre Dame de l'Assomption in Boma, the contemporary cathedral right next to its historic prefabricated predecessor, is one of twenty-two cathedrals in the six Roman Catholic archdioceses of the DRC. The handsomest of them is at Kisantu, on the Inkisi River. Together the twenty-two and many smaller churches serve a population of communicants estimated at 35 million, every second Congolese. Another fifth or more are Protestants. Some among the latter adhere to home-grown Christian sects, like those who follow the teachings of the most popular native prophet, the late Simon Kimbangu. City streets are thick with rickety storefront chapels, whose names and colorful hand-painted signage promise grace and salvation to passersby in Jesus' name. In the country it's the same. Even tiny villages reserve some space for worship. Jason and I woke early one morning on the river to the sounds of an enthusiastic prayer service and fell asleep one evening at Maongi, our fifth camp, while a men's choir practiced multipart hymns prettily while night fell.

We left Boma at nine the next morning for Banana Point under a low deck of clouds but in dry weather. Hugging the bank of the river, an hour or so out, our new pilot followed a lead north and got us lost for an hour or so in a mangrove swamp. Earlier he'd explained that water levels on the river were unusually low and nothing looked exactly the same as he remembered. I watched on the GPS while we headed 90° off course and meandered through the leads until emerging back onto the river very near from where we'd gone wrong. The reappearance in front of us around noon of a small transport laboring downriver that we'd passed soon after departure from Boma in the morning gave away what had happened, and cost our pilot pro tem some status with Frederick. But the day had cleared, and beneath cornflower blue skies the mangroves were beautiful. The GPS scaled up had showed us where Banana was the entire time, and so the diversion was a treat.

A little less than five hours after departing Boma and 1,407 miles downriver from Kisangani we disembarked at Banana Point, once—bizarrely—the focus of the world's attention and now a forgotten sand spit. Two separate marine, customs, and immigration inspections—one on each side of the water approach to the point, the marine inspectors looking like a party of marooned beachcombers or bankrupt pirates—had slowed our arrival slightly, but finally standing very near where Emory Taunt had seen the Congo for his first and last time, Jason and I were elated. Nearby a boatload of Congolese refugees, caught by authorities sneaking into Angola and being forcibly returned home loudly protesting, reminded us that not everyone at Banana was happy to be there.

Acknowledgments

I'm grateful to Beth Miles and Colleen Houlahan of Houlahan Travel in Evanston, Illinois, and to Michel Van Roten of Go Congo in Kinshasa for organizing an astonishing expedition into Equatorial Africa in late summer 2011. My son, Jason, and I rode the length of the Congo River in a small boat with Alain Mawuba, coxswain, and Reverend Frederick Lombe, our interpreter. Jean Batanga Lifafu and Wivene Akomba Mokaka were also crew for the first 1,100 of those miles.

Our guide at Kisangani was Mabamvu Soleil. At the Bamanya Mission Village in Mbandaka, archivist Guillaume Essalo introduced us to the Bibliotheque Aequatoria's documents collection. François Lenta Mofiki drove us around the extensive Congo River cataracts between Kinshasa and Matadi. At Matadi, where the National Transportation Office's Paul Kunga Talula Sena showed us the railroad station he manages before we boarded an even smaller open boat for Boma and Banana, our guide was Terence Mwanza Ngombo.

Throughout our weeks-long adventure Evelyn Makita in Kinshasa worked tirelessly and successfully to clear away bureaucratic obstructions to travel in her country.

In the United States I owe a special debt to August Imholtz of Beltsville, Maryland, who first introduced me to Emory Taunt in 2006 and has, since then, continued to share his interest in and his sources about Taunt generously with me. More generally, Anita Barrett (Loudoun County, Virginia, Public Library), Rose Chou (National Anthropological Archive, Smithsonian Institution), Michael Brooks (University of Central Florida), Jennifer Bryan (Nimitz Library, U.S. Naval Academy), Julie Bushong (Culpeper County, Virginia, Public Library), Joan Green (Episcopal Diocese of Central New York), Halima Khanom (Royal Geographical Society), Mary Markey (Smithsonian Institution Archives), Judy McCary (Cong. Frank Wolf's staff, U.S. House of Representatives), Mark Mollan and Charles Johnson (National Archives and Records Administration, Washington, D.C.), John Sullivan (Fuller Evolutionary Biology Program, Cornell University), Lissa Schneider-Rebozo (University of Wisconsin, River Falls), Alicia Clarke

(Sanford Museum, Sanford, Florida), André Sobocinski (Navy Medicine Institute for the Medical Humanities, Washington, D.C.), Rick Swart (U.S. Department of State), John Stacey (Nanjemoy, Maryland), Meredith Wisner (Brooklyn Navy Yard), and Cynthia Van Ness (Buffalo and Erie County Historical Society) also helped.

Jim Burk (Oak Hill, Virginia), Alicia Clarke, Bart Houlahan (Devon, Pennsylvania), Mike Pestorius (Austin, Texas), and Lissa Schneider-Rebozo read the manuscript in draft and commented on it. Their generous help has improved it, for which I thank them. My thanks, too, to Karin Kaufman, who has copyedited all five of my books and made each one of them a better read.

Jason, our son (a former U.S. Army medic and now a veteran emergency room nurse—useful skill sets in Congo), joined me on the river. The trip would have been impossible without him, and I am especially grateful to him for taking days out of his life and away from his family to humor and watch over his father with great grace. My wife, Suzy, made his trip with me possible, as she makes possible many other good things. She also prepared the illustrations in this book and read the manuscript many times.

Andrew C. A. Jampoler
Outremer Farm
Leesburg, Virginia

Notes

Chapter 1. The Congo

1. Including 120 tons of ivory. The estimate is from the first draft of *The Congo-Railway from Matadi to the Stanley-Pool: Results of Survey* (Brussels: P. Weissenbruch, 1889), 83.

2. Tisdel to Bayard, June 29, 1885, Foreign Relations of the United States (No. 228) (hereafter cited as FRUS, followed by the number), 300, 49th Cong., 1st sess.

3. E. J. Glave, "The Congo River of Today," *Century Illustrated Magazine* 39, no. 4 (February 1890): 619.

4. John Reader, *Africa: A Biography of a Continent* (New York: Knopf, 1998), 239–241.

Chapter 2. The U.S. Navy in West African Waters

1. Taunt's February 1886 report of his journey up and down the Congo said that one of the station chiefs he met claimed American citizenship. It's likely that man was Augustus Sparhawk of Boston, since February 1880 the chief of Vivi Station. Henry Morton Stanley had met Sparhawk in 1871 during Stanley's first transit of Zanzibar, where Sparhawk was working for John Bertram and Company.

2. W. F. Lynch, "Report of an Examination of the Dead Sea, 1848–9," Senate Ex. Doc. 34, vol. 4, 30th Cong., 2nd sess.

3. James M. Gilliss, "The U.S. Naval Astronomical Expedition to the Southern Hemisphere during the Years 1849–52," House Ex. Doc. 121, 2 vols., 33rd Cong., 1st sess.

4. W. L. Herndon and L. Gibbon, "Exploration of the Valley of the Amazon made under the direction of the Navy Dept," Senate Ex. Docs., vol. 6, 2 pts., 32nd Cong., 2nd sess.

5. The Battle of the Barrier Forts, four Chinese garrisons commanding the Pearl River between the anchorage at Whampoa and the city of Canton, was fought in November 1856 between Marines and sailors from the three ships of the U.S. East Indies Squadron and the Chinese army garrisons manning the forts. The squadron had been deployed in October to protect Americans living in Canton. Despite official American neutrality in the war between China and France and

England, a battle over the forts erupted following the usual inevitable incidents between opposing armed forces pressed too close together. All four forts were captured and their guns spiked at a cost to the U.S. Navy believed to be six sailors killed and twenty-two sailors and Marines wounded. English appears to have been be the only officer casualty, and his injury might not have been in combat. Hundreds, perhaps thousands, of Chinese are thought to have been killed or wounded in the battle.

6. Gilliland, *Voyage to a Thousand Cares*, 24–25. The entry was for November 22, 1844. Lawrence died fourteen months later, on January 20, 1846, after eight days of fever. He was buried at sea off the ex-slaver *Pons*, 197 tons and once a transport for 850 slaves, then en route to Philadelphia as a prize.

7. Before Lucy's marriage to Chandler, she'd also been linked romantically to President Lincoln's son, Robert Todd; to Lincoln's secretary, John Hay, years later a secretary of state; and also to Oliver Wendell Holmes Jr., later a U.S. Supreme Court justice. Looking today at pictures of Lucy, it's not easy to understand her allure, but she was reputed to be a wit and a charmer. Lucy's father reappears later in this chapter, further demonstrating how small a world official Washington was in the nineteenth century.

8. NARA RG 45, E23, vol. 12 of 13, 386–484.

9. Braisted and Bell, *Life Story of Presley Marion Rixey*, 216–217. In September 1901 then–medical inspector Presley Rixey, USN, White House physician, was one of the many doctors standing the death watch over President William McKinley, shot by the assassin Leon Czolgosz. Rixey was the author of the medical reports describing the treatment administered to McKinley that were released to the public during the nine days between the attack and McKinley's death. A year later, Sunday, September 28, Surgeon General Rixey operated on President Roosevelt, badly injured in the leg three weeks earlier during a carriage and trolley car accident that might have killed him. A first operation in Indianapolis by local surgeons proved insufficient; Rixey, in Washington, restored the president to health after a weeks-long convalescence.

10. Whitney (1841–1904), educated at Yale and Harvard Law School, was active in New York Democratic politics and played an important role in Grover Cleveland's 1882 and 1884 gubernatorial and presidential campaigns in the state. His reward was a cabinet position as secretary of the navy, which he took over from Chandler near the Navy's post–Civil War nadir. Credited with shepherding more than 67,000 tons of new ship construction through Congress, he left office (to return to an enormously lucrative legal practice) proudly tagged as "the father of the new navy." Whitney had the good sense in 1869 to marry a wealthy Cleveland heiress, Flora Payne, the daughter of Henry Payne, Ohio's "Democratic patriarch." His father-in-law, at age seventy-four, was a first-term senator while Whitney was the navy secretary.

11. *Annual Report of the Secretary of the Navy for the Year 1884*, 2 vols. (Washington, D.C.: Government Printing Office, 1884), 15.

12. In 1984 CSS *Alabama*'s shattered, 122-year-old hull was discovered on the bottom by *Circé* (M715), lead ship of the French navy's *Circé*-class coastal minehunters. Although artifacts from the wreck are in museums of both countries, *Alabama*'s legacy has been preserved most memorably by Edouard Manet's famous oil painting of the battle now hanging in the Philadelphia Museum of Art, a seminal work in the history of French impressionism.

    Little remains of *Kearsarge* other than a section of her sternpost, with an embedded, dud shell from one of *Alabama*'s guns, exhibited on the floor of the U.S. Navy Museum at the Washington Navy Yard. All that is left of *Lancaster* is wood carver John Bellamy's handsome figurehead, now dominating the front gallery of the Mariners' Museum in Newport News, Virginia.

13. Some six months after her arrival off the Brazils, USS *Lancaster* left Montevideo, Uruguay, on December 17, 1885, for a cruise in the southern Indian Ocean, calling at the Comoro Islands, Zanzibar, Madagascar, and Mozambique. In part *Lancaster*'s mission was to succor New England merchants trading in these distant islands, who after the Civil War had found themselves increasingly losing an important traditional market to sharp competition from Indian textile mills.

14. *New York Times*, September 16, 1891. Admiral English didn't make *Lancaster*'s 1886 Indian Ocean deployment. He'd shifted his flag to the gunboat USS *Nipsic* before *Lancaster* sailed and then in November 1885, after barely half a year in his new command, he was detached from the South Atlantic Squadron and ordered home. English's retirement in February 1886 was scheduled by law, not forced by a cunning Walker maneuver, but his reassignment from the prestigious European Squadron command might have been.

15. Almost 7.5 million African Americans were enumerated in the census of 1890. Despite that daunting number, repatriation and emigration ideas had remarkable staying power. In his 1895 consular report, Dorsey Mohun wrote that "the Kongo Free State offers the best advantages possible to any intending negro emigrants from the United States. . . . I was led to believe the State would be willing to offer special inducements to the American negro to settle in the country in the way of reduction of duty on their imports and exports, assisted transportation to the interior to the points selected for settlement, and a grant of land upon which to commence farming. The Government is just and I can assure all intending settlers they will receive fair and liberal treatment."

16. The description of Banana Point in the mid-1880s is drawn from W. P. Tisdel, "My Trip to the Congo," *Century Illustrated Monthly Magazine* 39, no. 4 (February 1890): 609–618; Glave, *In Savage Africa*, 24; and R. E. Dennet, "From Banana, at the Mouth of the Congo, to Boma," *Journal of the Manchester Geographical Society*, 112–123.

Chapter 3. "Colonel" Willard Tisdel, U.S. Commercial Agent

1. "Colonel" was an honorific. Willard Tisdel served in the 7th Ohio Volunteer Infantry Regiment during the Civil War, rising to the rank of regimental sergeant

major. A biographic sketch is in Lawrence Wilson, ed., *Itinerary of the Seventh Ohio Volunteer Infantry, 1861–1864* (New York: Neale Publishing, 1907). A later sketch is in the *Bulletin of the Pan American Union*, September 1911, 596–597.

A *New York Times* obituary published June 22, 1911, said that Tisdel, "one of the leading commercial experts of the United States," died at his home in Washington of heart disease on June 21. At the time of his death he was the chief of the Guatemala Central Railroad.

2. Sickles' biographer, Thomas Keneally, aptly titled his book *American Scoundrel: The Life of the Notorious Civil War General Dan Sickles* (New York: Doubleday, 2002). In 1859 Sickles had been the first defendant successfully to use a temporary insanity defense in an American murder trial. (His victim was Philip Barton Key, his wife Teresa's lover and the late Francis Scott Key's son.) The European assignment ten years later, wrote Keneally, gave Sickles an opportunity to seduce the deposed queen of Spain, Isabella II, which he eagerly grasped.

3. Arthur's speech was delivered December 4, 1883. Its relevant paragraph:

> The rich and populous Valley of the Kongo is being opened to commerce by a society called the International African Association, of which the King of the Belgians is the president and a citizen of the United States the chief executive officer. Large tracts of territory have been ceded to the association by native chiefs, roads have been opened, steamboats placed on the river, and the nuclei of states established at twenty-two stations under one flag which offers freedom to commerce and prohibits the slave trade. The objects of the society are philanthropic. It does not aim at permanent political control, but seeks the neutrality of the valley. The United States cannot be indifferent to this work nor to the interests of their citizens involved in it. It may become advisable for us to cooperate with other commercial powers in promoting the rights of trade and residence in the Kongo Valley free from the interference or political control of any one nation.

4. Joe M. Richardson, "The Florida Excursion of President Chester A. Arthur," *Tequesta* 24 (1964): 41–47.

5. Mark Twain, *King Leopold's Soliloquy: A Defense of His Congo Rule* (Boston: P. R. Warren, 1905), 31.

6. United States Consular Reports, House Misc. Doc. 29, 69, 49th Cong., 1st sess.

7. "Commercial aptitudes of the negroes" was the subject of Schedule 20 of the Congo Railway's Survey Report, in which "the negroes' ardour for trade" was described as the best chance for the success of the enterprise. Unlike the fierce native races of America, the text observed, "the negro, incited by his highly developed commercial faculty, is naturally disposed to approach the white, to enter into connexion with him, to become his auxiliary. Thus by the frequentation of races we shall in the end not extirpate the black race, but rather on the contrary, fortify, civilize, and later on emancipate them."

8. Kasson, "Congo Conference and the President's Message," 122.

9. "Proposed" because the Congo Free State was not formally established until the following August. On August 1, 1885, King Leopold wrote his "Very Dear and Great Friend," President Cleveland, to tell him that "the possessions of the International Association of the Congo will hereafter form the Independent State of the Congo. I have at the same time the honor to inform you and the Government of the Republic of the United States of America that, authorized by the Belgian Legislative Chambers to become the chief of the new State, I have taken ... the title of Sovereign of the Independent State of the Congo."

10. Kasson, "Congo Conference and the President's Message," 121.

11. Despite General Paul von Lettow-Vorbeck's leadership commanding a 2,500-man-strong native Schutztruppe in strategic German East Africa, the colonies proved to be indefensible after the Great War began in 1914. Once fighting started, Germany was slowly chivvied out of its African holdings, expulsions confirmed in June 1919 by the Treaty of Versailles, which assigned these former colonies as League of Nations "mandates" to Great Britain, France, Belgium, Portugal, and the Union of South Africa.

12. Not everyone was convinced that a railroad around the rapids was the solution to the Congo's transportation infrastructure problem. On August 27, 1888, Roger Casement, who was then employed by the railroad survey, wrote Henry Sanford suggesting "a good road with bullock and mule teams would meet every requirement for Congo commerce for the next twenty years."

13. *New York Herald*, December 9, 1884, p. 7.

14. Stanley's British citizenship was restored May 26, 1892, in the service of his new wife's political ambitions for her husband. Regrooved as a subject of the queen and a Liberal Unionist politician, Stanley lost the chance to represent Lambeth North in Parliament in general elections that year, but won a second try three years later, having been driven into both campaigns by Dorothy Stanley, his wife, over his own great reluctance.

15. Bayard (1828–1898), a Democrat and former four-term U.S. senator from Delaware, took office in President Cleveland's cabinet March 7, 1885. He replaced Frelinghuysen, who left office with President Arthur in early March and then died in May. Bayard is remarkable for having been the grandson, son, and father of a U.S. senator from Delaware. All took their seats in the days before the direct election of senators. During Cleveland's second term, Bayard served as the U.S. ambassador to Great Britain.

16. Tisdel to Bayard, June 29, 1885, U.S. Bureau of Foreign Commerce, United States Consular Reports, Issues 53–56 (Washington, D.C.: Government Printing Office, 1885), 542.

17. The idea that Leopold II was entirely ignorant, and therefore innocent of the crimes being committed in his name and service, had astonishing staying power. In late April 1895 (and just days before his death), Edward Glave wrote from Matadi to his publisher, the *Century Magazine*, and reported on the abuse of

enslaved African orphans riding on a river boat with him. Glave then observed, "It is his [Leopold II's] duty to learn the true facts of things in the domain in which he is sovereign." For years no charge of bad governance adhered to the king.

18. Tisdel, "My Trip to the Congo," 618.

19. The quotation from Pechuel-Loesche is from a review of his *Herr Stanley und das Kongo-Unternehmen* and *Herr Stanley's Partisane und meine offiziellen Berichte vom Kongolande* in the August 12, 1886, issue of the *Nation*, 142–143.

20. Stanley, *Congo and the Founding of Its Free State* 1:448–449.

Chapter 4. Lieutenant Emory Taunt, U.S. Navy

1. If the 1880 census data are correct, Taunt's mother, Marie, was born in France in 1838 (both her parents were French) and was only fourteen or fifteen when she gave birth to her son. His father was twenty or twenty-one when Taunt was born. An Emory Taunt had a cabinet- and chair-making business, Taunt and Baldwin, in Buffalo at 213 Main Street for a while in the mid-1800s. His partnership with James Baldwin broke up in 1856. It's unclear what family connection this Taunt shared with Rev. Frederick Taunt or with his son, Emory H. Taunt.

2. Jeal, *Stanley*, 43.

3. The 1892 edition was the first. Osler's original text was revised fifteen times in new editions published, some posthumously, for the next fifty-five years. Through its first forty years *The Principles and Practice of Medicine* was a reliable guide to the current state of American medical art and science. Osler (1849–1919) is perhaps best known as one of the four physicians who founded the Johns Hopkins Medical School. He died of influenza at age seventy in December 1919.

4. In the early 1870s, the U.S. Navy mounted ten separate surveys of possible routes for a trans-isthmus canal under the general supervision of Commo. Daniel Ammen, USN, then chief of the Bureau of Navigation—the notorious Rear Adm. John Walker's immediate predecessor. Ammen described these surveys for a ship canal, identified their leadership, and summarized their conclusions in an October 1876 letter to the president of the American Geographical Society of New York, published in the society's annual report for that year. Ammen's purpose was to catalogue for members what had been done and to debunk French claims to superior knowledge of a practicable route.

5. Some of what follows first appeared in Jampoler, "Disaster at Lady Franklin Bay," *Naval History Magazine* 24, no. 4 (August 2010).

6. Appropriations for the protected cruisers *Atlanta*, *Boston*, and *Chicago* and the dispatch steamer *Dolphin* had passed Congress in 1883, procuring for the navy its first new ships in more than a decade, but renewed political acrimony on the Hill halted further acquisitions until after Schley's return.

7. June 1892 the boat in which Mohun was riding got caught in the whirlpools a mile below Vivi and capsized. "It was as much as I could do to save myself,"

he wrote to the State Department, in explanation for the fact that his accounts submitted for the first half of the year lacked required vouchers, which had been lost in the water.

8. Several hours' march from Matadi and very near the current site of Dupagne's vandalized *porteurs* sculpture.

9. A beautiful strip map of their route of march marks the many obstacles to river navigation between Vivi and the Pool. Their map located thirteen named waterfalls (one, Yelala, Bentley described as "a struggle of water not to be surpassed on the face of the earth"), more than a dozen other unnamed falls and rapids, and three "whirlpools."

10. Bentley, *Pioneering on the Congo* 1:137.

11. Major Edmund Barttelot, who sailed with Tib around the Cape of Good Hope in 1887 at the start of the Emin Pasha relief expedition, described him as "an oldish-looking man about 6ft. 2 in.—a fine, powerful, intelligent face." In February 1887, cynically adjusting to the local balance of power, Leopold elevated Tib (nominally a subordinate of the sultan of Zanzibar) to salaried governor of the Free State's Stanley Falls Station.

    Tib's several failures later that year to provide Stanley, as agreed, with six hundred porters to move expedition stores between Stanley Falls and Lake Albert, at six pounds sterling round trip "per loaded head," triggered a collapse of morale and discipline in the base camp at Yambuya that ended in horrific crimes, terrible suffering, and eventually the deaths of many members of the misbegotten relief expedition.

12. Nathaniel Philbrick, *Sea of Glory: America's Voyage of Discovery, The U.S. Exploring Expedition, 1838–1842* (New York: Penguin, 2003), 303.

13. At the end of 1848, Lt. William Lynch returned home with specimens from his expedition to the Dead Sea. Unfortunately, thanks to inept preservation—he'd put his unschooled young son in charge of preparing the collection—they were largely unusable, a problem so common that in 1854 the museum published *Directions for Collecting, Preserving, and Transporting Natural History Specimens*, a do-it-yourself handbook for the amateur collector.

14. *Harper's New Monthly Magazine* 72, no. 438 (March 1886): 546–559.

Chapter 5. The Sanford Exploring Expedition

1. In her review of Rev. François Bontinck's *Aux Origines de L'État Indépendent du Congo: Documents tirés d'Archives Américaines* (Louvain: Nauwelaerts for l'Université Lovanium, 1966) in *Catholic Historical Review* 55, no. 3 (October 1969): 516–517.

2. Fry, *Henry S. Sanford*, 170.

3. Harry believed himself a poet, and to advance that career he affected a monocle and eccentric costumes, leading an American classmate to explain "his dress savors a bit of the Anglomaniac." Harry failed to graduate with the Harvard class of 1888. He seems to have briefly studied "fruiticulture" at the Bussey Institute

in Jamaica Plain, and when that effort proved fruitless he was exiled to "Belair," the 145-acre family citrus grove in central Florida under threat of having his allowance cut off if he didn't go. There was an expectation in the family that Harry would be elected mayor of Sanford (his father had briefly flirted with a political career in Florida; his Republican identity made that impossible), thus making a small place for himself in the world. Some twenty years after the Civil War, however, local citizens were not prepared to vote for a young, carpetbagging "Anglomaniac," even if his father owned the heart of their downtown. Harry lost what must have been a very slow race and settled back down to brooding over his parents' iniquities.

4. Conan Doyle, *Crime of the Congo*, 85.

5. Quotations from Stevens' letters to Sanford are from Gifford A. Cochran's unpublished biography of Sanford, "Mr. Lincoln's Many-Faceted Minister and Entrepreneur Extraordinary," 360–365. The manuscript is in the archives of the Sanford Museum.

6. These he edited into *B. F. Stevens's Facsimiles,* published in a limited edition of two hundred by Malby and Sons of London and issued to subscribers in 1889.

7. The current edition of Bowditch's in the mid-1880s, titled *The American Practical Navigator, Being an Epitome of Navigation and Nautical Astronomy*, was published under the aegis of the Navy Department's Bureau of Navigation in 1883. The volume included over four hundred pages of reference tables, and it is these that Taunt required together with navigation instruments to "establish the lat. and long. of the different points on the Congo and its affluents."

8. The reference was to *Le Mouvement Géographique, Journal Populaire des Sciences Géographique. Organe des Intérêts Belges au Congo*, a biweekly, tabloid-sized magazine edited by M. Alphonse-Jules Wauters, from offices on Rue Bréderode in Brussels. The first issue appeared April 6, 1884, and subsequent copies came out every other Sunday. At least until 1890 *Le Mouvement Géographique* shamelessly boosted Leopold II's ambitions in the Congo.

9. São Tomé, St. Thomas, just north of the equator between 6° and 7° east longitude, was the largest Portuguese island possession in the Bight of Benin, and a stop on the steamer route between Lisbon and San Antonio, across from Banana at the mouth of the river in Portuguese Angola. The island merited lengthy descriptions in the sailing directions of the day because it was a good place to water and provision and because it had no natural harbors and required ships drawing more than ten feet to defy baffling winds and currents and use exposed anchorages.

10. Casement to Sanford, August 27, 1888, Box 22, Sanford Archive.

11. In April 1887 Janssens' post was retitled "governor-general."

12. Taunt to Sanford, December 27, 1888, Box 22, Sanford Archive.

13. Members of Taunt's promotion examination board in 1876 judged his knowledge of French as inadequate.

14. In *Stanley*, author Tim Jeal describes Anthony Swinburne as one of Henry Stanley's "two favorite whites." Swinburne's connection to Stanley went back to

1874, when he was fifteen, and to the Ashanti Wars on the West African Gold Coast. Six years later, and now a great man, Stanley drew Swinburne back into his orbit at the start of his years-long, two-phase station-building effort along the Congo in Leopold's employ. Swinburne began his career in the Congo as Stanley's clerk, went on to become a storekeeper, and eventually was chief of the stations at Isangila and Kinshasa, where he first met Taunt.

15. Neither Ward's biography, *A Valiant Gentleman* (London: Chapman and Hall, 1927), by his wife, Sarita Ward, nor admiring obituaries mention his employment with the S.E.E. Tim Butcher, author of *Blood River*, put the first Ward book on his list of top ten about the Congo.

16. In 1889 at Banana, Taunt met Ward, who was then leaving for Europe escorting some invalids from Stanley's "rear guard" and learned that "every African obstacle" had obstructed Stanley's progress on his last African mission, during which nearly five hundred of the expedition's men died or deserted in three years. Ward (1863–1919) wrote about the experience in *My Life with Stanley's Rear Guard* (Charles L. Webster, 1891). He was the author of two other books about his experiences in Africa, *Five Years with the Congo Cannibals* (Chatto and Windus, 1890) and *A Voice from the Congo* (Charles Scribner's Sons, 1911).

17. The reading public was fascinated by the Congo. Charles (he apparently went by "Latrobe," a middle name) Bateman's contribution to this evergreen library was *The First Ascent of the Kasai: Being Some Records of Service Under the Lone Star* (George Philip & Son, 1889). It appears that no European who could find a publisher failed to write a book about his experiences in central Africa, some less well received than others. Bateman's book, one reviewer wrote, "was disfigured here and there by some faulty sentences, due to haste or literary inexperience."

18. Casement's eloquent speech from the dock after his conviction, charging the court had no jurisdiction, changed nothing. After conviction, his supporters seeking clemency were embarrassed and abruptly silenced by the appearance of two "Black Diaries" that purported to show Casement was a promiscuous homosexual, a crime in that era. He was hanged in Petonville Prison on August 3, 1916. For decades many suspected the diaries to be forgeries, but in 2002 a forensic handwriting analysis sponsored by the BBC and RTÉ (Ireland's national radio and TV broadcaster) concluded the books were authentic.

19. Sanford Exploring Expedition Memoranda, Box 32, Sanford Archive.

20. At its peak the Belgian flag steamship fleet in the 1880s numbered about sixty vessels operating from two ports, Antwerp on the River Schelde and Ghent. Two large carriers, Cockerill and the Société de Navigation Royale Belge Sud américaine, sailed a third of these between them, and the other forty or so merchant ships belonged to eight smaller companies. Walford operated only two ships, the steamers *Brabo* and *Schelde*.

21. Poor Sanford. If the problem wasn't flood it was fire: Not long thereafter he learned that Manyanga Station had been the target of thieves and arsonists.

Three hundred loads of trade stocks in storage at the station were saved, thanks to Herbert Ward's quick work, and the three malefactors (or reasonable facsimiles of them) were caught, made to confess, and promptly hanged. The station was then returned to the state at Valcke's insistence.

22. Van Eetveld to Tree, December 31, 1887, in Tree to Bayard, January 6, 1888, FRUS (No. 289).

23. The 1,850-ton steamer *Lualaba* was built in 1878 by Cunliffe and Dunlop of Port Glasgow, on the Clyde River, and scrapped in Spain in 1934. She was named for the Lualaba River, the headwaters of the Congo beginning immediately upstream from Stanley Falls Station. She sailed for the B&ASN Company for seventeen years and was sold to Spanish interests in 1895. Notably, in June 1889 SS *Lualaba* was the first steamer up the Congo River to Matadi.

   Livingstone once believed that the Lualaba River might feed into the Nile, but in 1876–77 Stanley's great transcontinental trek proved that the north-flowing river ran into the Congo.

24. Taunt to Sanford, April 11, 1887, Box 28, Sanford Archive.

25. Arthur Hodister died miserably in an Arab ambush in May 1892, a few months after this mention, while he was trying to open an ivory collection station in Katanga. The *New York Times* reported August 14, 1892, that before being beheaded, he'd been tortured for three days. Only after Hodister's death did stories emerge of his character's dark side. Norman Sherry has suggested at length that Hodister was the model for Conrad's Kurtz, one among a number of candidates for that juicy role. *Conrad's Western World*, 95–118.

Chapter 6. The Court-Martial

1. Convicted and sentenced to life in prison in July for second-degree murder, young John Walworth was released four years later, following a successful pardon campaign by his mother, Ellen, which had kept the crime, and the hotel, in the news. After the four Leland brothers sold their hotel, it began to decline. By the mid-1890s Sturtevant House wasn't even numbered among the fifteen best hotels list in Moses King's self-published *King's Handbook of New York City* (1893). When the hotel was sold for the last time in 1903, newspaper headlines still identified the property as "the Scene of the Walworth Murder."

2. In February 1898 then–lieutenant commander Marix (1848–1919) was the judge advocate on the Navy board of inquiry that first investigated the explosion and sinking of the second-rate battleship USS *Maine* in Havana Harbor, the first of five such investigations. He went on to have an interesting career, remarkable in that he was born in Dresden, in Saxony, and was Jewish, in the early 1900s an unusual lineage for a U.S. Navy flag officer. Adolphus Marix retired as a rear admiral in 1910, at the statutory age of sixty-two after forty-seven years of Navy service, twenty-four of them spent at sea.

3. "To Try Lieutenant Taunt, the Naval Court martial Begin Their Work in the Lyceum," *New York Herald*, November 18, 1887.

4. On September 5, 1909, the *New York Times* reported that Lemly, fifty-six, had died in the Government Hospital for the Insane at Anacostia the day before, five years after he'd been relieved as the Navy's JAG and retired prematurely.

5. In fact, in 1905 *Nipsic* was converted into a prison ship and stationed at Naval Station Puget Sound to house court-martial convicts. She was finally broken up in 1913.

6. Winthrop, *Military Law and Precedents*, 455.

7. Weber to Sanford, April 14, 1887, Box 23, File 9, Henry Shelton Sanford Papers.

8. The note, handwritten on three plain pages, is signed "G C." No letterhead, nothing else other than the perspective, subject matter, and signature initials identify it as possibly from President Cleveland's hand, but I believe it to be. NARA RG 125, Records of the Proceedings of Naval and Marine Examining Boards, Box 74, File No. 1694, Records of the Office of the Judge Advocate General (Navy).

9. Quoted in the *New York Times*, April 23, 1889.

10. *Dennis W. Mullan, Appt., v. United States*, 212 U.S. 516 (29 S. Ct. 330), 53 L.Ed 632, No. 82, argued: January 20, 1909, decided: February 23, 1909.

Chapter 7. Emory Taunt, U.S. Commercial Agent

1. 25 Stat. 247, Chap. 614, 50th Cong., 1st sess. On February 28, 1889, Congress passed the appropriation for the Consular and Diplomatic Service for the next fiscal year, 1890. It contained the same language about the commercial agency in Boma and the same dollar appropriation. 25 Stat. 696, Chap. 278, 50th Cong., 2nd sess. The appropriation was increased to five thousand dollars in fiscal years 1891 and 1892. 26 Stat. 272, Chap. 706, 51st Cong., 1st sess., and 26 Stat. 1063, Chap. 545, 51st Cong., 2nd sess.

2. "Though he has always been recognized as a thorough Republican," Thomas Quinn wrote greasily in *Massachusetts of Today* (Columbia Publishing, 1892) about Wharton, "he is regarded by his political opponents as one whose manliness and independence are sufficient to cause him to be governed by his sense of right, irrespective of the demands of party."

3. Taunt's accounts for the six months between mid-November 1888 and mid-May 1889 show some $2,100 in expenditures, including $684 for camp equipment, guns, and ammunition; $313 for trade goods, including beads, cloth, brass wire, and notions; $440 for porters to Stanley Pool; and $579 for two caravans into the lower Congo watershed.

4. *Regulations Prescribed for the Use of the Consular Service of the United States (1888)* (Washington, D.C.: Government Printing Office, 1888), art. 402.

5. Morris, *Theodore Rex*, 162.

6. Smallpox was in the Congo earlier. It was present in 1873, wreaking "sad havoc" among the natives, when Royal Navy lieutenant W. R. Grandy's expedition to aid Livingstone, sponsored by the Royal Geographical Society of London, left Ambriz for the interior to find the missionary. Grandy was hiking generally

east into central Africa from the Atlantic Coast; another RGS expedition was moving inland west from the Indian Ocean coast. News of Livingstone's death concluded both.

7. After Mohun resigned in May 1895, the post was vacant until October 1906. The next three official Americans in Boma (Clarence Slocum, James Smith, and William Handley) enjoyed the rank of consul general. All three moved on after a year or so to other diplomatic posts. After a years-long gap, Harry McBride of Michigan was assigned to Boma in 1917.

8. Quoted in Leopold, "Guide to Early African Collections," 15–16. There's nothing in the Smithsonian Institution Archives, Record Units 33 and 34, the Secretary's Outgoing Correspondence, that indicates Langley replied to Camp.

9. [A Belgian], *Truth about Civilization in Congoland*, 171.

10. Kathryn Barrett-Gaines, "Travel Writing, Experiences and Silences . . . the Case of Richard D. Mohun," *History in Africa* 24 (1997): 53.

11. According to county records, Frankie died on either June 14 or 15, 1883. The *Washington Post* of June 16, 1888, said the fifteenth. She was twenty-seven. The Russell-Smith family plot in Oak Hill Cemetery in Georgetown (No. 150) where Frankie (1863–1888) lies with her husband and her older sister, Mary, also contains the remains of an unnamed female infant, buried June 18, 1888.

12. *Exponent* (Culpeper, Va.), July 25, 1946, 1.

Chapter 8. Heart of Darkness

1. Williams was born in 1849 in Bedford Springs, Pennsylvania, and died in 1891 in Liverpool, England, not long after his return from the Congo. His biographer, discoverer really, the late Professor John Hope Franklin (1915–2009), was the author of several journal essays about Williams that were part of a huge body of scholarly work. Williams' description of the king is quoted from Franklin, *George Washington Williams*, 181. Professor Franklin's papers are held at Duke University.

2. A report that Williams sent to President Harrison from Luanda that October, at the end of a month-long trip through Portuguese Angola and before leaving for Zanzibar, was no less tough. Leopold's Congo, Williams told the president, was "an absolute monarchy, a cruel and oppressive government, an exclusive Belgian colony."

3. Tim Jeal, Stanley's most recent biographer and the first one with access to all the Stanley family papers now held in archives of the Musée Royal de l'Afrique Centrale in Tervuren, Belgium, has found in his research evidence not of the nineteenth century's most brutal explorer but of "a sensitive and wounded man" incapable of the land acquisition scams Stanley was accused of by Williams. In a fundamental reappraisal of the great explorer's character based on these newly available materials, Jeal describes Stanley as initially opposed to European sovereignty in central Africa and as seeking only the right to rent riverfront tracts for use in trade. The confiscatory treaties unknowing Congo chiefs consented

to that gave away tribal lands to Leopold, Jeal says, were the work of a retired British general and others in the king's employ and kept secret by Leopold from Stanley.

4. See Richard White's *Railroaded: The Transcontinentals and the Making of America* (New York: W. W. Norton, 2011).

5. Freiesleben was killed on January 29, 1890. When his bones were recovered on March 23, 1890, grass was reportedly growing through the skeleton. Robert Hampson, ed., *Heart of Darkness with the Congo Dairy* (New York: Penguin Books, 1995), 130. "The grass growing through his ribs," Charlie Marlow tells his shipmates on board the yawl *Nellie* in the Thames, as Conrad's *Heart of Darkness* begins, "was tall enough to hide his bones."

6. Joseph Conrad's replacement, the real "Carlier," seems to have actually been named "Galhier." That's what Rev. William Sheppard and Rev. Samuel Lapsley called *Florida*'s master when they rode his steamboat for four weeks in March–April 1891 up the Kwa-Kasai to Luebo Station, where they were going to establish the first and principal central African mission of the Presbyterian Church in the United States. Lapsley (a white Alabaman) died of malaria in 1892, but Sheppard (a black Virginian) lived to spend most of the next twenty years doing missionary work in the valley of the Kasai. Sheppard, *Presbyterian Pioneers in the Congo*.

Chapter 9. Exposing the Crime of the Congo

1. "Liverpool Steamship Lines," *Weekly Northwestern Miller* (Minneapolis) 77, no. 3 (January 18, 1899).

2. During the years 1899–1902, for example, less than £900,000 worth of goods was imported into the Congo Free State to pay for more than £7 million of exports, mostly rubber. From a total of £3,529,317 in Congo Free State imports, Morel subtracted £2,636, 000, representing payments for state administrative costs, leaving only £893,317 worth of trade goods to pay for more than eight times that amount in exports, including more than £6 million of rubber. Cocks, *E. D. Morel*.

3. Allen Sinclair Will, *Life of Cardinal Gibbons, Archbishop of Baltimore* (New York: E. P. Dutton, 1922), 2:951.

4. Gibbons' letter was quoted in 1904 as an editorial in the *Messenger*, a Jesuit monthly magazine published in 1902–9, in 1909 renamed *America*.

5. Peter Duignan and Lewis H. Gann, *The United States and Africa: A History* (Cambridge: Cambridge University Press, 1987), 194.

6. Wack (1869–1954) was the author of *The Congo Free State: Social, Political, and Economic Aspects of the Belgian System of Government in Central Africa* (New York: G. P. Putnam's Sons, 1905), a 640-page whitewash of Leopold's Congo. Setting a low standard for objectivity in print, the *New York Times* had Consul Whiteley review Wack's book in its issue of March 4, 1905. Predictably Whiteley endorsed it, announcing that "the verdict of every fair-minded man who

goes out there and sees in this new country so many evidences of civilization, of good government, and of progress" will be "there is much to praise in the Congo and very little to blame."

7. Eventually fired by Baron Moncheur, Kowalsky got revenge by selling his confidential Congo papers to the Star Publishing Company's *New York American*. The revelations on December 10, 1906, under a headline screaming "King Leopold's Amazing Attempt to Corrupt Our Congress Exposed," outed the secretary of the Senate's Committee on Foreign Relations as a bribe taker. While Kowalsky covered his tracks by pretending the letters were stolen from his office, the inflammatory exposures continued, tarring government officials, academics, and others as Leopold's paid agents.

8. An effervescent remedy for constipation, named after a spa in Bohemia.

9. Quoted in Miller, *Adventures of Arthur Conan Doyle*, 75.

10. The most colorful foreign investigation of the Congo Free State was probably the one begun in June 1903 by an Italian navy physician, Captain Eduardo Baccari. Baccari (1871–1952) was sent to Africa by King Victor Emmanuel III either to explore the potential for Italian emigration despite endemic disease (the usual contemporary description of his mission) or to examine "the condition and conduct" of the sixty to seventy Italian officers then working for Leopold in the Congo (the occasional other explanation).

    In July 1904, a year after he disembarked at Boma, Baccari claimed that he had been the target of an assassination attempt by agents of the state in an effort to silence his forthcoming report about Belgian abuses. His breakfast wine, he said, had been dosed with "corrosive sublimate" by a suborned servant, nearly killing him. The failed murder was followed up with a whispering campaign alleging Baccari had lost his mind in the Congo and anything he said could not be believed.

    Baccari's bizarre reports after his return were a sensation in Italy, where the foreign minister announced an investigation of his charges and the end of the emigration scheme. They naturally got a lot of press attention elsewhere in Europe, and in the United States, too.

11. "Affairs in the Congo, Message from the President of the U.S. Transmitting a Report by the Secretary of State Accompanying Correspondence, Touching the Condition of Affairs in the Kongo," Senate Doc. 147, 61st Cong., 1st sess. (Washington, D.C.: Government Printing Office, 1909). Slocum's report quoted, his seventh dispatch to the department, is the first of thirty-nine papers, spanning December 1906–December 1909, forwarded to Congress by President Taft in this document.

12. According to Reverend Bentley, the ground root was made into pudding-like dough and sun dried, then boiled or baked into a hard dumpling, kwanga. He described kwanga in *Pioneering on the Congo* as "a tough, glutinous mass, with a slightly sour taste, and . . . very nutritious." The product was edible for up to twelve days "with care and occasional sunning."

13. Among them the most interesting, albeit not the largest, might have been the American Congo Company, chartered in New York and owned by Guggenheim, Rockefeller, Baruch, Payne, Aldrich, and Whitney, names to conjure with in that century.

Concessionary companies in the Congo dated back twenty years to the first, Sanford's failed Exploring Expedition. The American Congo Company was born in November 1906, the product of Leopold's tactical decision the year before to get powerful Americans on his side in the debate over the Free State's future by seducing them with the prospect of vast wealth. His incentives to them were a half-share in the International Congo Forestry and Mining Company, which granted rights to prospect and mine for minerals for six and ninety-nine years, respectively, and rubber collection rights in an area, according to the *New York Times*, "larger than all of New England, New York, New Jersey, Delaware, and half of Pennsylvania."

14. John Daniels, "The Congo Question and the 'Belgian Solution,'" *North American Review* 188 (December 1908): 891–902.

Epilogue

1. Twelve days after Perdicaris was abducted from his elegant home in the hills outside of Tangiers, early on May 30, the cruiser USS *Brooklyn* steamed into the port. That day and the next, six additional American cruisers and gunboats joined *Brooklyn*. On June 22, with this threatening force still resting at anchor and collecting its strength near the Arab capital, Secretary of State Hay delivered a public ultimatum to the sultan of Morocco: Perdicaris alive or his kidnapper, Ahmed ben Mohammed el Raisuli, dead. Two days later, after Raisuli's ransom and political demands were quietly met in full by the sultan, Perdicaris and his stepson were released unharmed.

2. The CIA's population estimate for July 2012 is 73.6 million, but it's possible that's too high by some 5–6 million. No census has been conducted in the post-independence DRC since the first in 1984. An ambitious $176 million effort was planned to begin in mid-2011, employing 70,000 enumerators to do the head count. As I write this in December 2012, that count hasn't begun.

Selected Bibliography

Primary Sources

National Archives and Records Administration, Washington, D.C.

RG 24. Records of the Bureau of Naval Personnel. Entry 118, Logs of U.S. Ships and Stations. Deck logs of USS *Lancaster,* vols. 37–41; USS *Kearsarge,* vols. 47–51; and USS *Nipsic,* vol. 46.

RG 45. Naval Records Collection of the Office of Naval Records and Library. Correspondence 1798–1918. Confidential and other Letters, Telegrams and Cables sent to COs of Squadrons and Vessels. September 12, 1843–November 6, 1886.

RG 59. General Records of the Department of State. Consular Despatches Boma 1888–1895, T-47; Papers of R. Dorsey Mohun, 1892–1913, T-294.

RG 125. Records of the Office of the Judge Advocate General (Navy). Box 72, GCM No. 5518; Box 74, File No. 1694; Box 134, GCM No. 6956; Box 135, Records of the Proceedings of Naval and Marine Examining Boards.

U.S. Congressional Papers

"Affairs in the Congo, Message from the President of the U.S. Transmitting a Report by the Secretary of State Accompanying Correspondence, Touching the Condition of Affairs in the Kongo." Senate Doc. 147. 61st Cong., 1st sess. Washington, D.C.: Government Printing Office, 1909. (The "accompanying correspondence" includes ninety-nine diplomatic documents dated from December 1, 1906, to June 12, 1909.)

"Congo Conference. Message from the President of the United States transmitting a communication from the Secretary of State in relation to the Congo Conference. February 19, 1885." House Ex. Doc. 247. Serial Set vol. 2304. Session vol. 29, 48th Cong., 2nd sess.

"Occupation of the Congo Country in Africa." March 26, 1884. Senate Report 393. 48th Cong., 1st sess.

Papers Relating to the Foreign Relations of the United States. Serial Set vol. 2368. Session vol. 1, 49th Cong., 1st sess.

"The Proceedings of the 'Proteus' Court of Inquiry on the Greely Relief Expedition of 1883." Senate Ex. Doc. 100, 48th Cong., 1st sess. Washington, D.C.: Government Printing Office, 1884.

"Report of Lieutenant Taunt of a journey on the river Congo." Ex. Doc. 77. 49th Cong., 2nd sess.

"Reports from the Consuls of the United States, the Lower Congo," 206–214. House Misc. Doc. 232. Serial Set vol. 2784. Session vol. 25, 51st Cong. 1st sess.

"United States Consular Reports . . . on the commerce, manufactures, etc., of their consular districts . . ." House Misc. Doc. 29. Serial Set vol. 2413. Session vol. 8, 49th Congress, 1st sess.

Sanford Museum, Sanford, Florida

Henry Shelton Sanford's papers, comprising approximately 50,000 documents, are at the museum of the City of Sanford, Florida. Those relating to Sanford's business and other interests in Africa are held in Boxes 21–32. Papers specifically related to the Sanford Exploring Expedition and to Lieutenant Emory Taunt are in Boxes 26–32.

National Anthropological Archives, Suitland, Maryland

Smithsonian Museum curator emeritus Gordon Gibson's papers are held in the National Anthropological Archives. From 1958 to 1983, Gibson (1915–2007) was the curator of the museum's collection of African artifacts. Boxes 76 and 77 contain research material and the unfinished chapters of a book Gibson was writing on the first contributors to the museum's African collection.

Maps and Charts

Carta do curso do Rio Zaire de Stanley Pool ao Oceano. Ca. 1:500,000. Portugal: Commissão de Cartografia Junto do Ministério da Marinha e Ultramar, 1883. Perry-Casteñeda Library, University of Texas at Austin.

Journey to Stanley Pool of H. E. Crudgington and W. H. Bentley. 1:550,000. London: F. Cartwright, 1881. Published in the *Missionary Herald*, August 1881.

Kiepert, Richard. *Carte du Bassin du Congo*. 1:4,000,000. Berlin: Dietrich Reimer, 1886.

Lauwers, J. *Fleuve Congo Leopoldville–Stanleyville*. 1:50,000. Congo Belge Service Hydrographique Section de Haut Congo, 1916. Bibliothèque Aequatoria, Bamanya, Mbandaka.

———. *République Démocratique du Congo*. 1:2,000,000. Louvain: Université Catholique de Louvain, 2006.

Letts's Intermediate Atlas. London: Mason and Payne, 1889.

Letts's Popular Atlas, being a series of maps delineating the whole surface of the globe . . . London: Letts, Son & Company, 1883.

Plan of the US Navy Yard N.Y. including Cob Dock, Ordnance Dock, Marine Barracks and Hospital Grounds. Y&D No. 4266, November 23, 1882.

Wauters, A. J. *Carte de L'État Indépendent du Congo*. 13th ed. Brussels: Institute National de Geographie, 1891.

Period Secondary Sources

Annual Report of the Secretary of the Navy. Washington, D.C.: Government Printing Office, 1885.

Annual Report of the Secretary of the Navy. Washington, D.C.: Government Printing Office, 1889.

Bartlett, J. R., trans. *The West Coast of Africa, Part III, Cape Lopez to the Cape of Good Hope*. U.S. Hydrographic Office No. 48. Washington, D.C.: Government Printing Office, 1877.

Barttelot, Walter George. *The Life of Edmund Musgrave Barttelot*. 2nd ed. London: Richard Bentley and Son, 1890.

[A Belgian]. *The Truth about Civilization in Congoland*. Brussels: J. Lebeque, 1903.

Bentley, Rev. W. Holman. *Pioneering on the Congo*. 2 vols. London: Religious Tract Society, 1900.

Braisted, Rear Adm. William C., M.C., USN, and Capt. William Hemphill Bell, M.C., USN. *The Life Story of Presley Marion Rixey, Surgeon General, U.S. Navy, 1902–1910*. Strasburg, Va.: Shenandoah Publishing House, 1930. Written in 1910.

Brown, Robert. *The Story of Africa and Its Explorers*. 4 vols. London: Cassell, 1892–95.

Bryson, Alexander. *Report on the Climate and Principal Diseases of the African Station*. London: William Clowes and Sons, 1847.

Bulens, A., and G. Bulens, eds. *An Answer to Mark Twain*. Brussels: A & G Bulens Brothers, c. 1907.

Burton, Sir Richard F. *Two Trips to Gorilla Land and the Cataracts of the Congo.* London: Sampson Low, 1876.

Cocks, F. Seymour. *E. D. Morel, the Man and his Works.* London: George Allen & Unwin, 1920.

[Compagnie du Congo pour Le Commerce at L'Industrie]. *The Congo-Railway from Matadi to the Stanley-Pool.* Brussels: P. Weissenbruch, 1889.

Conan Doyle, Arthur. *The Crime of the Congo.* New York: Doubleday, Page, 1909.

Cummings, Henry. *A Synopsis of the Cruise of the U.S.S. "Tuscarora" from the date of her Commission to Her Arrival in San Francisco, California, September 2d, 1874.* Privately printed, 1874.

Delcommune, Alexandre. *Vingt années de vie africaine: Récits de voyages, d'adventures et d'exploration au Congo Belge, 1874–1893.* Brussels: Larcier, 1922.

Dennett, R. E. "From Banana, at the Mouth of the Congo, to Boma." *Journal of the Manchester Geographical Society* 3, nos. 1–6 (January–June 1877): 112–123.

De Winton, Francis. "The Congo Free State." *Proceedings of the Royal Geographic Society and Monthly Record of Geography* 8, no. 10 (October 1886): 609–627.

Dorman, Marcus R. P. *A Journal of a Tour in the Congo Free State.* Brussels: J. Lebègue, 1905.

Edwards, Richard, ed. *New York's Great Industries.* New York: Historical Publishing, 1884.

Fenn, G. Manville. *Memoir of Benjamin Franklin Stevens.* London: Chiswick Press, 1903.

Fox-Bourne, H. R. *Civilisation in Congoland: A Story of International Wrong-doing.* London: P. S. King & Son, 1903.

Glave, E. J. *In Savage Africa; or, Six Years of Adventure in Congo-land.* New York: R. H. Russell & Son, 1892.

Goldsmid, F. J. "My Recent Visit to the Congo." *Proceedings of the Royal Geographic Society and Monthly Record of Geography* 6, no. 4 (April 1884): 177–183.

Greely, Adolphus W. *Three Years of Arctic Service: An Account of the Lady Franklin Bay Expedition of 1881–1884 and the Attainment of Farthest North.* 2 vols. New York: Charles Scribner's Sons, 1886.

Hamersly, Lewis R. *The Records of Living Officers of the U.S. Navy and Marine Corps.* 4th ed. Philadelphia: L. R. Hamersly, 1890.

Hawker, George. *The Life of George Grenfell, Congo Missionary and Explorer*. New York: Fleming H. Revell, 1909.

Hensey, Andrew F. *A Master-Builder of the Congo*. New York: Fleming H. Revell, 1916.

Johnston, H. H. *The River Congo from Its Mouth to Bolobo, with a General Description of the Natural History and Anthropology of Its Western Basin*. 4th ed. London: Sampson, Low, Marston, 1895.

———. "A Visit to Mr. Stanley's Stations on the Congo." In *Report of the Fifty-third Meeting of the British Association for the Advancement of Science*, 593–594. London: John Murray, 1884.

Kasson, John A. "The Congo Conference and the President's Message." *North American Review* 351 (February 1886): 119–133.

Keith, Arthur Berriedale. *The Belgian Congo and the Berlin Act*. Oxford: Oxford University Press, 1919.

Kowalski, Henry I. *Brief of Henry I. Kowalski, of the New York Bar, attorney and counsellor to Leopold II, King of the Belgians and Sovereign of the Independent State of the Congo, in matters touching his rights and possessions abroad, in reply to [the] memorial presented to the President of the United States of America concerning affairs in the Congo State by the Congo Reform Association, supported by the British and Foreign Anti-slavery Society and the Aborigines' Protection Society*. Privately printed, March 1905.

Low, Sidney. "Henry Morton Stanley." *Cornhill Magazine* 17 (July–December 1904): 26–42.

Mohun, R. Dorsey. "The Kongo Free State." *Consular Reports, Commerce, Manufactures, Etc.* 52 (September 1896), no. 192. House Doc. 24, pt. 1, 54th Cong., 2nd sess. Washington, D.C.: Government Printing Office, 1–22.

Morgan, E. Delmar. "The Free State of the Congo." *Proceedings of the Royal Geographic Society and Monthly Record of Geography* 7, no. 4 (April 1885): 223–230.

———. "Notes on the Lower Congo, from Its Mouth to Stanley Pool." *Proceedings of the Royal Geographic Society and Monthly Record of Geography* 6, no. 4 (April 1884): 183–196.

Myers, Rev. John Brown. *The Congo for Christ*. New York: Fleming H. Revell, 1895.

Osler, William. *The Principles and Practice of Medicine*. New York: D. Appleton, 1892.

Parke, Thomas Heazle. *My Personal Experiences in Equatorial Africa as Medical Officer of the Emin Pasha Relief Expedition*. New York: Charles Scribner's Sons, 1891.

Phillips, Henry Jr. "An Account of the Congo Free State." *Proceedings of the American Philosophical Society* 26, no. 130 (July–December 1889): 459–476.

"The Recent Journey of Messrs. Crudgington and Bentley to Stanley Pool, on the Congo." *Proceedings of the Royal Geographical Society* 3, no. 9 (September 1881): 553–560.

Schley, W. S., and J. R. Soley. *The Rescue of Greely.* New York: Charles Scribner's Sons, 1885.

Sheppard, William H. *Presbyterian Pioneers in Congo.* Richmond, Va.: Presbyterian Committee of Publication, 1917.

Stanley, Dorothy, ed. *The Autobiography of Sir Henry Morton Stanley.* Boston: Houghton Mifflin, 1909.

Stanley, Henry M. *The Congo and the Founding of Its Free State: A Story of Work and Exploration.* 2 vols. New York: Harper & Brothers, 1885.

———. *How I Found Livingstone, Travels, Adventures and Discoveries in Central Africa* . . . New York: Scribner, Armstrong, 1874.

———. *In Darkest Africa.* New York: Charles Scribner's Sons, 1890.

———. *Through the Dark Continent.* 2 vols. New York: Harper & Brothers, 1879.

Stevens, B. F. *B. F. Stevens's Facsimiles of Manuscripts in European Archives Relating to America, 1773–1783, with Descriptions, Editorial Notes, etc.* London: Malby & Sons, 1889–95.

Taunt, Lt. Emory H., USN. *Young Sailor's Assistant in Practical Seamanship, including Rules of the Road, Directions for Resuscitating the Apparently Drowned, etc., etc.* Washington, D.C., 1883.

Wack, Henry Wellington. *The Story of the Congo Free State.* New York: Putnam, 1905.

Winthrop, Col. Williams, USA. *Military Law and Precedents.* Boston: Little, Brown, 1886.

Selected Modern Secondary Sources

Amundson, Richard J. "The Florida Land and Colonization Company." *Florida Historical Quarterly* 44, no. 3 (January 1966): 153–158.

Ascherson, Neal. *The King Incorporated.* London: George, Allen & Unwin, 1963.

Benedetto, Robert. *Presbyterian Reformers in Central Africa: a Documentary Account of the American Presbyterian Congo Mission and the Human Rights Struggle in the Congo.* Leiden: E. J. Brill, 1997.

Bontinck, François. *Aux Origines de L'État Independant du Congo: Documents tirés d'Archives Américaines*. Leopoldville: L'Université Louvanium de Leopoldville, 1966.

Butcher, Thomas. *Blood River: The Terrifying Journey Through the World's Most Dangerous Country*. New York: Grove Press, 2008.

Conrad, Joseph. *Heart of Darkness*. New York: W. W. Norton, 2005.

Curle, Richard, ed. "Conrad's Diary." *Yale Review* 15 (January 1926), 254–266.

De Gramont, Sanche. *The Strong Brown God: The Story of the Niger River*. Boston: Houghton Mifflin, 1976.

Dugard, Martin. *Into Africa: The Epic Adventures of Stanley and Livingstone*. New York: Doubleday, 2003.

Fernandez-Armesto, Felipe. *Pathfinders: A Global History of Exploration*. New York: W. W. Norton, 2006.

Firchow, Peter Edgerly. *Envisioning Africa: Race and Imperialism in Conrad's Heart of Darkness*. Lexington: University Press of Kentucky, 2000.

Franklin, John Hope. *George Washington Williams: A Biography*. Durham, N.C.: Duke University Press, 1998.

Fry, Joseph A. *Henry S. Sanford: Diplomacy and Business in Nineteenth-Century America*. Reno: University of Nevada Press, 1982.

Gilliland, C. Herbert. *Voyage to a Thousand Cares: Master's Mate Lawrence with the African Squadron, 1844–46*. Annapolis: Naval Institute Press, 2004.

Hawkins, Hunt. "Joseph Conrad, Roger Casement, and the Congo Reform Movement." *Journal of Modern Literature* 9, no. 1 (1981–82): 65–80.

———. "Mark Twain's Involvement with the Congo Reform Movement: 'A Fury of Generous Indignation.'" *New England Quarterly* 51, no. 2 (June 1978): 147–175.

Herderschee, Johannes, Kai-Alexander Kaiser, and Daniel Mukoko Samba. *Resilience of an African Giant, Boosting Growth and Development in the Democratic Republic of Congo*. Washington, D.C.: World Bank, 2012.

Hochschild, Adam. *King Leopold's Ghost: A Story of Greed, Terror, and Heroism in Colonial Africa*. New York: Houghton, Mifflin, Harcourt, 1998.

Jeal, Tim. *Stanley: The Impossible Life of Africa's Greatest Explorer*. London: Farber and Farber, 2007.

Karl, Frederick J., ed. *The Collected Letters of Joseph Conrad*. Cambridge: Cambridge University Press, 1983.

Liebowitz, Daniel, and Charles Pearson. *The Last Expedition, Stanley's Mad Journey Through the Congo.* New York: W. W. Norton, 2005.

Mangiafico, Luciano. "Garibaldi in Blue?" *Foreign Service Journal* (July–August 2010): 51–54.

Meyer, Lysle E. *The Farther Frontier: Six Case Studies of Americans and Africa, 1848–1936.* Cranbury, N.J.: Associated University Presses, 1992.

———. "Henry S. Sanford and the Congo: A Reassessment." *African Historical Studies* 4, no. 1 (1971): 19–39.

Miller, Russell. *The Adventures of Arthur Conan Doyle: A Biography.* New York: St. Martin's Press, 2008.

Molloy, Leo T. *Henry Shelton Sanford (1823–1891).* Derby, Conn.: Valley Historical Research Committee, 2009.

Morris, Edmund. *Colonel Roosevelt.* New York: Random House, 2010.

———. *Theodore Rex.* New York: Random House, 2001.

Naipaul, V. S. *A Bend in the River.* New York: Vintage Books, 1989.

Newman, James L. *Imperial Footprints: Henry Morton Stanley's African Journeys.* Washington, D.C.: Potomac Books, 2006.

Nicolai, Henri. "The Geographical Movement, a Newspaper and a Geographer in the Service of Colonization of the Congo." *Civilisations* [online], April 1993.

Phipps, William E. *William Sheppard: Congo's African American Livingstone.* Louisville, Ky.: Geneva Press, 2002.

Pletcher, David M. *The Awkward Years: American Foreign Relations under Garfield and Arthur.* Columbia: University of Missouri Press, 1962.

Porter, Roy. *The Greatest Benefit to Mankind: A Medical History of Humanity.* New York: W. W. Norton, 1997.

Richardson, Leon Burr. *William E. Chandler, Republican.* New York: Dodd, Mead, 1940.

Roark, James L. "American Expansionism vs. European Imperialism: Henry S. Sanford and the Congo Episode, 1883–1885." *Mid-America Historical Review* 60, no. 1 (January 1978): 21–33.

Robert, Stephen S. "An Indicator of Informal Empire: Patterns of U.S. Navy Cruising on Overseas Stations, 1869–1897." *Professional Paper* 295. Alexandria, Va.: Center for Naval Analysis, 1980.

Sherry, Norman. *Conrad's Western World.* Cambridge: Cambridge University Press, 1971.

Slade, Ruth. *King Leopold's Congo.* London: Oxford University Press, 1962.

Smith, Woodruff D. *The German Colonial Empire*. Chapel Hill: University of North Carolina Press, 1978

Stevens, Harold Ray, and J. H. Stape. *Last Essays*. Cambridge: Cambridge University Press, 2010.

Tayler, Jeffrey. *Facing the Congo: A Modern-day Journey into the Heart of Darkness*. New York: Three Rivers Press, 2000.

White, James P. "The Sanford Exploring Expedition," *Journal of African History* 8, no. 2 (1967): 291–301.

Unpublished Secondary Sources

Cochran, Gifford A. "Mr. Lincoln's Many-faceted Minister and Entrepreneur Extraordinary Henry Shelton Sanford, 1823–1891." Unpublished manuscript. Sanford Museum.

Gibson, Gordon D. "Early African Collections in the Smithsonian and their Collectors." N.d. Department of Anthropology, National Museum of Natural History, Smithsonian Institution.

Leopold, Robert S. "A Guide to Early African Collections in the Smithsonian Institution." August 1994. Anthropology.si.edu/Leopold /pubs/early_african_collections.pdf/. Accessed June 1, 2011.

Index

About the Author

Andrew C. A. Jampoler lives in the Lost Corner of Loudoun County, Virginia, with his wife, Susan, a professional geographer, and their two golden retrievers. They have children and grandchildren in Pennsylvania and Iowa. He is an alumnus of Columbia College and the School of International and Public Affairs, both of Columbia University, in New York City, and of the Foreign Service Institute's School of Language Study.

Earlier in life he commanded a maritime patrol aircraft squadron and an air station during twenty-four years on active duty as an aviator in the U.S. Navy. Later he was a senior sales and marketing executive in the international aerospace industry. *Congo* is Jampoler's fifth book. He has been writing about maritime history for the past dozen years.

R. Congo
Marunja
Mbundgu R.
Ikombo
Bangala Statⁿ
Mangala Villages
Mui Lutongo
Lulanga
Ochiokanga
Okanga (de Brazza 1878)
yeba or Fan
Amboco
Equator Statⁿ (Nganda)
Ikengo
Buena
Uriki
Licona
Ubangi Ikengo
kanda
Mbokondi
Boue
Fall
Iviado
Dilo
Osyeba
Ndolo
Zabure
Sjake
Mosjebe
Djumba
Bundji
Banguinda
Adima
Mbamba
Plake Kompaka
Umboti
Bababo
Mantumba
Trebu
Ngombe
L. Mohimba
Kedubeka
Obamba
Ngoma Ndumbi
Lukolela
Opove
Amangi Bakola
Brangue
Mt Abeki
Allala
 Neeny
Neenv
Madumbo
Andjiani
Livuangi
Libossi
Mpoka Fall
Mbete
Batéke
Njabi Apfuru
Uyanzi
Barumbi
Njavi
Nyadis
Mimbumbo Njavole
Franceville
Amp
Alima
Mbamba
Biabinna
Livako
Acuo
Levi Hills
Bacham
Ngambo
Yoadi
Obira
Lalo
Moïé
Bolobo
Kombo
Bucanda
Ongomo
Npimi
Nquara
Mpaka
L. King Leopold II.
Niombuli
Ascikuya Plateau
Ngango
Ainya
Djamballa
Ngamfuru
C O
Zolo
Bantu
Ogowe
Bankoto
Aboma
Lefinel
Laighi
Lekarighi
Ngantalli
Miebo
Fafa
Mpu
Ngampu
Chumbiri
Kimba
Mbana
Nantere Hill
Bapuno
Ncandu
Balali
Okoto Buali
Baala
Djua
Makoko
Ngampey
Misongo
Wabuma
Bakinu
Bekisonga
Madembe
Makalka
Nganchimo
Kwamouth
Msuta
Mbita
Ndondejoka
Balumbo
Bayaka
Ngodi
Magonso
Nkolo
Batéke
Bagongo
Kitabi
Stanley Niadi
R. Djue
Buama Nzulu
Brazzaville
Kimpoko
STANLEY POOL
Mavombe
Vuduvuio
Stephanieville
Philippeville
Moanda
Rubifu
Leopoldville & Kinshasha
Ngoma
Mutiti
Manli
Kalga
Nkula
Bulangongu
Nzadi
Gombi
Wabuno
Mbako Songlo
Inkissi Cat.
Mohita Masesse Fall
Lutete
Mpumbu
Bakundi
Kingungi Catt (Mechow 1880)
Masyomb
Maniam
Kibindika
Buballa Cat.
Junzimba Cat.
Mempimbo
Kamalambo
Issangila
Ndambi Mbore
Banesville
Makuta
Banza Pango
Lusanga Muamba
Cungo
Kakongo
Sadika Banza
Ikungula
Banza Manteka
Ruby Tn
Kinsuka
Nydinga
Ngoio
Bomma
Praia
Pallaballa
Banza Mputu
Quanza
Moila
Quite
Sanbung
Maiakka
Chima Bikua
Mussorongos
San Salvador
Congo da Lemba
Mbangu
Muene Putu Kassango
Banana
Antonio
Padron
Chinga Plana
Kung Kala
Sonho
Muxicongos
Madimba
Bamba
Mujolo
Bembe
Sosso